MARTIN LUTHER'S

COMMENTARY ON

GALATIANS

TRANSLATED BY
THEODORE GRAEBNER

Vintage Puritan
GLH Publishing
LOUISVILLE, KY

Originally titled *A Commentary on St. Paul's Epistle to the Galatians*.
Translated by Theodore Graebner. Grand Rapids: Zondervan, 1939.
Public Domain.

Reprinted by GLH Publishing, 2021

ISBN:
  Paperback 978-1-64863-088-0
  Epub 978-1-64863-089-7

*For information on new releases, weekly deals,
and free ebooks visit
www.GLHpublishing.com*

CONTENTS

In my heart reigns this one article, faith in my dear Lord Christ, the beginning, middle and end of whatever spiritual and divine thoughts I may have, whether by day or by night.

From Luther's 1538 Introduction

Preface

The preparation of this edition of Luther's Commentary on Galatians was first suggested to me by Mr. P. J. Zondervan, of the firm of publishers, in March, 1937. The consultation had the twofold merit of definiteness and brevity.

"Luther is still the greatest name in Protestantism. We want you to help us publish some leading work of Luther's for the general American market. Will you do it?"

"I will, on one condition."

"And what is that?"

"The condition is that I will be permitted to make Luther talk American, 'streamline' him, so to speak—because you will never get people, whether in or outside the Lutheran Church, actually to read Luther unless we make him talk as he would talk today to Americans."

I illustrated the point by reading to Mr. Zondervan a few sentences from an English translation lately reprinted by an American publisher, of one of Luther's outstanding reformatory essays.

The demonstration seemed to prove convincing for it was agreed that one may as well offer Luther in the original German or Latin as expect the American church-member to read any translations that would adhere to Luther's German or Latin constructions and employ the Mid-Victorian type of English characteristic of the translations now on the market.

"And what book would be your choice?"

"There is one book that Luther himself like better than any other. Let us begin with that: his Commentary on Galatians..."

The undertaking, which seemed so attractive when viewed as a literary task, proved a most difficult one, and at times became oppressive. The Letter to the Galatians consists of six short chapters. Luther's commentary fills seven hundred and thirty-three octavo pages in the Weidman Edition of his works. It was written in Latin. We were resolved not to present this entire mass of exegesis. It would have run to more than fifteen hundred pages, ordinary octavo (like this), since it is impossible to use the compressed structure of sentences which is characteristic of Latin, and particularly of Luther's Latin. The work had to be condensed. German and English translations are available, but the most acceptable English version, besides laboring under the handicaps of an archaic style, had to be condensed into half its volume in order to accomplish the "streamlining" of the book. Whatever merit the translation now presented to the reader

may possess should be written to the credit of Rev. Gerhardt Mahler of
Geneva, N.Y., who came to my assistance in a very busy season by making
a rough draft of the translation and later preparing a revision of it, which
forms the basis of the final draft submitted to the printer. A word should
now be said about the origin of Luther's Commentary on Galatians.

The Reformer had lectured on this Epistle of St. Paul's in 1519 and
again in 1523. It was his favorite among all the Biblical books. In his table
talks the saying is recorded: "The Epistle to the Galatians is my epistle. To
it I am as it were in wedlock. It is my Katherine." Much later when a friend
of his was preparing an edition of all his Latin works, he remarked to his
home circle: "If I had my way about it they would republish only those of
my books which have doctrine. My Galatians, for instance. "The lectures
which are preserved in the works herewith submitted to the American
public were delivered in 1531. They were taken down by George Roerer,
who held something of a deanship at Wittenberg University and who was
one of Luther's aids in the translation of the Bible. Roerer took down Luther's lectures and this manuscript has been preserved to the present day,
in a copy which contains also additions by Veit Dietrich and by Cruciger,
friends of Roerer's, who with him attended Luther's lectures. In other
words, these three men took down the lectures which Luther addressed
to his students in the course of Galatians, and Roerer prepared the manuscript for the printer. A German translation by Justus Menius appeared in
the Wittenberg Edition of Luther's writings, published in 1539.

The importance of this Commentary on Galatians for the history of
Protestantism is very great. It presents like no other of Luther's writings
the central thought of Christianity, the justification of the sinner for the
sake of Christ's merits alone. We have permitted in the final revision of the
manuscript many a passage to stand which seemed weak and ineffectual
when compared with the trumpet tones of the Latin original. But the essence of Luther's lectures is there. May the reader accept with indulgence
where in this translation we have gone too far in modernizing Luther's
expression—making him "talk American."

At the end of his lectures in 1531, Luther uttered a brief prayer and
then dictated two Scriptural texts, which we shall inscribe at the end of
these introductory remarks: "The Lord who has given us power to teach
and to hear, let Him also give us the power to serve and to do."

Glory to God in the highest,
And on earth peace,
Good will to men.
—Luke 2

The Word of our God shall stand forever.
—Isaiah 40

Theodore Graebner
St. Louis, Missouri

GALATIANS 1:1-3

VERSE 1. Paul, an apostle, (not of men, neither by man, but by Jesus Christ, and God the Father, who raised him from the dead).

St. Paul wrote this epistle because, after his departure from the Galatian churches, Jewish-Christian fanatics moved in, who perverted Paul's Gospel of man's free justification by faith in Christ Jesus.

The world bears the Gospel a grudge because the Gospel condemns the religious wisdom of the world. Jealous for its own religious views, the world in turn charges the Gospel with being a subversive and licentious doctrine, offensive to God and man, a doctrine to be persecuted as the worst plague on earth.

As a result we have this paradoxical situation: The Gospel supplies the world with the salvation of Jesus Christ, peace of conscience, and every blessing. Just for that the world abhors the Gospel.

These Jewish-Christian fanatics who pushed themselves into the Galatian churches after Paul's departure, boasted that they were the descendants of Abraham, true ministers of Christ, having been trained by the apostles themselves, that they were able to perform miracles.

In every way they sought to undermine the authority of St. Paul. They said to the Galatians: "You have no right to think highly of Paul. He was the last to turn to Christ. But we have seen Christ. We heard Him preach. Paul came later and is beneath us. It is possible for us to be in error—we who have received the Holy Ghost? Paul stands alone. He has not seen Christ, nor has he had much contact with the other apostles. Indeed, he persecuted the Church of Christ for a long time."

When men claiming such credentials come along, they deceive not only the naive, but also those who seemingly are well-established in the faith. This same argument is used by the papacy. "Do you suppose that God for the sake of a few Lutheran heretics would disown His entire Church? Or do you suppose that God would have left His Church floundering in error all these centuries?" The Galatians were taken in by such arguments with the result that Paul's authority and doctrine were drawn in question.

Against these boasting, false apostles, Paul boldly defends his apostolic authority and ministry. Humble man that he was, he will not now take a back seat. He reminds them of the time when he opposed Peter to his face and reproved the chief of the apostles.

3

Paul devotes the first two chapters to a defense of his office and his Gospel, affirming that he received it, not from men, but from the Lord Jesus Christ by special revelation, and that if he or an angel from heaven preach any other gospel than the one he had preached, he shall be accursed.

THE CERTAINTY OF OUR CALLING

Every minister should make much of his calling and impress upon others the fact that he has been delegated by God to preach the Gospel. As the ambassador of a government is honored for his office and not for his private person, so the minister of Christ should exalt his office in order to gain authority among men. This is not vain glory, but needful glorying.

Paul takes pride in his ministry, not to his own praise but to the praise of God. Writing to the Romans, he declares, "Inasmuch as I am the apostle of the Gentiles, I magnify mine office," i.e., I want to be received not as Paul of Tarsus, but as Paul the apostle and ambassador of Jesus Christ, in order that people might be more eager to hear. Paul exalts his ministry out of the desire to make known the name, the grace, and the mercy of God.

VERSE 1. Paul, an apostle, (not of men, etc.)

Paul loses no time in defending himself against the charge that he had thrust himself into the ministry. He says to the Galatians: "My call may seem inferior to you. But those who have come to you are either called of men or by man. My call is the highest possible, for it is by Jesus Christ, and God the Father."

When Paul speaks of those called "by men," I take it he means those whom neither God nor man sent, but who go wherever they like and speak for themselves.

When Paul speaks of those called "by man" I take it he means those who have a divine call extended to them through other persons. God calls in two ways. Either He calls ministers through the agency of men, or He calls them directly as He called the prophets and apostles. Paul declares that the false apostles were called or sent neither by men, nor by man. The most they could claim is that they were sent by others. "But as for me I was called neither of men, nor by man, but directly by Jesus Christ. My call is in every respect like the call of the apostles. In fact I am an apostle."

Elsewhere Paul draws a sharp distinction between an apostleship and lesser functions, as in I Corinthians 12:28: "And God hath set some in the church; first, apostles; secondarily, prophets; thirdly, teachers." He mentions the apostles first because they were appointed directly by God.

Matthias was called in this manner. The apostles chose two candidates and then cast lots, praying that God would indicate which one He would have. To be an apostle he had to have his appointment from God. In the same manner Paul was called as the apostle of the Gentiles.

The call is not to be taken lightly. For a person to possess knowledge is not enough. He must be sure that he is properly called. Those who operate without a proper call seek no good purpose. God does not bless their labors. They may be good preachers, but they do no edify. Many of the fanatics of our day pronounce words of faith, but they bear no good fruit, because their purpose is to turn men to their perverse opinions. On the other hand, those who have a divine call must suffer a good deal of opposition in order that they may become fortified against the running attacks of the devil and the world.

This is our comfort in the ministry, that ours is a divine office to which we have been divinely called. Reversely, what an awful thing it must be for the conscience if one is not properly called. It spoils one's best work. When I was a young man I thought Paul was making too much of his call. I did not understand his purpose. I did not then realize the importance of the ministry. I knew nothing of the doctrine of faith because we were taught sophistry instead of certainty, and nobody understood spiritual boasting. We exalt our calling, not to gain glory among men, or money, or satisfaction, or favor, but because people need to be assured that the words we speak are the words of God. This is no sinful pride. It is holy pride.

VERSE 1. *And God the Father, who raised him from the dead.*

Paul is so eager to come to the subject matter of his epistle, the righteousness of faith in opposition to the righteousness of works, that already in the title he must speak his mind. He did not think it quite enough to say that he was an apostle "by Jesus Christ"; he adds, "and God the Father, who raised him from the dead."

The clause seems superfluous on first sight. Yet Paul had a good reason for adding it. He had to deal with Satan and his agents who endeavored to deprive him of the righteousness of Christ, who was raised by God the Father from the dead. These perverters of the righteousness of Christ resist the Father and the Son, and the works of them both.

In this whole epistle Paul treats of the resurrection of Christ. By His resurrection Christ won the victory over law, sin, flesh, world, devil, death, hell, and every evil. And this His victory He donated unto us. These many tyrants and enemies of ours may accuse and frighten us, but they dare not condemn us, for Christ, whom God the Father has raised from the dead is our righteousness and our victory.

Do you notice how well suited to his purpose Paul writes? He does not say, "By God who made heaven and earth, who is Lord of the angels," but Paul has in mind the righteousness of Christ, and speaks to the point, saying, "I am an apostle, not of men, neither by man, but by Jesus Christ, and God the Father, who raised him from the dead."

VERSE 2. And all the brethren which are with me.

This should go far in shutting the mouths of the false apostles. Paul's intention is to exalt his own ministry while discrediting theirs. He adds for good measure the argument that he does not stand alone, but that all the brethren with him attest to the fact that his doctrine is divinely true. "Although the brethren with me are not apostles like myself, yet they are all of one mind with me, think, write, and teach as I do."

VERSE 2. Unto the churches of Galatia.

Paul had preached the Gospel throughout Galatia, founding many churches which after his departure were invaded by the false apostles. The Anabaptists in our time imitate the false apostles. They do not go where the enemies of the Gospel predominate. They go where the Christians are. Why do they not invade the Catholic provinces and preach their doctrine to godless princes, bishops, and doctors, as we have done by the help of God? These soft martyrs take no chances. They go where the Gospel has a hold, so that they may not endanger their lives. The false apostles would not go to Jerusalem of Caiaphas, or to the Rome of the Emperor, or to any other place where no man had preached before as Paul and the other apostles did. But they came to the churches of Galatia, knowing that where men profess the name of Christ they may feel secure.

It is the lot of God's ministers not only to suffer opposition at the hand of a wicked world, but also to see the patient indoctrination of many years quickly undone by such religious fanatics. This hurts more than the persecution of tyrants. We are treated shabbily on the outside by tyrants, on the inside by those whom we have restored to the liberty of the Gospel, and also by false brethren. But this is our comfort and our glory, that being called of God we have the promise of everlasting life. We look for that reward which "eye hath not seen, nor ear heard, neither hath entered into the heart of man."

Jerome raises the question why Paul called them churches that were no churches, inasmuch as the Galatians had forsaken the grace of Christ for the law of Moses. The proper answer is: Although the Galatians had fallen away from the doctrine of Paul, baptism, the Gospel, and the name of Christ continued among them. Not all the Galatians had become perverted. There were some who clung to the right view of the Word and the Sacraments. These means cannot be contaminated. They remain divine regardless of men's opinion. Wherever the means of grace are found, there is the Holy Church, even though Antichrist reigns there. So much for the title of the epistle. Now follows the greeting of the apostle.

VERSE 3. Grace be to you, and peace, from God the Father, and from our
Lord Jesus Christ.

The terms of grace and peace are common terms with Paul and are now pretty well understood. But since we are explaining this epistle, you will not mind if we repeat what we have so often explained elsewhere. The article of justification must be sounded in our ears incessantly because the frailty of our flesh will not permit us to take hold of it perfectly and to believe it with all our heart.

The greeting of the Apostle is refreshing. Grace remits sin, and peace quiets the conscience. Sin and conscience torment us, but Christ has overcome these fiends now and forever. Only Christians possess this victorious knowledge given from above. These two terms, grace and peace, constitute Christianity. Grace involves the remission of sins, peace, and a happy conscience. Sin is not canceled by lawful living, for no person is able to live up to the Law. The Law reveals guilt, fills the conscience with terror, and drives men to despair. Much less is sin taken away by man-invented endeavors. The fact is, the more a person seeks credit for himself by his own efforts, the deeper he goes into debt. Nothing can take away sin except the grace of God. In actual living, however, it is not so easy to persuade oneself that by grace alone, in opposition to every other means, we obtain the forgiveness of our sins and peace with God.

The world brands this a pernicious doctrine. The world advances free will, the rational and natural approach of good works, as the means of obtaining the forgiveness of sin. But it is impossible to gain peace of conscience by the methods and means of the world. Experience proves this. Various holy orders have been launched for the purpose of securing peace of conscience through religious exercises, but they proved failures because such devices only increase doubt and despair. We find no rest for our weary bones unless we cling to the word of grace.

The Apostle does not wish the Galatians grace and peace from the emperor, or from kings, or from governors, but from God the Father. He wishes them heavenly peace, the kind of which Jesus spoke when He said, "Peace I leave unto you: my peace I give unto you." Worldly peace provides quiet enjoyment of life and possessions. But in affliction, particularly in the hour of death, the grace and peace of the world will not deliver us. However, the grace and peace of God will. They make a person strong and courageous to bear and to overcome all difficulties, even death itself, because we have the victory of Christ's death and the assurance of the forgiveness of our sins.

MEN SHOULD NOT SPECULATE ABOUT THE NATURE OF GOD

The Apostle adds to the salutation the words, "and from our Lord Jesus Christ." Was it not enough to say, "from God the Father"?

It is a principle of the Bible that we are not to inquire curiously into the nature of God. "There shall no man see me, and live," Exodus 33:20. All who trust in their own merits to save them disregard this principle and lose sight of the Mediator, Jesus Christ.

True Christian theology does not inquire into the nature of God, but into God's purpose and will in Christ, whom God incorporated in our flesh to live and to die for our sins. There is nothing more dangerous than to speculate about the incomprehensible power, wisdom, and majesty of God when the conscience is in turmoil over sin. To do so is to lose God altogether because God becomes intolerable when we seek to measure and to comprehend His infinite majesty.

We are to seek God as Paul tells us in I Corinthians 1:23, 24: "We preach Christ crucified, unto the Jews a stumbling block, and unto the Greeks foolishness; but unto them which are called, both Jews and Greeks, Christ the power of God, and the wisdom of God." Begin with Christ. He came down to earth, lived among men, suffered, was crucified, and then He died, standing clearly before us, so that our hearts and eyes may fasten upon Him. Thus we shall be kept from climbing into heaven in a curious and futile search after the nature of God.

If you ask how God may be found, who justifies sinners, know that there is no other God besides this man Christ Jesus. Embrace Him, and forget about the nature of God. But these fanatics who exclude our Mediator in their dealings with God, do not believe me. Did not Christ Himself say: "I am the way, and the truth, and the life: no man cometh unto the Father, but by me"? Without Christ there is no access to the Father, but futile rambling; no truth, but hypocrisy; no life, but eternal death.

When you argue about the nature of God apart from the question of justification, you may be as profound as you like. But when you deal with conscience and with righteousness over against the law, sin, death, and the devil, you must close your mind to all inquiries into the nature of God, and concentrate upon Jesus Christ, who says, "Come unto me, all ye that labor and are heavy laden, and I will give you rest." Doing this, you will recognize the power, and majesty condescending to your condition according to Paul's statement to the Colossians, "In Christ are hid all the treasures of wisdom and knowledge," and, "In him dwelleth all the fulness of the Godhead bodily." Paul in wishing grace and peace not alone from God the Father, but also from Jesus Christ, wants to warn us against the curious incursions into the nature of God. We are to hear Christ, who has been appointed by the Father as our divine Teacher.

CHRIST IS GOD BY NATURE

At the same time, Paul confirms our creed, "that Christ is very God." We need such frequent confirmation of our faith, for Satan will not fail to attack it. He hates our faith. He knows that it is the victory which overcometh him and the world. That Christ is very God is apparent in that Paul ascribes to Him divine powers equally with the Father, as for instance, the power to dispense grace and peace. This Jesus could not do unless He were God.

To bestow peace and grace lies in the province of God, who alone can create these blessings. The angels cannot. The apostles could only distribute these blessings by the preaching of the Gospel. In attributing to Christ the divine power of creating and giving grace, peace, everlasting life, righteousness, and forgiveness of sins, the conclusion is inevitable that Christ is truly God. Similarly, St. John concludes from the works attributed to the Father and the Son that they are divinely One. Hence, the gifts which we receive from the Father and from the Son are one and the same. Otherwise Paul should have written: "Grace from God the Father, and peace from our Lord Jesus Christ." In combining them he ascribes them equally to the Father and the Son. I stress this on account of the many errors emanating from the sects.

The Arians were sharp fellows. Admitting that Christ had two natures, and that He is called "very God of very God," they were yet able to deny His divinity. The Arians took Christ for a noble and perfect creature, superior even to the angels, because by Him God created heaven and earth. Mohammed also speaks highly of Christ. But all their praise is mere palaver to deceive men. Paul's language is different. To paraphrase him: "You are established in this belief that Christ is very God because He gives grace and peace, gifts which only God can create and bestow."

GALATIANS 1:4-6

VERSE 4. Who gave himself for our sins.

Paul sticks to his theme. He never loses sight of the purpose of his epistle. He does not say, "Who received our works," but "who gave." Gave what? Not gold, or silver, or paschal lambs, or an angel, but Himself. What for? Not for a crown, or a kingdom, or our goodness, but for our sins. These words are like so many thunderclaps of protest from heaven against every kind and type of self-merit. Underscore these words, for they are full of comfort for sore consciences.

How may we obtain remission of our sins? Paul answers: "The man who is named Jesus Christ and the Son of God gave himself for our sins." The heavy artillery of these words explodes papacy, works, merits, superstitions. For if our sins could be removed by our own efforts, what need was there for the Son of God to be given for them? Since Christ was given for our sins it stands to reason that they cannot be put away by our own efforts.

This sentence also defines our sins as great, so great, in fact, that the whole world could not make amends for a single sin. The greatness of the ransom, Christ, the Son of God, indicates this. The vicious character of sin is brought out by the words "who gave himself for our sins." So vicious is sin that only the sacrifice of Christ could atone for sin. When we reflect that the one little word "sin" embraces the whole kingdom of Satan, and that it includes everything that is horrible, we have reason to tremble. But we are careless. We make light of sin. We think that by some little work or merit we can dismiss sin.

This passage, then, bears out the fact that all men are sold under sin. Sin is an exacting despot who can be vanquished by no created power, but by the sovereign power of Jesus Christ alone.

All this is of wonderful comfort to a conscience troubled by the enormity of sin. Sin cannot harm those who believe in Christ, because He has overcome sin by His death. Armed with this conviction, we are enlightened and may pass judgment upon the papists, monks, nuns, priests, Mohammedans, Anabaptists, and all who trust in their own merits, as wicked and destructive sects that rob God and Christ of the honor that belongs to them alone.

Note especially the pronoun "our" and its significance. You will readily grant that Christ gave Himself for the sins of Peter, Paul, and others who were worthy of such grace. But feeling low, you find it hard to believe that Christ gave Himself for your sins. Our feelings shy at a personal application of the pronoun "our," and we refuse to have anything to do with God until we have made ourselves worthy by good deeds.

This attitude springs from a false conception of sin, the conception that sin is a small matter, easily taken care of by good works; that we must present ourselves unto God with a good conscience; that we must feel no sin before we may feel that Christ was given for our sins.

This attitude is universal and particularly developed in those who consider themselves better than others. Such readily confess that they are frequent sinners, but they regard their sins as of no such importance that they cannot easily be dissolved by some good action, or that they may not appear before the tribunal of Christ and demand the reward of eternal life for their righteousness. Meantime they pretend great humility and acknowledge a certain degree of sinfulness for which they soulfully join in the publican's prayer, "God be merciful to me a sinner." But the real significance and comfort of the words "for our sins" is lost upon them.

The genius of Christianity takes the words of Paul "who gave himself for our sins" as true and efficacious. We are not to look upon our sins as insignificant trifles. On the other hand, we are not to regard them as so terrible that we must despair. Learn to believe that Christ was given, not for picayune and imaginary transgressions, but for mountainous sins; not for one or two, but for all; not for sins that can be discarded, but for sins that are stubbornly ingrained.

Practice this knowledge and fortify yourself against despair, particularly in the last hour, when the memory of past sins assails the conscience. Say with confidence: "Christ, the Son of God, was given not for the righteous, but for sinners. If I had no sin I should not need Christ. No, Satan, you cannot delude me into thinking I am holy. The truth is, I am all sin. My sins are not imaginary transgressions, but sins against the first table, unbelief, doubt, despair, contempt, hatred, ignorance of God, ingratitude towards Him, misuse of His name, neglect of His Word, etc.; and sins against the second table, dishonor of parents, disobedience of government, coveting of another's possessions, etc. Granted that I have not committed murder, adultery, theft, and similar sins in deed, nevertheless I have committed them in the heart, and therefore I am a transgressor of all the commandments of God.

"Because my transgressions are multiplied and my own efforts at self-justification rather a hindrance than a furtherance, therefore Christ the Son of God gave Himself into death for my sins." To believe this is to have eternal life.

Let us equip ourselves against the accusations of Satan with this and similar passages of Holy Scripture. If he says, "Thou shalt be damned," you tell him: "No, for I fly to Christ who gave Himself for my sins. In accusing me of being a damnable sinner, you are cutting your own throat, Satan. You are reminding me of God's fatherly goodness toward me, that

He so loved the world that He gave His only-begotten Son that whosoever believeth in Him should not perish, but have everlasting life. In calling me a sinner, Satan, you really comfort me above measure." With such heavenly cunning we are to meet the devil's craft and put from us the memory of sin.

St. Paul also presents a true picture of Christ as the virgin-born Son of God, delivered into death for our sins. To entertain a true conception of Christ is important, for the devil describes Christ as an exacting and cruel judge who condemns and punishes men. Tell him that his definition of Christ is wrong, that Christ has given Himself for our sins, that by His sacrifice He has taken away the sins of the whole world.

Make ample use of this pronoun "our." Be assured that Christ has canceled the sins, not of certain persons only, but your sins. Do not permit yourself to be robbed of this lovely conception of Christ. Christ is no Moses, no law-giver, no tyrant, but the Mediator for sins, the Giver of grace and life.

We know this. Yet in the actual conflict with the devil, when he scares us with the Law, when he frightens us with the very person of the Mediator, when he misquotes the words of Christ, and distorts for us our Savior, we so easily lose sight of our sweet High-Priest.

For this reason I am so anxious for you to gain a true picture of Christ out of the words of Paul "who gave himself for our sins." Obviously, Christ is no judge to condemn us, for He gave Himself for our sins. He does not trample the fallen but raises them. He comforts the broken-hearted. Otherwise Paul should lie when he writes "who gave himself for our sins."

I do not bother my head with speculations about the nature of God. I simply attach myself to the human Christ, and I find joy and peace, and the wisdom of God in Him. These are not new truths. I am repeating what the apostles and all teachers of God have taught long ago. Would to God we could impregnate our hearts with these truths.

VERSE 4. *That he might deliver us from this present evil world.*

Paul calls this present world evil because everything in it is subject to the malice of the devil, who reigns over the whole world as his domain and fills the air with ignorance, contempt, hatred, and disobedience of God. In this devils's kingdom we live.

As long as a person is in the world he cannot by his own efforts rid himself of sin, because the world is bent upon evil. The people of the world are the slaves of the devil. If we are not in the Kingdom of Christ, it is certain we belong to the kingdom of Satan and we are pressed into his service with every talent we possess.

Take the talents of wisdom and integrity. Without Christ, wisdom is double foolishness and integrity double sin, because they not only fail to perceive the wisdom and righteousness of Christ, but hinder and blaspheme the salvation of Christ. Paul justly calls it the evil or wicked world, for when the world is at its best the world is at its worst. The grossest vices are small faults in comparison with the wisdom and righteousness of the world. These prevent men from accepting the Gospel of the righteousness of Christ. The white devil of spiritual sin is far more dangerous than the black devil of carnal sin because the wiser, the better men are without Christ, the more they are likely to ignore and oppose the Gospel.

With the words, "that he might deliver us," Paul argues that we stand in need of Christ. No other being can possibly deliver us from this present evil world. Do not let the fact disturb you that a great many people enjoy excellent reputations without Christ. Remember what Paul says, that the world with all its wisdom, might, and righteousness is the devil's own. God alone is able to deliver us from the world.

Let us praise and thank God for His mercy in delivering us from the captivity of Satan, when we were unable to do so by our own strength. Let us confess with Paul that all our work-righteousness is loss and dung. Let us condemn as filthy rags all talk about free will, all religious orders, masses, ceremonies, vows, fastings, and the like.

In branding the world the devil's kingdom of iniquity, ignorance, error, sin, death, and everlasting despair, Paul at the same time declares the Kingdom of Christ to be a kingdom of equity, light, grace, remission of sin, peace, saving health, and everlasting life into which we are translated by our Lord Jesus Christ, to whom be glory forever.

In this passage Paul contends against the false apostles for the article of Justification. Christ, says Paul, has delivered us from this wicked kingdom of the devil and the world according to the good will, the pleasure and commandment of the Father. Hence we are not delivered by our own will, or shrewdness, or wisdom, but by the mercy and love of God, as it is written, I John 4:10, "Herein is love, not that we loved God, but that he loved us, and sent his Son to be the propitiation for our sins."

Another reason why Paul, like John, emphasizes the Father's will is Christ's habit of directing attention to the Father. For Christ came into the world to reconcile God with us and to draw us to the Father.

Not by curious inquiries into the nature of God shall we know God and His purpose for our salvation, but by taking hold of Christ, who according to the will of the Father has given Himself into death for our sins. When we understand this to be the will of the Father in Christ, then shall we know God to be merciful, and not angry. We shall realize that He loved us wretched sinners so much indeed that He gave us His only-begotten Son into death for us.

The pronoun "our" refers to both God and Father. He is our God and our Father. Christ's Father and our Father are one and the same. Hence Christ said to Mary Magdalene: "Go to my brethren, and say unto them, I ascend unto my Father, and your Father; and to my God, and your God." God is our Father and our God, but only in Christ Jesus.

Verse 5. To whom be glory for ever and ever. Amen.

Hebrew writing is interspersed with expressions of praise and gratitude. This peculiarity can be traced in the apostolic writings, particularly in those of Paul. The name of the Lord is to be mentioned with great reverence and thanksgiving.

Verse 6. I marvel.

How patiently Paul deals with his seduced Galatians! He does not pounce on them but, like a father, he fairly excuses their error. With motherly affection he talks to them yet he does it in a way that at the same time he also reproves them. On the other hand, he is highly indignant at the seducers whom he blames for the apostasy of the Galatians. His anger bursts forth in elemental fury at the beginning of his epistle. "If any may," he cries, "preach any other gospel unto you than that ye have received, let him be accursed." Later on, in the fifth chapter, he threatens the false apostles with damnation. "He that troubleth you shall bear his judgment, whosoever he be." He pronounces a curse upon them. "I would they were even cut off which trouble you."

He might have addressed the Galatians after this fashion: "I am ashamed of you. Your ingratitude grieves me. I am angry with you." But his purpose was to call them back to the Gospel. With this purpose in his mind he speaks very gently to them. He could not have chosen a milder expression than this, "I marvel." It indicates his sorrow and his displeasure.

Paul minds the rule which he himself lays down in a later chapter where he says: "Brethren, if a man be overtaken in a fault, ye which are spiritual, restore such an one in the spirit of meekness; considering thyself, lest thou also be tempted." Toward those who have been misled we are to show ourselves parentally affectionate, so that they may perceive that we seek not their destruction but their salvation. Over against the devil and his missionaries, the authors of false doctrines and sects, we ought to be like the Apostle, impatient, and rigorously condemnatory, as parents are with the dog that bites their little one, but the weeping child itself they soothe.

The right spirit in Paul supplies him with an extraordinary facility in handling the afflicted consciences of the fallen. The Pope and his bishops, inspired by the desire to lord it over men's souls, crack out thunders and curses upon miserable consciences. They have no care for the saving of men's souls. They are interested only in maintaining their position.

Verse 6. That ye are so soon.

Paul deplores the fact that it is difficult for the mind to retain a sound and steadfast faith. A man labors for a decade before he succeeds in training his little church into orderly religion, and then some ignorant and vicious poltroon comes along to overthrow in a minute the patient labor of years. By the grace of God we have effected here in Wittenberg the form of a

Christian church. The Word of God is taught as it should be, the Sacraments are administered, and everything is prosperous. This happy condition, secured by many years of arduous labors, some lunatic might spoil in a moment. This happened in the churches of Galatia which Paul had brought into life in spiritual travail. Soon after his departure, however, these Galatian churches were thrown into confusion by the false apostles.

The church is a tender plant. It must be watched. People hear a couple of sermons, scan a few pages of Holy Writ, and think they know it all. They are bold because they have never gone through any trials of faith. Void of the Holy Spirit, they teach what they please as long as it sounds good to the common people who are ever ready to join something new.

We have to watch out for the devil lest he sow tares among the wheat while we sleep. No sooner had Paul turned his back on the churches of Galatia, than the false apostles went to work. Therefore, let us watch over ourselves and over the whole church.

VERSE 6. I marvel that ye are so soon removed.

Again the Apostle puts in a gentle word. He does not berate the Galatians, "I marvel that ye are so unsteady, unfaithful." He says, "I marvel that ye are so soon removed." He does not address them as evildoers. He speaks to them as people who have suffered great loss. He condemns those who removed them rather than the Galatians. At the same time he gently reproves them for rather themselves to be removed. The criticism is implied that they should have been permitting a little more settled in their beliefs. If they had taken better hold of the Word they could not have been removed so easily.

Jerome thinks that Paul is playing upon the name Galatians, deriving it from the Hebrew word Galath, which means fallen or carried away, as though Paul wanted to say, "You are true Galatians, i.e., fallen away in name and in fact." Some believe that the Germans are descended from the Galatians. There may be something to that. For the Germans are not unlike the Galatians in their lack of constancy. At first we Germans are very enthusiastic, but presently our emotions cool and we become slack. When the light of the Gospel first came to us many were zealous, heard sermons greedily, and held the ministry of God's Word in high esteem. But now that religion has been reformed, many who formerly were such earnest disciples have discarded the Word of God, have become sow-bellies like the foolish and inconsistent Galatians.

VERSE 6. From him that called you into the grace of Christ.

The reading is a little doubtful. The sentence may be construed to read: "From that Christ that called you into grace"; or it may be construed to read: "From God that called you into the grace of Christ." I prefer the former for it seems to me that Paul's purpose is to impress upon us the benefits of Christ. This reading also preserves the implied criticism that the Galatians withdrew themselves from that Christ who had called them not unto the law, but unto grace. With Paul we decry the blindness and perverseness of men in that they will not receive the message of grace and salvation, or having received it they quickly let go of it, in spite of the fact that the Gospel bestows all good things spiritual: forgiveness of sins, true righteousness, peace of conscience, everlasting life; and all good things temporal: good judgment, good government and peace.

Why does the world abhor the glad tidings of the Gospel and the blessings that go with it? Because the world is the devil's. Under his direction the world persecutes the Gospel and would if it could nail again Christ, the Son of God, to the Cross although He gave Himself into death for the sins of the world. The world dwells in darkness. The world is darkness.

Paul accentuates the point that the Galatians had been called by Christ unto grace. "I taught you the doctrine of grace and of liberty from the Law, from sin and wrath, that you should be free in Christ, and not slaves to the hard laws of Moses. Will you allow yourselves to be carried away so easily from the living fountain of grace and life?"

Verse 6. Unto another gospel.

Note the resourcefulness of the devil. Heretics do not advertise their errors. Murderers, adulterers, thieves disguise themselves. So the devil masquerades all his devices and activities. He puts on white to make himself look like an angel of light. He is astoundingly clever to sell his patent poison for the Gospel of Christ. Knowing Satan's guile, Paul sardonically calls the doctrine of the false apostles "another gospel," as if he would say, "You Galatians have now another gospel, while my Gospel is no longer esteemed by you."

We infer from this that the false apostles had depreciated the Gospel of Paul among the Galatians on the plea that it was incomplete. Their objection to Paul's Gospel is identical to that recorded in the fifteenth chapter of the Book of Acts to the effect that it was not enough for the Galatians to believe in Christ, or to be baptized, but that it was needful to circumcise them, and to command them to keep the law of Moses, for "except ye be circumcised after the manner of Moses, ye cannot be saved." As though Christ were a workman who had begun a building and left it for Moses to finish.

Today the Anabaptists and others, finding it difficult to condemn us, accuse us Lutherans of timidity in professing the whole truth. They grant that we have laid the foundation in Christ, but claim that we have failed to go through with the building. In this way these perverse fanatics parade their cursed doctrine as the Word of God, and, flying the flag of God's name, they deceive many. The devil knows better than to appear ugly and black. He prefers to carry on his nefarious activities in the name of God. Hence the German proverb: "All mischief begins in the name of God."

When the devil sees that he cannot hurt the cause of the Gospel by destructive methods, he does it under the guise of correcting and advancing the cause of the Gospel. He would like best of all to persecute us with fire and sword, but this method has availed him little because through the blood of martyrs the church has been watered. Unable to prevail by force, he engages wicked and ungodly teachers who at first make common cause with us, then claim that they are particularly called to teach the hidden mysteries of the Scriptures to superimpose upon the first principles of Christian doctrine that we teach. This sort of thing brings the Gospel into trouble. May we all cling to the Word of Christ against the wiles of the devil, "for we wrestle not against flesh and blood, but against principalities, against powers, against the rulers of the darkness of this world, against spiritual wickedness in high places."

GALATIANS 1:7-24

VERSE 7. Which is not another; but there be some that trouble you.

Here again the apostle excuses the Galatians, while he blames the false apostles for disturbing their consciences and for stealing them out of his hand. How angry he gets at these deceivers! He calls them troublemakers, seducers of poor consciences.

This passage adduces further evidence that the false apostles defamed Paul as an imperfect apostle and a weak and erroneous preacher. They condemn Paul, Paul condemns them. Such warfare of condemnation is always going on in the church. The papists and the fanatics hate us, condemn our doctrine, and want to kill us. We in turn hate and condemn their cursed doctrine. In the meanwhile the people are uncertain whom to follow and which way to turn, for it is not given to everybody to judge these matters. But the truth will win out. So much is certain, we persecute no man, neither does our doctrine trouble men. On the contrary, we have the testimony of many good men who thank God on their knees for the consolation that our doctrine has brought them. Like Paul, we are not to blame that the churches have trouble. The fault lies with the Anabaptists and other fanatics.

Every teacher of work-righteousness is a trouble-maker. Has it never occurred to you that the pope, cardinals, bishops, monks, and that the whole synagogue of Satan are trouble-makers? The truth is, they are worse than false apostles. The files apostles taught that in addition to faith in Christ the works of the Law of God were necessary unto salvation. But the papists omit faith altogether and teach self-devised traditions and works that are not commanded of God, indeed are contrary to the Word of God, and for these traditions they demand preferred attention and obedience.

Paul calls the false apostles troublers of the church because they taught circumcision and the keeping of the Law as needful unto salvation. They insisted that the Law must be observed in every detail. They were supporters in this contention by the Jews, with the result that those who were not firmly established in faith were easily persuaded that Paul was not a sincere teacher of God because he ignored the Law. The Jews were offended at the idea that the Law of God should be entirely ignored by Paul and that the Gentiles, former idol-worshippers, should gratuitously attain to the station of God's people without circumcision, without the penitentiary performance of the law, by grace alone through faith in Christ Jesus.

18

These criticisms were amplified by the false apostles. They accused Paul of designs to abolish the law of God and the Jewish dispensation, contrary to the law of God, contrary to their Jewish heritage, contrary to apostolic example, contrary to Paul's own example. They demanded that Paul be shunned as a blasphemer and a rebel, while they were to be heard as true teachers of the Gospel and authentic disciples of the apostles. Thus Paul stood defamed among the Galatians. He was forced to attack the false apostles. He did so without hesitation.

VERSE 7. And would pervert the gospel of Christ.

To paraphrase this sentence: "These false apostles do not merely trouble you, they abolish Christ's Gospel. They act as if they were the only true Gospel-preachers. For all that they muddle Law and Gospel. As a result they pervert the Gospel. Either Christ must live and the Law perish, or the Law remains and Christ must perish; Christ and the Law cannot dwell side by side in the conscience. It is either grace or law. To muddle the two is to eliminate the Gospel of Christ entirely."

It seems a small matter to mingle the Law and Gospel, faith and works, but it creates more mischief than man's brain can conceive. To mix Law and Gospel not only clouds the knowledge of grace, it cuts out Christ altogether.

The words of Paul, "and would pervert the gospel of Christ," also indicate how arrogant these false apostles were. They were shameless boasters. Paul simply had to exalt his own ministry and Gospel.

VERSE 8. But though we, or an angel from heaven, preach any other gospel unto you than that which we have preached unto you, let him be accursed.

Paul's zeal for the Gospel becomes so fervent that it almost leads him to curse angels. "I would rather that I, my brethren, yes, the angels of heaven be anathematized than that my gospel be overthrown."

The Greek word *anathema*, Hebrew *herem*, means to accurse, execrate, to damn. Paul first (hypothetically) curses himself. Knowing persons first find fault with themselves in order that they may all the more earnestly reprove others.

Paul maintains that there is no other gospel besides the one he had preached to the Galatians. He preached, not a gospel of his own invention, but the very same Gospel God had long ago prescribed in the Sacred Scriptures. No wonder Paul pronounces curses upon himself and upon others, upon the angels of heaven, if anyone should dare to preach any other gospel than Christ's own.

VERSE 9. As we said before, so say I now again. If any man preach any other gospel unto you than that ye have received, let him be accursed.

Paul repeats the curse, directing it now upon other persons. Before, he cursed himself, his brethren, and an angel from heaven. "Now," he says, "if there are any others who preach a gospel different from that you have received from us, let them also be accursed." Paul herewith curses and excommunicates all false teachers including his opponents. He is so worked up that he dares to curse all who pervert his Gospel. Would to God that this terrible pronouncement of the Apostle might strike fear into the hearts of all who pervert the Gospel of Paul.

The Galatians might say: "Paul, we do not pervert the Gospel you have brought unto us. We did not quite understand it. That is all. Now these teachers who came after you have explained everything so beautifully."

This explanation the Apostle refuses to accept. They must add nothing; they must correct nothing. "What you received from me is the genuine Gospel of God. Let it stand. If any man brings any other gospel than the one I brought you, or promises to deliver better things than you have received from me, let him be accursed."

In spite of this emphatic denunciation so many accept the pope as the supreme judge of the Scriptures. "The Church," they say, "chose only four gospels. The Church might have chosen more. Ergo the Church is above the Gospel." With equal force one might argue: "I approve the Scriptures. Ergo I am above the Scriptures. John the Baptist confessed Christ. Hence he is above Christ." Paul subordinates himself, all preachers, all the angels of heaven, everybody to the Sacred Scriptures. We are not the masters, judges, or arbiters, but witnesses, disciples, and confessors of the Scriptures, whether we be pope, Luther, Augustine, Paul, or an angel from heaven.

VERSE 10. For do I now persuade men, or God?

With the same vehemence Paul continues: "You Galatians ought to be able to tell from my preaching and from the many afflictions which I have endured, whether I serve men or God. Everybody can see that my preaching has stirred up persecution against me everywhere, and has earned for me the cruel hatred of my own people, in fact the hatred of all men. This should convince you that by my preaching I do not seek the favor and praise of men, but the glory of God."

No man can say that we are seeking the favor and praise of men with our doctrine. We teach that all men are naturally depraved. We condemn man's free will, his strength, wisdom, and righteousness. We say that we obtain grace by the free mercy of God alone for Christ's sake. This is no preaching to please men. This sort of preaching procures for us the hatred and disfavor of the world, persecutions, excommunications, murders, and curses.

"Can't you see that I seek no man's favor by my doctrine?" asks Paul. "If I were anxious for the favor of men I would flatter them. But what do I do? I condemn their works. I teach things only that I have been commanded to teach from above. For that I bring down upon my head the wrath of Jews and Gentiles. My doctrine must be right. It must be divine. Any other doctrine cannot be better than mine. Any other doctrine must be false and wicked."

With Paul we boldly pronounce a curse upon every doctrine that does not agree with ours. We do not preach for the praise of men, or the favor of princes. We preach for the favor of God alone whose grace and mercy we proclaim. Whosoever teaches a gospel contrary to ours, or different from ours, let us be bold to say that he is sent of the devil.

VERSE 10. Or do I seek to please men?

"Do I serve men or God?" Paul keeps an eye on the false apostles, those flatterers of men. They taught circumcision to avoid the hatred and persecution of men.

To this day you will find many who seek to please men in order that they may live in peace and security. They teach whatever is agreeable to men, no matter whether it is contrary to God's Word or their own conscience. But we who endeavor to please God and not men, stir up hell itself. We must suffer reproach, slanders, death.

For those who go about to please men we have a word from Christ recorded in the fifth chapter of St. John: "How can ye believe, which receive honor one of another, and seek not the honor that cometh from God alone?"

VERSE 10. For if I yet pleased men, I should not be the servant of Christ.

Observe the consummate cleverness with which the false apostles went about to bring Paul into disrepute. They combed Paul's writings for contradictions (our opponents do the same) to accuse him of teaching contradictory things. They found that Paul had circumcised Timothy according to the Law, that Paul had purified himself with four other men in the Temple at Jerusalem, that Paul had shaven his head at Cenchrea. The false apostles slyly suggested that Paul had been constrained by the other apostles to observe these ceremonial laws. We know that Paul observed these *decora* out of charitable regard for the weak brethren. He did not want to offend them. But the false apostles turned Paul's charitable regard to his disadvantage. If Paul had preached the Law and circumcision, if he had commended the strength and free will of man, he would not have been so obnoxious to the Jews. On the contrary they would have praised his every action.

VERSES 11, 12. But I certify you, brethren, that the gospel which was preached of me is not after man. For I neither received it of man, neither was I taught it, but by the revelation of Jesus Christ.

This passage constitutes Paul's chief defense against the accusations of his opponents. He maintains under oath that he received his Gospel not from men, but by the revelation of Jesus Christ.

In declaring that his Gospel is not after man, Paul does not merely wish to state that his Gospel is not mundane. The false apostles made the same claim for their gospel. Paul means to say that he learned his Gospel not in the usual and accepted manner through the agency of men by hearing, reading, or writing. He received the Gospel by special revelation directly from Jesus Christ.

Paul received his Gospel on the way to Damascus when Christ appeared to him. St. Luke furnishes an account of the incident in the ninth chapter of the Book of Acts. "Arise," said Christ to Paul, "and go into the city, and it shall be told thee what thou must do." Christ did not send Paul into the city to learn the Gospel from Ananias. Ananias was only to baptize Paul, to lay his hands on Paul, to commit the ministry of the Word unto Paul, and to recommend him to the Church. Ananias recognized his limited assignment when he said to Paul: "Brother Saul, the Lord, even Jesus, that appeared unto thee in the way as thou camest, hath sent me, that thou mightest receive thy sight, and be filled with the Holy Ghost." Paul did not receive instruction from Ananias. Paul had already been called, enlightened, and taught by Christ in the road. His contact with Ananias was merely a testimonial to the fact that Paul had been called by Christ to preach the Gospel.

Paul was forced to speak of his conversion to combat the slanderous contention of the false apostles to the effect that this apostleship was inferior to that of the other apostles.

If it were not for the example of the Galatian churches I would never have thought it possible that anybody who had received the Word of God with such eagerness as they had, could so quickly let go of it. Good Lord, what terrible mischief one single false statement can create.

The article of justification is fragile. Not in itself, of course, but in us. I know how quickly a person can forfeit the joy of the Gospel. I know in what slippery places even those stand who seem to have a good footing in the matters of faith. In the midst of the conflict when we should be consoling ourselves with the Gospel, the Law rears up and begins to rage all over our conscience. I say the Gospel is frail because we are frail.

What makes matters worse is that one-half of ourselves, our own reason, stands against us. The flesh resists the spirit, or as Paul puts it, "The flesh lusteth against the Spirit." Therefore we teach that to know Christ and to believe in Him is no achievement of man, but the gift of God. God alone can create and preserve faith in us. God creates faith in us through the Word. He increases, strengthens and confirms faith in us through His word. Hence the best service that anybody can render God is diligently to hear and read God's Word. On the other hand, nothing is more perilous than to be weary of the Word of God. Thinking he knows enough, a person begins little by little to despise the Word until he has lost Christ and the Gospel altogether.

Let every believer carefully learn the Gospel. Let him continue in humble prayer. We are molested not by puny foes, but by mighty ones, foes who never grow tired of warring against us. These, our enemies, are many: Our own flesh, the world, the Law, sin, death, the wrath and judgment of God, and the devil himself.

The arguments which the false apostles advanced impress people to this day. "Who are you to dissent from the fathers and the entire Church, and to bring a contradictory doctrine? Are you wiser than so many holy men, wiser than the whole Church?" When Satan, abetted by our own reason, advances these arguments against us, we lose heart, unless we keep on saying to ourselves: "I don't care if Cyprian, Ambrose, Augustine, Peter, Paul, John, or an angel from heaven, teaches so and so. I know that I teach the truth of God in Christ Jesus."

When I first took over the defense of the Gospel, I remembered what Doctor Staupitz said to me. "I like it well," he said, "that the doctrine which you proclaim gives glory to God alone and none to man. For never can too much glory, goodness, and mercy be ascribed unto God." These words of the worthy Doctor comforted and confirmed me. The Gospel is true because it deprives men of all glory, wisdom, and righteousness and turns over all honor to the Creator alone. It is safer to attribute too much glory unto God than unto man.

You may argue that the Church and the fathers are holy. Yet the Church is compelled to pray: "Forgive us our trespasses," I am not to be believed, nor is the Church to be believed, or the fathers, or the apostles, or an angel from heaven, if they teach anything contrary to the Word of God. Let the Word of God abide forever.

Peter erred in life and in doctrine. Paul might have dismissed Peter's error as a matter of no consequence. But Paul saw that Peter's error would lead to the damage of the whole Church unless it were corrected. Therefore he withstood Peter to his face. The Church, Peter, the apostles, angels from heaven, are not to be heard unless they teach the genuine Word of God.

This argument is not always to our advantage. People ask: "Whom then shall we believe?" Our opponents maintain that they teach the pure Word of God. We do not believe them. They in turn hate and persecute us for vile heretics. What can we do about it? With Paul we glory in the Gospel of Jesus Christ. What do we gain? We are told that our glorying is idle vanity and unadulterated blasphemy. The moment we abase ourselves and give in to the rage of our opponents, Papists and Anabaptists grow arrogant. The Anabaptists hatch out some new monstrosity. The Papists revive their old abominations. What to do? Let everybody become sure of his calling and doctrine, that he may boldly say with Paul: "But though we, or an angel from heaven, preach any other gospel unto you than ye have received, let him be accursed."

VERSES 13, 14. For ye have heard of my conversation in time past in the Jews' religion, how that beyond measure I persecuted the church of God, and wasted it: And profited in the Jews' religion above many my equals in mine own nation.

This passage does not contain doctrine. Paul adduces his own case for an example. "I have," he says, "at one time defended the traditions of the Pharisees more fiercely than any of your false apostles. Now, if the righteousness of the Law had been worth anything I would never have forsaken it. So carefully did I live up to the Law that I excelled many of my companions. So zealous was I in defense of the Law that I wasted the church of God."

VERSE 14. Being more exceedingly zealous of the traditions of my fathers.

Speaking now of the Mosaic Law, Paul declares that he was wrapped up in it. To the Philippians he wrote: "As touching the law, a Pharisee; concerning zeal, persecuting the church; touching the righteousness which is in the law, blameless." He means to say, "I can compare myself with the best and holiest of all those who are of the circumcision. Let them show me if they can, a more earnest defender of the Mosaic Law than I was at one time. This fact, O Galatians, should have put you on your guard against these deceivers who make so much of the Law. If anybody ever had reason to glory in the righteousness of the Law, it was I."

I too may say that before I was enlightened by the Gospel, I was as zealous for the papistical laws and traditions of the fathers as ever a man was. I tried hard to live up to every law as best I could. I punished myself with fasting, watching, praying, and other exercises more than all those who today hate and persecute me. I was so much in earnest that I imposed upon my body more than it could stand. I honored the pope as a matter of conscience. Whatever I did, I did with a single heart to the glory of God. But our opponents, well-fed idlers that they are, will not believe what I and many others have endured.

VERSES 15, 16, 17. But when it pleased God, who separated me from my mother's womb, and called me by his grace. To reveal his Son in me, that I might preach him among the heathen; immediately I conferred not with flesh and blood: Neither went I up to Jerusalem to them which were apostles before me; but I went into Arabia, and returned again unto Damascus.

Here Paul relates that immediately upon being called by God to preach the Gospel to the Gentiles, he went into Arabia without consulting a single person. "When it had pleased God," he writes, "I did not deserve it. I had been an enemy of Christ. I had blasphemed His Gospel. I had shed innocent blood. In the midst of my frenzy I was called. Why? On account of my outrageous cruelty? Indeed not. My gracious God who shows mercy unto whom He will, pardoned all mine iniquities. He bestowed His grace upon me, and called me for an apostle."

We also have come to the knowledge of the truth by the same kindness of God. I crucified Christ daily in my cloistered life, and blasphemed God by my wrong faith. Outwardly I kept myself chaste, poor, and obedient. I was much given to fasting, watching, praying, saying of masses, and the like. Yet under the cloak of my outward respectability I continually mistrusted, doubted, feared, hated, and blasphemed God. My righteousness was a filthy puddle. Satan loves such saints. They are his darlings, for they quickly destroy their body and soul by depriving them of the blessings of God's generous gifts.

I tell you I stood in awe of the pope's authority. To dissent from him I considered a crime worthy of eternal death. I thought of John Huss as a cursed heretic. I counted it a sin even to think of him. I would gladly have furnished the wood to burn him. I would have felt I had done God a real service.

In comparison with these sanctimonious hypocrites of the papacy, publicans and harlots are not bad. They at least feel remorse. They at least do not try to justify their wicked deeds. But these pretended saints, so far from acknowledging their errors, justify them and regard them as acceptable sacrifices unto God.

Verse 15a. When it pleased God.

"By the favor of God I, a wicked and cursed wretch, a blasphemer, persecutor, and rebel, was spared. Not content to spare me, God granted unto me the knowledge of His salvation, His Spirit, His Son, the office of an apostle, everlasting life." Paul speaking.

God not only pardoned our iniquities, but in addition overwhelmed us with blessings and spiritual gifts. Many, however, are ungrateful. Worse, by opening again a window to the devil many begin to loathe God's Word, and end by perverting the Gospel.

Verse 15. Who separated me from my mother's womb.

This is a Hebrew expression, meaning to sanctify, ordain, prepare. Paul is saying, "When I was not yet born God ordained me to be an apostle, and in due time confirmed my apostleship before the world. Every gift, be it small or great, spiritual or temporal, and every good thing I should ever do, God has ordained while I was yet in my mother's womb where I could neither think nor perform any good thing. After I was born God supported me. Heaping mercy upon mercy, He freely forgave my sins, replenishing me with His grace to enable me to learn what great things are ours in Christ. To crown it all, He called me to preach the Gospel to others."

Verse 15. And called me by his grace.

"Did God call me on account of my holy life? Or on account of my pharisaical religion? Or on account of my prayers, fastings, and works? Never. Well, then, it is certain God did not call me on account of my blasphemies, persecutions, oppressions. What prompted Him to call me? His grace alone."

VERSE 16. To reveal his Son to me.

We now hear what kind of doctrine was committed to Paul: The doctrine of the Gospel, the doctrine of the revelation of the Son of God. This doctrine differs greatly from the Law. The Law terrorizes the conscience. The Law reveals the wrath and judgment of God. The Gospel does not threaten. The Gospel announces that Christ is come to forgive the sins of the world. The Gospel conveys to us the inestimable treasures of God.

VERSE 16. That I might preach him among the heathen.

"It pleased God," says the Apostle, "to reveal himself in me. Why? For a twofold purpose. That I personally should believe in the Son of God, and that I should reveal Him to the Gentiles."

Paul does not mention the Jews, for the simple reason that he was the called and acknowledged apostle of the Gentiles, although he preached Christ also to the Jews.

We can hear the Apostle saying to himself: "I will not burden the Gentiles with the Law, because I am their apostle and not their lawgiver. Not once did you Galatians hear me speak of the righteousness of the Law or of works. My job was to bring you the Gospel. Therefore you ought to listen to no teachers of the Law, but the Gospel: not Moses, but the Son of God; not the righteousness of works, but the righteousness of faith must be proclaimed to the Gentiles. That is the right kind of preaching for Gentiles."

VERSE 16. Immediately I conferred not with flesh and blood.

Once Paul had received the Gospel from Christ, he conferred with nobody in Damascus. He asked no man to teach him. He did not go up to Jerusalem to sit at the feet of Peter and the other apostles. At once he preached Jesus Christ in Damascus.

VERSE 17. Neither went I up to Jerusalem to them which were apostles before me; but I went into Arabia, and returned again unto Damascus.

"I went to Arabia before I saw any of the apostles. I took it upon myself to preach the Gospel to the Gentiles without delay, because Christ had called me for that purpose." This statement refutes the assertion of the false apostles that Paul had been a pupil of the apostles, from which the false apostles inferred that Paul had been instructed in the obedience of the Law, that therefore the Gentiles also ought to keep the Law and submit to circumcision.

VERSES 18, 19. Then after three years I went up to Jerusalem to see Peter, and abode with him fifteen days. But other of the apostles saw I none, save James the Lord's brother.

Paul minutely recounts his personal history to stop the cavil of the false apostles. Paul does not deny that he had been with some of the apostles. He went to Jerusalem uninvited, not to be instructed, but to visit with Peter. Luke reports the occasion in the ninth chapter of the Book of Acts. Barnabas introduced Paul to the apostles and related to them how Paul had met the Lord Jesus on the way to Damascus, also how Paul had preached boldly at Damascus in the name of Jesus. Paul says that he saw Peter and James, but he denies that he learned anything from them.

Why does Paul harp on this seemingly unimportant fact? To convince the churches of Galatia that his Gospel was the true Word of Christ which he learned from Christ Himself and from no man. Paul was forced to affirm and re-affirm this fact. His usefulness to all the churches that had used him as their pastor and teacher was at stake.

VERSE 20. Now the things which I write unto you, behold, before God, I lie not.

Was it necessary for Paul to go under oath? Yes. Paul is reporting personal history. How else would the churches believe him? The false apostles might say, "Who knows whether Paul is telling the truth?" Paul, the elect vessel of God, was held in so little esteem by his own Galatians to whom he had preached Christ that it was necessary for him to swear an oath that he spoke the truth. If this happened to Paul, what business have we to complain when people doubt our words, or hold us in little regard, we who cannot begin to compare ourselves with the Apostle?

VERSE 21. Afterwards I came into the regions of Syria and Cilicia.

Syria and Cilicia are adjacent countries. Paul traces his movements carefully in order to convince the Galatians that he had never been the disciple of any apostle.

VERSE 22, 23, 24. And was unknown by face unto the churches of Judaea which were in Christ: But they had heard only, that he which persecuted us in times past now preacheth the faith which once he destroyed. And they glorified God in me.

In Syria and Cilicia Paul won the indorsement of all the churches of Judea, by his preaching. All the churches everywhere, even those of Judea, could testify that he had preached the same faith everywhere. "And," Paul adds, "these churches glorified God in me, not because I taught that circumcision and the law of Moses should be observed, but because I urged upon all faith in the Lord Jesus Christ."

GALATIANS 2:1-3

VERSE 1. Then fourteen years after I went up again to Jerusalem.

Paul taught justification by faith in Christ Jesus, without the deeds of the Law. He reported this to the disciples at Antioch. Among the disciples were some that had been brought up in the ancient customs of the Jews. These rose against Paul in quick indignation, accusing him of propagating a gospel of lawlessness.

Great dissension followed. Paul and Barnabas stood up for the truth. They testified: "Wherever we preached to the Gentiles, the Holy Ghost came upon those who received the Word. This happened everywhere. We preached not circumcision, we did not require observance of the Law. We preached faith in Jesus Christ. At our preaching of faith, God gave to the hearers the Holy Ghost." From this fact Paul and Barnabas inferred that the Holy Ghost approved the faith of the Gentiles without the Law and circumcision. If the faith of the Gentiles had not pleased the Holy Ghost, He would not have manifested His presence in the uncircumcised hearers of the Word.

Unconvinced, the Jews fiercely opposed Paul, asserting that the Law ought to be kept and that the Gentiles ought to be circumcised, or else they could not be saved.

When we consider the obstinacy with which Romanists cling to their traditions, we can very well understand the zealous devotion of the Jews for the Law. After all, they had received the Law from God. We can understand how impossible it was for recent converts from Judaism suddenly to break with the Law. For that matter, God did bear with them, as He bore with the infirmity of Israel when the people halted between two religions. Was not God patient with us also while we were blindfolded by the papacy? God is longsuffering and full of mercy. But we dare not abuse the patience of the Lord. We dare no longer continue in error now that the truth has been revealed in the Gospel.

The opponents of Paul had his own example to prefer against him. Paul had circumcised Timothy. Paul defended his action on the ground that he had circumcised Timothy, not from compulsion, but from Christian love, lest the weak in faith should be offended. His opponents would not accept Paul's explanation.

When Paul saw that the quarrel was getting out of hand he obeyed the direction of God and left for Jerusalem, there to confer with the other apostles. He did this not for his own sake, but for the sake of the people.

VERSE 1. With Barnabas, and took Titus with me also.

Paul chose two witnesses, Barnabas and Titus. Barnabas had been Paul's preaching companion to the Gentiles. Barnabas was an eye-witness of the fact that the Holy Ghost had come upon the Gentiles in response to the simple preaching of faith in Jesus Christ. Barnabas stuck to Paul on this point, that it was unnecessary for the Gentiles to be bothered with the Law as long as they believed in Christ.

Titus was superintendent of the churches in Crete, having been placed in charge of the churches by Paul. Titus was a former Gentile.

VERSE 2. And I went up by revelation.

If God had not ordered Paul to Jerusalem, Paul would never have gone there.

VERSE 2. And communicated unto them that gospel.

After an absence of fourteen years, respectively eighteen years, Paul returned to Jerusalem to confer with the other apostles.

VERSE 2. Which I preach among the Gentiles.

Among the Jews Paul allowed Law and circumcision to stand for the time being. So did all the apostles. Nevertheless Paul held fast to the liberty of the Gospel. On one occasion he said to the Jews: "Through this man (Christ) is preached unto you forgiveness of sins; and by him all that believe are justified from all things, from which ye could not be justified by the law of Moses." (Acts 13:39.) Always remembering the weak, Paul did not insist that they break at once with the Law.

Paul admits that he conferred with the apostles concerning his Gospel. But he denies that the conference benefited or taught him anything. The fact is he resisted those who wanted to force the practice of the Law upon the Gentiles. They did not overcome him, he overcame them. "Your false apostles lie, when they say that I circumcised Timothy, shaved my head in Cenchrea, and went up to Jerusalem, at the request of the apostles. I went to Jerusalem at the request of God. What is more, I won the indorsement of the apostles. My opponents lost out."

The matter upon which the apostles deliberated in conference was this: Is the observance of the Law requisite unto justification? Paul answered: "I have preached faith in Christ to the Gentiles, and not the Law. If the Jews want to keep the Law and be circumcised, very well, as long as they do so from a right motive."

VERSE 2. But privately to them which were of reputation.

This is to say, "I conferred not only with the brethren, but with the leaders among them."

VERSE 2. Lest by any means I should run, or had run, in vain.

Not that Paul himself ever thought he had run in vain. However, many did think that Paul had preached the Gospel in vain, because he kept the Gentiles free from the yoke of the Law. The opinion that obedience to the Law was mandatory unto salvation was gaining ground. Paul meant to remedy this evil. By this conference he hoped to establish the identity of his Gospel with that of the other apostles, to stop the talk of his opponents that he had been running around in vain.

VERSE 3. But neither Titus, who was with me, being a Greek, was compelled to be circumcised.

The word "compelled" acquaints us with the outcome of the conference. It was resolved that the Gentiles should not be compelled to be circumcised.

Paul did not condemn circumcision in itself. Neither by word nor deed did he ever inveigh against circumcision. But he did protest against circumcision being made a condition for salvation. He cited the case of the Fathers. "The fathers were not justified by circumcision. It was to them a sign and seal of righteousness. They looked upon circumcision as a confession of their faith."

The believing Jews, however, could not get it through their heads that circumcision was not necessary for salvation. They were encouraged in their wrong attitude by the false apostles. The result was that the people were up in arms against Paul and his doctrine.

Paul did not condemn circumcision as if it were a sin to receive it. But he insisted, and the conference upheld him, that circumcision had no bearing upon salvation and was therefore not to be forced upon the Gentiles. The conference agreed that the Jews should be permitted to keep their ancient customs for the time being, so long as they did not regard those customs as conveying God's justification of the sinner.

The false apostles were dissatisfied with the verdict of the conference. They did not want to rest circumcision and the practice of the Law in Christian liberty. They insisted that circumcision was obligatory unto salvation.

As the opponents of Paul, so our own adversaries [Luther's, the enemies of the Reformation] contend that the traditions of the Fathers dare not be neglected without loss of salvation. Our opponents will not agree with us on anything. They defend their blasphemies. They go as far to enforce them with the sword.

Paul's victory was complete. Titus, who was with Paul, was not compelled to be circumcised, although he stood in the midst of the apostles when this question of circumcision was debated. This was a blow to the false apostles. With the living fact that Titus was not compelled to be circumcised Paul was able to squelch his adversaries.

GALATIANS 2:4-13

VERSES 4,5. And that because of false brethren unawares brought in, who came in privily to spy out our liberty which we have in Christ Jesus, that they might bring us into bondage: To whom we gave place by subjection, no, not for an hour; that the truth of the gospel might continue with you.

Paul here explains his motive for going up to Jerusalem. He did not go to Jerusalem to be instructed or confirmed in his Gospel by the other apostles. He went to Jerusalem in order to preserve the true Gospel for the Galatian churches and for all the churches of the Gentiles.

When Paul speaks of the truth of the Gospel he implies by contrast a false gospel. The false apostles also had a gospel, but it was an untrue gospel. "In holding out against them," says Paul, "I conserved the truth of the pure Gospel."

Now the true Gospel has it that we are justified by faith alone, without the deeds of the Law. The false gospel has it that we are justified by faith, but not without the deeds of the Law. The false apostles preached a conditional gospel.

So do the papists. They admit that faith is the foundation of salvation. But they add the conditional clause that faith can save only when it is furnished with good works. This is wrong. The true Gospel declares that good works are the embellishment of faith, but that faith itself is the gift and work of God in our hearts. Faith is able to justify, because it apprehends Christ, the Redeemer.

Human reason can think only in terms of the Law. It mumbles: "This I have done, this I have not done." But faith looks to Jesus Christ, the Son of God, given into death for the sins of the whole world. To turn one's eyes away from Jesus means to turn them to the Law.

True faith lays hold of Christ and leans on Him alone. Our opponents cannot understand this. In their blindness they cast away the precious pearl, Christ, and hang onto their stubborn works. They have no idea what faith is. How can they teach faith to others?

Not satisfied with teaching an untrue gospel, the false apostles tried to entangle Paul. "They went about," says Paul, "to spy out our liberty which we have in Christ Jesus, that they might bring us into bondage."

When Paul saw through their scheme, he attacked the false apostles. He says, "We did not let go of the liberty which we have in Christ Jesus. We routed them by the judgment of the apostles, and we would not give in to them, no, not an inch."

We too were willing to make all kinds of concessions to the papists. Yes, we are willing to offer them more than we should. But we will not give up the liberty of conscience which we have in Christ Jesus. We refuse to have our conscience bound by any work or law, so that by doing this or that we should be righteous, or leaving this or that undone we should be damned.

Since our opponents will not let it stand that only faith in Christ justifies, we will not yield to them. On the question of justification we must remain adamant, or else we shall lose the truth of the Gospel. It is a matter of life and death. It involves the death of the Son of God, who died for the sins of the world. If we surrender faith in Christ, as the only thing that can justify us, the death and resurrection of Jesus are without meaning; that Christ is the Savior of the world would be a myth. God would be a liar, because He would not have fulfilled His promises. Our stubbornness is right, because we want to preserve the liberty which we have in Christ. Only by preserving our liberty shall we be able to retain the truth of the Gospel inviolate.

Some will object that the Law is divine and holy. Let it be divine and holy. The Law has no right to tell me that I must be justified by it. The Law has the right to tell me that I should love God and my neighbor, that I should live in chastity, temperance, patience, etc. The Law has no right to tell me how I may be delivered from sin, death, and hell. It is the Gospel's business to tell me that. I must listen to the Gospel. It tells me, not what I must do, but what Jesus Christ, the Son of God, has done for me.

To conclude, Paul refused to circumcise Titus for the reason that the false apostles wanted to compel him to circumcise Titus. Paul refused to accede to their demands. If they had asked it on the plea of brotherly love, Paul would not have denied them. But because they demanded it on the ground that it was necessary for salvation, Paul defied them, and prevailed. Titus was not circumcised.

Verse 6. But of those who seemed to be somewhat, whatsoever they were, it maketh no matter to me.

This is a good point in Paul's refutation. Paul disparages the authority and dignity of the true apostles. He says of them, "Which seemed to be somewhat." The authority of the apostles was indeed great in all the churches. Paul did not want to detract from their authority, but he had to speak disparagingly of their authority in order to conserve the truth of the Gospel, and the liberty of conscience.

The false apostles used this argument against Paul: "The apostles lived with Christ for three years. They heard His sermons. They witnessed His miracles. They themselves preached and performed miracles while Christ was on earth. Paul never saw Jesus in the flesh. Now, whom ought you to believe: Paul, who stands alone, a mere disciple of the apostles, one of the last and least; or will you believe those grand apostles who were sent and confirmed by Christ Himself long before Paul?"

What could Paul say to that? He answered: "What they say has no bearing on the argument. If the apostles were angels from heaven, that would not impress me. We are not now discussing the excellency of the apostles. We are talking about the Word of God now, and the truth of the Gospel. That Gospel is more excellent than all apostles.

VERSE 6. God accepteth no man's person.

Paul is quoting Moses: "Thou shalt not respect the person of the poor, nor honor the person of the mighty." (Lev. 19:15) This quotation from Moses ought to shut the mouths of the false apostles. "Don't you know that God is no respecter of persons?" cries Paul. The dignity or authority of men means nothing to God. The fact is that God often rejects just such who stand in the odor of sanctity and in the aura of importance. In doing so God seems unjust and harsh. But men need deterring examples. For it is a vice with us to esteem personality more highly than the Word of God. God wants us to exalt His Word and not men.

There must be people in high office, of course. But we are not to deify them. The governor, the mayor, the preacher, the teacher, the scholar, father, mother, are persons whom we are to love and revere, but not to the extent that we forget God. Least we attach too much importance to the person, God leaves with important persons offenses and sins, sometimes astounding shortcomings, to show us that there is a lot of difference between any person and God. David was a good king. But when the people began to think too well of him, down he fell into horrible sins, adultery and murder. Peter, excellent apostle that he was, denied Christ. Such examples of which the Scriptures are full, ought to warn us not to repose our trust in men. In the papacy appearance counts for everything. Indeed, the whole papacy amounts to nothing more than a mere kowtowing of persons and outward mummery. But God alone is to be feared and honored.

I would honor the Pope, I would love his person, if he would leave my conscience alone, and not compel me to sin against God. But the Pope wants to be adored himself, and that cannot be done without offending God. Since we must choose between one or the other, let us choose God. The truth is we are commissioned by God to resist the Pope, for it is written, "We ought to obey God rather than men." (Acts 5:29)

We have seen how Paul refutes the argument of the false apostles concerning the authority of the apostles. In order that the truth of the Gospel may continue; in order that the Word of God and the righteousness of faith may be kept pure and undefiled, let the apostles, let an angel from heaven, let Peter, let Paul, let them all perish.

VERSE 6. For they who seemed to be somewhat in conference added nothing
to me.

The Apostle repeats: "I did not so confer with the apostles that they taught me anything. What could they possibly teach me since Christ by His revelation had taught me all things? It was but a conference, and no disputation. I learned nothing, neither did I defend my cause. I only stated what I had done, that I had preached to the Gentiles faith in Christ, without the Law, and that in response to my preaching the Holy Ghost came down upon the Gentiles. When the apostles heard this, they were glad that I had taught the truth."

If Paul would not give in to the false apostles, much less ought we to give in to our opponents. I know that a Christian should be humble, but against the Pope I am going to be proud and say to him: "You, Pope, I will not have you for my boss, for I am sure that my doctrine is divine." Such pride against the Pope is imperative, for if we are not stout and proud we shall never succeed in defending the article of the righteousness of faith.

If the Pope would concede that God alone by His grace through Christ justifies sinners, we would carry him in our arms, we would kiss his feet. But since we cannot obtain this concession, we will give in to nobody, not to all the angels in heaven, not to Peter, not to Paul, not to a hundred emperors, not to a thousand popes, not to the whole world. If in this matter we were to humble ourselves, they would take from us the God who created us, and Jesus Christ who has redeemed us by His blood. Let this be our resolution, that we will suffer the loss of all things, the loss of our good name, of life itself, but the Gospel and our faith in Jesus Christ—we will not stand for it that anybody take them from us.

> VERSES 7, 8. *But contrariwise, when they saw that the gospel of the uncircumcision was committed unto me, as the gospel of the circumcision was unto Peter; [For he that wrought effectually in Peter to the apostleship of the circumcision, the same was mighty in me toward the Gentiles.]*

Here the Apostle claims for himself the same authority which the false apostles attributed to the true apostles. Paul simply inverts their argument. "to bolster their evil cause," says he, "the false apostles quote the authority of the great apostles against me. I can quote the same authority against them, for the apostles are on my side. They gave me the right hand of fellowship. They approved my ministry. O my Galatians, do not believe the counterfeit apostles!"

What does Paul mean by saying that the gospel of the uncircumcision was committed unto him, and that of the circumcision to Peter? Did not Paul preach to the Jews, while Peter preached to the Gentiles also? Peter converted the Centurion. Paul's custom was to enter into the synagogues of the Jews, there to preach the Gospel. Why then should he call himself the apostle of the Gentiles, while he calls Peter the apostle of the circumcision?

Paul refers to the fact that the other apostles remained in Jerusalem until the destruction of the city became imminent. But Paul was especially called the apostle of the Gentiles. Even before the destruction of Jerusalem Jews dwelt here and there in the cities of the Gentiles. Coming to a city, Paul customarily entered the synagogues of the Jews and first brought to them as the children of the kingdom, the glad tidings that the promises made unto the fathers were fulfilled in Jesus Christ. When the Jews re-fused to hear these glad tidings, Paul turned to the Gentiles. He was the apostle of the Gentiles in a special sense, as Peter was the apostle of the Jews.

Paul reiterates that Peter, James, and John, the accepted pillars of the Church, taught him nothing, nor did they commit unto him the office of preaching the Gospel unto the Gentiles. Both the knowledge of the Gospel and the commandment to preach it to the Gentiles, Paul received directly from God. His case was parallel to that of Peter's, who was particularly commissioned to preach the Gospel to the Jews.

The apostles had the same charge, the identical Gospel. Peter did not proclaim a different Gospel, nor had he appointed his fellow apostles. They were equals. They were all taught of God. None was greater than the other, none could point to prerogatives above the other. To justify his usurped primacy in the Church the Pope claims that Peter was the chief of the apostles. This is an impudent falsehood.

VERSE 8. For he that wrought effectually in Peter.

With these words Paul refutes another argument of the false apostles. "What reason have the false apostles to boast that the Gospel of Peter was mighty, that he converted many, that he wrought great miracles, and that his very shadow healed the sick? These reports are true enough. But where did Peter acquire this power? God gave him the power. I have the same power. I received my power, not from Peter, but from the same God, the same Spirit who was mighty in Peter was mighty in me also." Luke corroborates Paul's statement in the words: "And God wrought special miracles by the hands of Paul, so that from his body were brought unto the sick handkerchiefs or aprons, and the diseases departed from them, and the evil spirits went out of them." (Acts 19:11, 12.)

To conclude, Paul is not going to be inferior to the rest of the apostles. Some secular writers put Paul's boasting down as carnal pride. But Paul had no personal interest in his boasting. It was with him a matter of faith and doctrine. The controversy was not about the glory of Paul, but the glory of God, the Word of God, the true worship of God, true religion, and the righteousness of faith.

VERSE 9. And when James, Cephas and John, who seemed to be pillars, perceived the grace that was given unto me, they gave to me and Barnabas the right hands of fellowship; that we should go unto the heathen, and they unto the circumcision.

"The fact is, when the apostles heard that I had received the charge to preach the Gospel to the Gentiles from Christ; when they heard that God had wrought many miracles through me; that great numbers of the Gen-tiles had come to the knowledge of Christ through my ministry; when they heard that the Gentiles had received the Holy Ghost without Law and circumcision, by the simple preaching of faith; when they heard all this they glorified God for His grace in me." Hence, Paul was justified in concluding that the apostles were for him, and not against him.

VERSE 9. The right hands of fellowship.

As if the apostles had said to him: "We, Paul, do agree with you in all things. We are companions in doctrine. We have the same Gospel with this difference, that to you is committed the Gospel for the uncircumcised, while the Gospel for the circumcision is committed unto us. But this difference ought not to hinder our friendship, since we preach one and the same Gospel."

VERSE 10. Only they would that we should remember the poor; the same which I also was forward to do.

Next to the preaching of the Gospel, a true and faithful pastor will take care of the poor. Where the Church is, there must be the poor, for the world and the devil persecute the Church and impoverish many faithful Christians.

Speaking of money, nobody wants to contribute nowadays to the maintenance of the ministry, and the erection of schools. When it comes to establishing false worship and idolatry, no cost is spared. True religion is ever in need of money, while false religions are backed by wealth.

VERSE 11. But when Peter was come to Antioch, I withstood him to the face, because he was to be blamed.

Paul goes on in his refutation of the false apostles by saying that in Antioch he withstood Peter in the presence of the whole congregation. As he stated before, Paul had no small matter in hand, but the chief article of the Christian religion. When this article is endangered, we must not hesitate to resist Peter, or an angel from heaven. Paul paid no regard to the dignity and position of Peter, when he saw this article in danger. It is written: "He that loveth father or mother or his own life, more than me, is not worthy of me." (Matt. 10:37.)

For defending the truth in our day, we are called proud and obstinate hypocrites. We are not ashamed of these titles. The cause we are called to defend, is not Peter's cause, or the cause of our parents, or that of the government, or that of the world, but the cause of God. In defense of that cause we must be firm and unyielding.

When he says, "to his face," Paul accuses the false apostles of slandering him behind his back. In his presence they dared not to open their mouths. He tells them, "I did not speak evil of Peter behind his back, but I withstood him frankly and openly."

Others may debate here whether an apostle might sin. I claim that we ought not to make Peter out as faultless. Prophets have erred. Nathan told David that he should go ahead and build the Temple of the Lord. But his prophecy was afterwards corrected by the Lord. The apostles erred in thinking of the Kingdom of Christ as a worldly state. Peter had heard the command of Christ, "Go ye into all the world, and preach the Gospel to every creature." But if it had not been for the heavenly vision and the special command of Christ, Peter would never have gone to the home of Cornelius. Peter also erred in this matter of circumcision. If Paul had not publicly censured him, all the believing Gentiles would have been compelled to receive circumcision and accept the Jewish law. We are not to attribute perfection to any man.

Luke reports "that the contention between Paul and Barnabas was so sharp that they departed asunder one from the other." The cause of their disagreement could hardly have been small since it separated these two, who had been joined together for years in a holy partnership. Such incidents are recorded for our consolation. After all, it is a comfort to know that even saints might and do sin.

Samson, David, and many other excellent men, fell into grievous sins. Job and Jeremiah cursed the day of their birth. Elijah and Jonah became weary of life and prayed for death. Such offenses on the part of the saints, the Scriptures record for the comfort of those who are near despair. No person has ever sunk so low that he cannot rise again. On the other hand, no man's standing is so secure that he may not fall. If Peter fell, I may fall. If he rose again, I may rise again. We have the same gifts that they had, the same Christ, the same baptism and the same Gospel, the same forgiveness of sins. They needed these saving ordinances just as much as we do.

VERSE 12. For before that certain came from James, he did eat with the Gentiles.

The Gentiles who had been converted to faith in Christ, ate meats forbidden by the Law. Peter, visiting some of these Gentiles, ate meat and drank wine with them, although he knew that these things were forbidden in the Law. Paul declared that he did likewise, that he became as a Jew to the Jews, and to them that were without law, as without law. He ate and drank with the Gentiles unconcerned about the Jewish Law. When he was with the Jews, however, he abstained from all things forbidden in the Law, for he labored to serve all men, that he "might by all means save some." Paul does not reprove Peter for transgressing the Law, but for disguising his attitude to the Law.

VERSE 12. But when they were come, he withdrew and separated himself, fearing them which were of the circumcision.

Paul does not accuse Peter of malice or ignorance, but of lack of principle, in that he abstained from meats, because he feared the Jews that came from James. Peter's weak attitude endangered the principle of Christian liberty. It is the deduction rather than the fact which Paul reproves. To eat and to drink, or not to eat and drink, is immaterial. But to make the deduction "If you eat, you sin; if you abstain you are righteous" — this is wrong.

Meats may be refused for two reasons. First, they may be refused for the sake of Christian love. There is no danger connected with a refusal of meats for the sake of charity. To bear with the infirmity of a brother is a good thing. Paul himself taught and exemplified such thoughtfulness. Secondly, meats may be refused in the mistaken hope of thereby obtaining righteousness. When this is the purpose of abstaining from meats, we say, let charity go. To refrain from meats for this latter reason amounts to a denial of Christ. If we must lose one or the other, let us lose a friend and brother, rather than God, our Father.

Jerome, who understood not this passage, nor the whole epistle for that matter, excuses Peter's action on the ground "that it was done in ignorance." But Peter offended by giving the impression that he was indorsing the Law. By his example he encouraged Gentiles and Jews to forsake the truth of the Gospel. If Paul had not reproved him, there would have been a sliding back of Christians into the Jewish religion, and a return to the burdens of the Law.

It is surprising that Peter, excellent apostle that he was, should have been guilty of such vacillation. In a former council at Jerusalem he practically stood alone in defense of the truth that salvation is by faith, without the Law. Peter at that time valiantly defended the liberty of the Gospel. But now by abstaining from meats forbidden in the Law, he went against his better judgment. You have no idea what danger there is in customs and ceremonies. They so easily tend to error in works.

VERSE 13. *And the other Jews dissembled likewise with him; insomuch that Barnabas also was carried away with their dissimulation.*

It is marvelous how God preserved the Church by one single person. Paul alone stood up for the truth, for Barnabas, his companion, was lost to him, and Peter was against him. Sometimes one lone person can do more in a conference than the whole assembly.

I mention this to urge all to learn how properly to differentiate between the Law and the Gospel, in order to avoid dissembling. When it come to the article of justification we must not yield, if we want to retain the truth of the Gospel.

When the conscience is disturbed, do not seek advice from reason or from the Law, but rest your conscience in the grace of God and in His Word, and proceed as if you had never heard of the Law. The Law has its place and its own good time. While Moses was in the mountain where he talked with God face to face, he had no law, he made no law, he administered no law. But when he came down from the mountain, he was a lawgiver. The conscience must be kept above the Law, the body under the Law.

Paul reproved Peter for no trifle, but for the chief article of Christian doctrine, which Peter's hypocrisy had endangered. For Barnabas and other Jews followed Peter's example. It is surprising that such good men as Peter, Barnabas, and others should fall into unexpected error, especially in a matter which they knew so well. To trust in our own strength, our own goodness, our own wisdom, is a perilous thing. Let us search the Scriptures with humility, praying that we may never lose the light of the Gospel. "Lord, increase our faith."

GALATIANS 2:14-16

VERSE 14. But when I saw that they walked not uprightly according to the truth of the gospel.

No one except Paul had his eyes open. Consequently it was his duty to reprove Peter and his followers for swerving from the truth of the Gospel. It was no easy task for Paul to reprimand Peter. To the honor of Peter it must be said that he took the correction. No doubt, he freely acknowledged his fault.

The person who can rightly divide Law and Gospel has reason to thank God. He is a true theologian. I must confess that in times of temptation I do not always know how to do it. To divide Law and Gospel means to place the Gospel in heaven, and to keep the Law on earth; to call the righteousness of the Gospel heavenly, and the righteousness of the Law earthly; to put as much difference between the righteousness of the Gospel and that of the Law, as there is difference between day and night. If it is a question of faith or conscience, ignore the Law entirely. If it is a question of works, then lift high the lantern of works and the righteousness of the Law. If your conscience is oppressed with a sense of sin, talk to your conscience. Say: "You are now groveling in the dirt. You are now a laboring ass. Go ahead, and carry your burden. But why don't you mount up to heaven? There the Law cannot follow you!" Leave the ass burdened with laws behind in the valley. But your conscience, let it ascend with Isaac into the mountain.

In civil life obedience to the law is severely required. In civil life Gospel, conscience, grace, remission of sins, Christ Himself, do not count, but only Moses with the lawbooks. If we bear in mind this distinction, neither Gospel nor Law shall trespass upon each other. The moment Law and sin cross into heaven, i.e., your conscience, kick them out. On the other hand, when grace wanders unto the earth, i.e., into the body, tell grace: "You have no business to be around the dreg and dung of this bodily life. You belong in heaven."

By his compromising attitude Peter confused the separation of Law and Gospel. Paul had to do something about it. He reproved Peter, not to embarrass him, but to conserve the difference between the Gospel which justifies in heaven, and the Law which justifies on earth.

The right separation between Law and Gospel is very important to know. Christian doctrine is impossible without it. Let all who love and fear God, diligently learn the difference, not only in theory but also in practice.

When your conscience gets into trouble, say to yourself: "There is a time to die, and a time to live; a time to learn the Law, and a time to un-learn the Law; a time to hear the Gospel, and a time to ignore the Gospel. Let the Law now depart, and let the Gospel enter, for now is the right time to hear the Gospel, and not the Law." However, when the conflict of con-science is over and external duties must be performed, close your ears to the Gospel, and open them wide to the Law.

VERSE 14. I said unto Peter before them all, If thou being a Jew, livest after the manner of Gentiles, and not as do the Jews, why compellest thou the Gentiles to live as do the Jews.

To live as a Jew is nothing bad. To eat or not to eat pork, what difference does it make? But to play the Jew, and for conscience' sake to abstain from certain meats, is a denial of Christ. When Paul saw that Peter's attitude tended to this, he withstood Peter and said to him: "You know that the observance of the law is not needed unto righteousness. You know that we are justified by faith in Christ. You know that we may eat all kinds of meats. Yet by your example you obligate the Gentiles to forsake Christ, and to return to the Law. You give them reason to think that faith is not sufficient unto salvation."

Peter did not say so, but his example said quite plainly that the obser-vance of the Law must be added to faith in Christ, if men are to be saved. From Peter's example the Gentiles could not help but draw the conclusion that the Law was necessary unto salvation. If this error had been permit-ted to pass unchallenged, Christ would have lost out altogether.

The controversy involved the preservation of pure doctrine. In such a controversy Paul did not mind if anybody took offense.

VERSE 15. We who are Jews by nature, and not sinners of the Gentiles.

"When we Jews compare ourselves with the Gentiles, we look pretty good. We have the Law, we have good works. Our rectitude dates from our birth, because the Jewish religion is natural to us. But all this does not make us righteous before God."

Peter and the others lived up to the requirements of the Law. They had circumcision, the covenant, the promises, the apostleship. But because of these advantages they were not to think themselves righteous before God. None of these prerogatives spell faith in Christ, which alone can justify a person. We do not mean to imply that the Law is bad. We do not condemn the Law, circumcision, etc., for their failure to justify us. Paul spoke dis-paragingly of these ordinances, because the false apostles asserted that mankind is saved by them without faith. Paul could not let this assertion stand, for without faith all things are deadly.

VERSE 16. Knowing that a man is not justified by the works of the law, but by the faith of Jesus Christ.

For the sake of argument let us suppose that you could fulfill the Law in the spirit of the first commandment of God: "Thou shalt love the Lord, thy God, with all thy heart." It would do you no good. A person simply is not justified by the works of the Law.

The works of the Law, according to Paul, include the whole Law, judicial, ceremonial, moral. Now, if the performance of the moral law cannot justify, how can circumcision justify, when circumcision is part of the ceremonial law?

The demands of the Law may be fulfilled before and after justification. There were many excellent men among the pagans of old, men who never heard of justification. They lived moral lives. But that fact did not justify them. Peter, Paul, all Christians, live up to the Law. But that fact does not justify them. "For I know nothing by myself," says Paul, "yet am I not hereby justified." (I Cor. 4:4.)

The nefarious opinion of the papists, which attributes the merit of grace and the remission of sins to works, must here be emphatically rejected. The papists say that a good work performed before grace has been obtained, is able to secure grace for a person, because it is no more than right that God should reward a good deed. When grace has already been obtained, any good work deserves everlasting life as a due payment and reward for merit. For the first, God is no debtor, they say; but because God is good and just, it is no more than right (they say) that He should reward a good work by granting grace for the service. But when grace has already been obtained, they continue, God is in the position of a debtor, and is in duty bound to reward a good work with the gift of eternal life. This is the wicked teaching of the papacy.

Now, if I could perform any work acceptable to God and deserving of grace, and once having obtained grace my good works would continue to earn for me the right and reward of eternal life, why should I stand in need of the grace of God and the suffering and death of Christ? Christ would be of no benefit to me. Christ's mercy would be of no use to me.

This shows how little insight the pope and the whole of his religious coterie have into spiritual matters, and how little they concern themselves with the spiritual health of their forlorn flocks. They cannot believe that the flesh is unable to think, speak, or do anything except against God. If they could see evil rooted in the nature of man, they would never entertain such silly dreams about man's merit or worthiness.

With Paul we absolutely deny the possibility of self merit. God never yet gave to any person grace and everlasting life as a reward for merit. The opinions of the papists are the intellectual pipe-dreams of idle pates, that serve no other purpose but to draw men away from the true worship of God. The papacy is founded upon hallucinations.

The true way of salvation is this. First, a person must realize that he is a sinner, the kind of a sinner who is congenitally unable to do any good thing. "Whatsoever is not of faith, is sin." Those who seek to earn the grace of God by their own efforts are trying to please God with sins. They mock God, and provoke His anger. The first step on the way to salvation is to repent.

The second part is this. God sent His only-begotten Son into the world that we may live through His merit. He was crucified and killed for us. By sacrificing His Son for us God revealed Himself to us as a merciful Father who donates remission of sins, righteousness, and life everlasting for Christ's sake. God hands out His gifts freely unto all men. That is the praise and glory of His mercy.

The scholastics explain the way of salvation in this manner. When a person happens to perform a good deed, God accepts it and as a reward for the good deed God pours charity into that person. They call it "charity infused." This charity is supposed to remain in the heart. They get wild when they are told that this quality of the heart cannot justify a person.

They also claim that we are able to love God by our own natural strength, to love God above all things, at least to the extent that we deserve grace. And, say the scholastics, because God is not satisfied with a literal performance of the Law, but expects us to fulfill the Law according to the mind of the Lawgiver, therefore we must obtain from above a quality above nature, a quality which they call "formal righteousness."

We say, faith apprehends Jesus Christ. Christian faith is not an inactive quality in the heart. If it is true faith it will surely take Christ for its object. Christ, apprehended by faith and dwelling in the heart, constitutes Christian righteousness, for which God gives eternal life.

In contrast to the doting dreams of the scholastics, we teach this: First a person must learn to know himself from the Law. With the prophet he will then confess: "All have sinned, and come short of the glory of God." And, "there is none that doeth good, no, not one." And, "against thee, thee only, have I sinned."

Having been humbled by the Law, and having been brought to a right estimate of himself, a man will repent. He finds out that he is so depraved, that no strength, no works, no merits of his own will ever deliver him from his guilt. He will then understand the meaning of Paul's words: "I am sold under sin"; and "they are all under sin."

At this state a person begins to lament: "Who is going to help me?" In due time comes the Word of the Gospel, and says: "Son, thy sins are forgiven thee. Believe in Jesus Christ who was crucified for your sins. Remember, your sins have been imposed upon Christ."

In this way are we delivered from sin. In this way are we justified and made heirs of everlasting life.

In order to have faith you must paint a true portrait of Christ. The scholastics caricature Christ into a judge and tormentor. But Christ is no law giver. He is the Lifegiver. He is the Forgiver of sins. You must believe that Christ might have atoned for the sins of the world with one single drop of His blood. Instead, He shed His blood abundantly in order that He might give abundant satisfaction for our sins.

Here let me say, that these three things, faith, Christ, and imputation of righteousness, are to be joined together. Faith takes hold of Christ. God accounts this faith for righteousness.

This imputation of righteousness we need very much, because we are far from perfect. As long as we have this body, sin will dwell in our flesh. Then, too, we sometimes drive away the Holy Spirit; we fall into sin, like Peter, David, and other holy men. Nevertheless we may always take recourse to this fact, "that our sins are covered," and that "God will not lay them to our charge." Sin is not held against us for Christ's sake. Where Christ and faith are lacking, there is no remission or covering of sins, but only condemnation.

After we have taught faith in Christ, we teach good works. "Since you have found Christ by faith," we say, "begin now to work and do well. Love God and your neighbor. Call upon God, give thanks unto Him, praise Him, confess Him. These are good works. Let them flow from a cheerful heart, because you have remission of sin in Christ."

When crosses and afflictions come our way, we bear them patiently. "For Christ's yoke is easy, and His burden is light." When sin has been pardoned, and the conscience has been eased of its dreadful load, a Christian can endure all things in Christ.

To give a short definition of a Christian: A Christian is not somebody chalks sin, because of his faith in Christ. This doctrine brings comfort to consciences in serious trouble. When a person is a Christian he is above law and sin. When the Law accuses him, and sin wants to drive the wits out of him, a Christian looks to Christ. A Christian is free. He has no master except Christ. A Christian is greater than the whole world.

VERSE 16. Even we have believed in Jesus Christ, that we might be justified.

The true way of becoming a Christian is to be justified by faith in Jesus Christ, and not by the works of the Law.

We know that we must also teach good works, but they must be taught in their proper turn, when the discussion is concerning works and not the article of justification.

Here the question arises by what means are we justified? We answer with Paul, "By faith only in Christ are we pronounced righteous, and not by works." Not that we reject good works. Far from it. But we will not allow ourselves to be removed from the anchorage of our salvation.

The Law is a good thing. But when the discussion is about justification, then is no time to drag in the Law. When we discuss justification we ought to speak of Christ and the benefits He has brought us.

Christ is no sheriff. He is "the Lamb of God, which taketh away the sin of the world." (John 1:29.)

VERSE 16. That we might be justified by the faith of Christ, and not by the works of the Law.

We do not mean to say that the Law is bad. Only it is not able to justify us. To be at peace with God, we have need of a far better mediator than Moses or the Law. We must know that we are nothing. We must understand that we are merely beneficiaries and recipients of the treasures of Christ.

So far, the words of Paul were addressed to Peter. Now Paul turns to the Galatians and makes this summary statement:

VERSE 16. For by the works of the law shall no flesh be justified.

By the term "flesh" Paul does not understand manifest vices. Such sins he usually calls by their proper names, as adultery, fornication, etc. By "flesh" Paul understands what Jesus meant in the third chapter of John, "That which is born of the flesh is flesh". (John 3:6.) "Flesh" here means the whole nature of man, inclusive of reason and instincts. "This flesh," says Paul, "is not justified by the works of the law."

The papists do not believe this. They say, "A person who performs this good deed or that, deserves the forgiveness of his sins. A person who joins this or that holy order, has the promise of everlasting life."

To me it is a miracle that the Church, so long surrounded by vicious sects, has been able to survive at all. God must have been able to call a few who in their failure to discover any good in themselves to cite against the wrath and judgment of God, simply took to the suffering and death of Christ, and were saved by this simple faith.

Nevertheless God has punished the contempt of the Gospel and of Christ on the part of the papists, by turning them over to a reprobate state of mind in which they reject the Gospel, and receive with gusto the abominable rules, ordinances, and traditions of men in preference to the Word of God, until they went so far as to forbid marriage. God punished them justly, because they blasphemed the only Son of God.

This is, then, our general conclusion: "By the works of the law shall no flesh be justified."

GALATIANS 2:17-21

VERSE 17. But if, while we seek to be justified by Christ, we ourselves also are found sinners, is therefore Christ the minister of sin? God forbid.

Either we are not justified by Christ, or we are not justified by the Law. The fact is, we are justified by Christ. Hence, we are not justified by the Law. If we observe the Law in order to be justified, or after having been justified by Christ, we think we must further be justified by the Law, we convert Christ into a legislator and a minister of sin.

"What are these false apostles doing?" Paul cries. "They are turning Law into grace, and grace into Law. They are changing Moses into Christ, and Christ into Moses. By teaching that besides Christ and His righteousness the performance of the Law is necessary unto salvation, they put the Law in the place of Christ, they attribute to the Law the power to save, a power that belongs to Christ only."

The papists quote the words of Christ: "If thou wilt enter into life, keep the commandments." (Matt. 19:17.) With His own words they deny Christ and abolish faith in Him. Christ is made to lose His good name, His office, and His glory, and is demoted to the status of a law enforcer, reproving, terrifying, and chasing poor sinners around.

The proper office of Christ is to raise the sinner, and extricate him from his sins.

Papists and Anabaptists deride us because we so earnestly require faith. "Faith," they say, "makes men reckless." What do these law-workers know about faith, when they are so busy calling people back from baptism, from faith, from the promises of Christ to the Law?

With their doctrine these lying sects of perdition deface the benefits of Christ to this day. They rob Christ of His glory as the Justifier of mankind and cast Him into the role of a minister of sin. They are like the false apostles. There is not a single one among them who knows the difference between law and grace.

We can tell the difference. We do not here and now argue whether we ought to do good works, or whether the Law is any good, or whether the Law ought to be kept at all. We will discuss these questions some other time. We are now concerned with justification. Our opponents refuse to make this distinction. All they can do is to bellow that good works ought to be done. We know that. We know that good works ought to be done, but we will talk about that when the proper time comes. Now we

47

are dealing with justification, and here good works should not be so much as mentioned.

Paul's argument has often comforted me. He argues: "If we who have been justified by Christ are counted unrighteous, why seek justification in Christ at all? If we are justified by the Law, tell me, what has Christ achieved by His death, by His preaching, by His victory over sin and death? Either we are justified by Christ, or we are made worse sinners by Him."

The Sacred Scriptures, particularly those of the New Testament, make frequent mention of faith in Christ. "Whosoever believeth in him is saved, shall not perish, shall have everlasting life, is not judged," etc. In open contradiction to the Scriptures, our opponents misquote, "He that believeth in Christ is condemned, because he has faith without works." Our opponents turn everything topsy-turvy. They make Christ over into a murderer, and Moses into a savior. Is not this horrible blasphemy?

VERSE 17. Is therefore Christ the minister of sin?

This is Hebrew phraseology, also used by Paul in II Corinthians, chapter 3. There Paul speaks of two ministers: The minister of the letter, and the minister of the spirit; the minister of the Law, and the minister of grace; the minister of death, and the minister of life. "Moses," says Paul, "is the minister of the Law, of sin, wrath, death, and condemnation."

Whoever teaches that good works are indispensable unto salvation, that to gain heaven a person must suffer afflictions and follow the example of Christ and of the saints, is a minister of the Law, of sin, wrath, and of death, for the conscience knows how impossible it is for a person to fulfill the Law. Why, the Law makes trouble even for those who have the Holy Spirit. What will not the Law do in the case of the wicked who do not even have the Holy Spirit?

The Law requires perfect obedience. It condemns all do not accomplish the will of God. But show me a person who is able to render perfect obedience. The Law cannot justify. It can only condemn according to the passage: "Cursed is every one that continueth not in all things which are written in the book of the law to do them."

Paul has good reason for calling the minister of the Law the minister of sin, for the Law reveals our sinfulness. The realization of sin in turn frightens the heart and drives it to despair. Therefore all exponents of the Law and of works deserve to be called tyrants and oppressors.

The purpose of the Law is to reveal sin. That this is the purpose of the Law can be seen from the account of the giving of the Law as reported in the nineteenth and twentieth chapters of Exodus. Moses brought the people out of their tents to have God speak to them personally from a cloud. But the people trembled with fear, fled, and standing aloof they begged Moses: "Speak thou with us, and we will hear: but let not God speak with us, lest we die." The proper office of the Law is to lead us out of our tents, in other words, out of the security of our self-trust, into the presence of God, that we may perceive His anger at our sinfulness.

All who say that faith alone in Christ does not justify a person, convert Christ into a minister of sin, a teacher of the Law, and a cruel tyrant who requires the impossible. All merit-seekers take Christ for a new lawgiver.

In conclusion, if the Law is the minister of sin, it is at the same time the minister of wrath and death. As the Law reveals sin it fills a person with the fear of death and condemnation. Eventually the conscience wakes up to the fact that God is angry. If God is angry with you, He will destroy and condemn you forever. Unable to stand the thought of the wrath and judgment of God, many a person commits suicide.

VERSE 17. God forbid.

Christ is not the minister of sin, but the Dispenser of righteousness and the Giver of life. Christ is Lord over law, sin and death. All who believe in Him are delivered from law, sin and death.

The Law drives us away from God, but Christ reconciles God unto us, for "He is the Lamb of God, that taketh away the sins of the world." Now if the sin of the world is taken away, it is taken away from me. If sin is taken away, the wrath of God and His condemnation are also taken away. Let us practice this blessed conviction.

VERSE 18. For if I build again the things which I destroyed, I make myself a transgressor.

"I have not preached to the end that I build again the things which I destroyed. If I should do so, I would not only be laboring in vain, but I would make myself guilty of a great wrong. By the ministry of the Gospel I have destroyed sin, heaviness of heart, wrath, and death. I have abolished the Law, so that it should not bother your conscience any more. Should I now once again establish the Law, and set up the rule of Moses? This is exactly what I should be doing, if I would urge circumcision and the performance of the Law as necessary unto salvation. Instead of righteousness and life, I would restore sin and death."

By the grace of God we know that we are justified through faith in Christ alone. We do not mingle law and grace, faith and works. We keep them far apart. Let every true Christian mark the distinction between law and grace, and mark it well.

We must not drag good works into the article of justification as the monks do who maintain that not only good works, but also the punishment which evildoers suffer for their wicked deeds, deserve everlasting life. When a criminal is brought to the place of execution, the monks try to comfort him in this manner: "You want to die willingly and patiently, and then you will merit remission of your sins and eternal life." What cruelty is this, that a wretched thief, murderer, robber should be so miserably misguided in his extreme distress, that at the very point of death he should be denied the sweet promises of Christ, and directed to hope for pardon of his sins in the willingness and patience with which he is about to suffer death for his crimes? The monks are showing him the paved way to hell.

These hypocrites do not know the first thing about grace, the Gospel, or Christ. They retain the appearance and the name of the Gospel and of Christ for a decoy only. In their confessional writings faith or the merit of Christ are never mentioned. In their writings they play up the merits of man, as can readily be seen from the following form of absolution used among the monks.

"God forgive thee, brother. The merit of the passion of our Lord Jesus Christ, and of the blessed Saint Mary, always a virgin, and of all the saints; the merit of thy order, the strictness of thy religion, the humility of thy profession, the contrition of thy heart, the good works thou hast done and shalt do for the love of our Lord Jesus Christ, be available unto thee for the remission of thy sins, the increase of thy worth and grace, and the reward of everlasting life. Amen."

True, the merit of Christ is mentioned in this formula of absolution. But if you look closer you will notice that Christ's merit is belittled, while monkish merits are aggrandized. They confess Christ with their lips, and at the same time deny His power to save. I myself was at one time entangled in this error. I thought Christ was a judge and had to be pacified by a strict adherence to the rules of my order. But now I give thanks unto God, the Father of all mercies, who has called me out of darkness into the light of His glorious Gospel, and has granted unto me the saving knowledge of Christ Jesus, my Lord.

We conclude with Paul, that we are justified by faith in Christ, without the Law. Once a person has been justified by Christ, he will not be unproductive of good, but as a good tree he will bring forth good fruit. A believer has the Holy Spirit, and the Holy Spirit will not permit a person to remain idle, but will put him to work and stir him up to the love of God, to patient suffering in affliction, to prayer, thanksgiving, to the habit of charity towards all men.

VERSE 19. For I through the law am dead to the law, that I might live unto God.

This cheering form of speech is frequently met with in the Scriptures, particularly in the writings of St. Paul, when the Law is set against the Law, and sin is made to oppose sin, and death is arrayed against death, and hell is turned loose against hell, as in the following quotations: "Thou hast led captivity captive," Psalm 68:18. "O death, I will be thy plagues; O grave, I will be thy destruction," Hosea 13:14. "And for sin, condemned sin in the flesh," Romans 8:3.

Here Paul plays the Law against the Law, as if to say: "The Law of Moses condemns me; but I have another law, the law of grace and liberty which condemns the accusing Law of Moses."

On first sight Paul seems to be advancing a strange and ugly heresy. He says, "I am dead to the law, that I might live unto God." The false apostles said the very opposite. They said, "If you do not live to the law, you are dead unto God."

The doctrine of our opponents is similar to that of the false apostles in Paul's day. Our opponents teach, "If you want to live unto God, you must live after the Law, for it is written, Do this and thou shalt live." Paul, on the other hand, teaches, "We cannot live unto God unless we are dead unto the Law." If we are dead unto the Law, the Law can have no power over us.

Paul does not only refer to the Ceremonial Law, but to the whole Law. We are not to think that the Law is wiped out. It stays. It continues to operate in the wicked. But a Christian is dead to the Law. For example, Christ by His resurrection became free from the grave, and yet the grave remains. Peter was delivered from prison, yet the prison remains. The Law is abolished as far as I am concerned, when it has driven me into the arms of Christ. Yet the Law continues to exist and to function. But it no longer exists for me.

"I have nothing to do with the Law," cries Paul. He could not have uttered anything more devastating to the prestige of the Law. He declares that he does not care for the Law, that he does not intend ever to be justified by the Law.

To be dead to the Law means to be free of the Law. What right, then, has the Law to accuse me, or to hold anything against me? When you see a person squirming in the clutches of the Law, say to him: "Brother, get things straight. You let the Law talk to your conscience. Make it talk to your flesh. Wake up, and believe in Jesus Christ, the Conqueror of Law and sin. Faith in Christ will lift you high above the Law into the heaven of grace. Though Law and sin remain, they no longer concern you, because you are dead to the Law and dead to sin."

Blessed is the person who knows how to use this truth in times of distress. He can talk. He can say: "Mr. Law, go ahead and accuse me as much as you like. I know I have committed many sins, and I continue to sin daily. But that does not bother me. You have got to shout louder, Mr. Law. I am deaf, you know. Talk as much as you like, I am dead to you. If you want to talk to me about my sins, go and talk to my flesh. Belabor that, but don't talk to my conscience. My conscience is a lady and a queen, and has nothing to do with the likes of you, because my conscience lives to Christ under another law, a new and better law, the law of grace."

We have two propositions: To live unto the Law, is to die unto God. To die unto the Law, is to live unto God. These two propositions go against reason. No law-worker can ever understand them. But see to it that you understand them. The Law can never justify and save a sinner. The Law can only accuse, terrify, and kill him. Therefore to live unto the Law is to die unto God. Vice versa, to die unto the Law is to live unto God. If you want to live unto God, bury the Law, and find life through faith in Christ Jesus.

We have enough arguments right here to conclude that justification is by faith alone. How can the Law effect our justification, when Paul so plainly states that we must be dead to the Law if we want to live unto God? If we are dead to the Law and the Law is dead to us, how can it possibly contribute anything to our justification? There is nothing left for us but to be justified by faith alone.

This nineteenth verse is loaded with consolation. It fortifies a person against every danger. It allows you to argue like this:

> *"I confess I have sinned."*
> *"Then God will punish you."*
> *"No, He will not do that."*
> *"Why not? Does not the Law say so?"*
> *"I have nothing to do with the Law."*
> *"How so?"*
> *"I have another law, the law of liberty."*
> *"What do you mean — 'liberty'?"*
> *"The liberty of Christ, for Christ has made me free from the Law that held me down. That Law is now in prison itself, held captive by grace and liberty."*

By faith in Christ a person may gain such sure and sound comfort, that he need not fear the devil, sin, death, or any evil. "Sir Devil," he may say, "I am not afraid of you. I have a Friend whose name is Jesus Christ, in whom I believe. He has abolished the Law, condemned sin, vanquished death, and destroyed hell for me. He is bigger than you, Satan. He has licked you, and holds you down. You cannot hurt me." This is the faith that overcomes the devil.

Paul manhandles the Law. He treats the Law as if it were a thief and a robber He treats the Law as contemptible to the conscience, in order that those who believe in Christ may take courage to defy the Law, and say: "Mr. Law, I am a sinner. What are you going to do about it?"

Or take death. Christ is risen from death. Why should we now fear the grave? Against my death I set another death, or rather life, my life in Christ.

Oh, the sweet names of Jesus! He is called my law against the Law, my sin against sin, my death against death. Translated, it means that He is my righteousness, my life, my everlasting salvation. For this reason was He made the law of the Law, the sin of sin, the death of death, that He might redeem me from the curse of the Law. He permitted the Law to accuse Him, sin to condemn Him, and death to take Him, to abolish the Law, to condemn sin, and to destroy death for me.

This peculiar form of speech sounds much sweeter than if Paul had said: "I through liberty am dead to the law." By putting it in this way, "I through the law am dead to the law," he opposes one law with another law, and has them fight it out.

In this masterly fashion Paul draws our attention away from the Law, sin, death, and every evil, and centers it upon Christ.

VERSE 20. I am crucified with Christ.

Christ is Lord over the Law, because He was crucified unto the Law. I also am lord over the Law, because by faith I am crucified with Christ.

Paul does not here speak of crucifying the flesh, but he speaks of that higher crucifying wherein sin, devil, and death are crucified in Christ and in me. By my faith in Christ I am crucified with Christ. Hence these evils are crucified and dead unto me.

VERSE 20. Nevertheless I live.

"I do not mean to create the impression as though I did not live before this. But in reality I first live now, now that I have been delivered from the Law, from sin, and death. Being crucified with Christ and dead unto the Law, I may now rise unto a new and better life."

We must pay close attention to Paul's way of speaking. He says that we are crucified and dead unto the Law. The fact is, the Law is crucified and dead unto us. Paul purposely speaks that way in order to increase the portion of our comfort.

VERSE 20. Yet not I.

Paul explains what constitutes true Christian righteousness. True Christian righteousness is the righteousness of Christ who lives in us. We must look away from our own person. Christ and my conscience must become one, so that I can see nothing else but Christ crucified and raised from the dead for me. If I keep on looking at myself, I am gone.

If we lose sight of Christ and begin to consider our past, we simply go to pieces. We must turn our eyes to the brazen serpent, Christ crucified, and believe with all our heart that He is our righteousness and our life. For Christ, on whom our eyes are fixed, in whom we live, who lives in us, is Lord over Law, sin, death, and all evil.

VERSE 20. But Christ liveth in me.

"Thus I live," the Apostle starts out. But presently he corrects himself, saying, "Yet not I, but Christ liveth in me." He is the form of my perfection. He embellishes my faith.

Since Christ is now living in me, He abolishes the Law, condemns sin, and destroys death in me. These foes vanish in His presence. Christ abiding in me drives out every evil. This union with Christ delivers me from the demands of the Law, and separates me from my sinful self. As long as I abide in Christ, nothing can hurt me.

Christ domiciling in me, the old Adam has to stay outside and remain subject to the Law. Think what grace, righteousness, life, peace, and salvation there is in me, thanks to that inseparable conjunction between Christ and me through faith!

Paul has a peculiar style, a celestial way of speaking. "I live," he says, "I live not; I am dead, I am not dead; I am a sinner, I am not a sinner; I have the Law, I have no Law." When we look at ourselves we find plenty of sin. But when we look at Christ, we have no sin. Whenever we separate the person of Christ from our own person, we live under the Law and not in Christ; we are condemned by the Law, dead before God.

Faith connects you so intimately with Christ, that He and you become as it were one person. As such you may boldly say: "I am now one with Christ. Therefore Christ's righteousness, victory, and life are mine." On the other hand, Christ may say: "I am that big sinner. His sins and his death are mine, because he is joined to me, and I to him."

Whenever remission of sins is freely proclaimed, people misinterpret it according to Romans 3:8, "Let us do evil, that good may come." As soon as people hear that we are not justified by the Law, they reason malicious-ly: "Why, then let us reject the Law. If grace abounds, where sin abounds, let us abound in sin, that grace may all the more abound." People who reason thus are reckless. They make sport of the Scriptures and slander the sayings of the Holy Ghost.

However, there are others who are not malicious, only weak, who may take offense when told that Law and good works are unnecessary for salvation. These must be instructed as to why good works do not justify, and from what motives good works must be done. Good works are not the cause, but the fruit of righteousness. When we have become righteous, then first are we able and willing to do good. The tree makes the apple; the apple does not make the tree.

VERSE 20. *And the life which I now live in the flesh I live by the faith of the Son of God.*

Paul does not deny the fact that he is living in the flesh. He performs the natural functions of the flesh. But he says that this is not his real life. His life in the flesh is not a life after the flesh.

"I live by the faith of the Son of God," he says. "My speech is no longer directed by the flesh, but by the Holy Ghost. My sight is no longer gov-erned by the flesh, but by the Holy Ghost. My hearing is no longer deter-mined by the flesh, but by the Holy Ghost. I cannot teach, write, pray, or give thanks without the instrumentality of the flesh; yet these activities do not proceed from the flesh, but from God."

A Christian uses earthly means like any unbeliever. Outwardly they look alike. Nevertheless there is a great difference between them. I may live in the flesh, but I do not live after the flesh. I do my living now "by the faith of the Son of God." Paul had the same voice, the same tongue, before and after his conversion. Before his conversion his tongue uttered blasphemies. But after his conversion his tongue spoke a spiritual, heav-enly language.

We may now understand how spiritual life originates. It enters the heart by faith. Christ reigns in the heart with His Holy Spirit, who sees, hears, speaks, works, suffers, and does all things in and through us over the protest and the resistance of the flesh.

VERSE 20. Who loved me, and gave himself for me.

The sophistical papists assert that a person is able by natural strength to love God long before grace has entered his heart, and to perform works of real merit. They believe they are able to fulfill the commandments of God. They believe they are able to do more than God expects of them, so that they are in a position to sell their superfluous merits to laymen, thereby saving themselves and others. They are saving nobody. On the contrary, they abolish the Gospel, they deride, deny, and blaspheme Christ, and call upon themselves the wrath of God. This is what they get for living in their own righteousness, and not in the faith of the Son of God.

The papists will tell you to do the best you can, and God will give you His grace. They have a rhyme for it:

"God will no more require of man, Than of himself perform he can."

This may hold true in ordinary civic life. But the papists apply it to the spiritual realm where a person can perform nothing but sin, because he is sold under sin.

Our opponents go even further than that. They say, nature is depraved, but the qualities of nature are untainted. Again we say: This may hold true in everyday life, but not in the spiritual life. In spiritual matters a person is by nature full of darkness, error, ignorance, malice, and perverseness in will and in mind.

In view of this, Paul declares that Christ began and not we. "He loved me, and gave Himself for me. He found in me no right mind and no good will. But the good Lord had mercy upon me. Out of pure kindness He loved me, loved me so that He gave Himself for me, that I should be free from the Law, from sin, devil, and death."

The words, "The Son of God who loved me, and gave Himself for me," are so many thunderclaps and lightning bolts of protest from heaven against the righteousness of the Law. The wickedness, error, darkness, ignorance in my mind and my will were so great, that it was quite impossible for me to be saved by any other means than by the inestimable price of Christ's death.

Let us count the price. When you hear that such an enormous price was paid for you, will you still come along with your cowl, your shaven pate, your chastity, your obedience, your poverty, your works, your merits? What do you want with all these trappings? What good are the works of all men, and all the pains of the martyrs, in comparison with the pains of the Son of God dying on the Cross, so that there was not a drop of His precious blood, but it was all shed for your sins. If you could properly evaluate this incomparable price, you would throw all your ceremonies, vows, works, and merits into the ash can. What awful presumption to imagine that there is any work good enough to pacify God, when to pacify God required the invaluable price of the death and blood of His own and only Son?

Verse 20. For me.

Who is this "me"? I, wretched and damnable sinner, dearly beloved of the Son of God. If I could by work or merit love the Son of God and come to Him, why should He have sacrificed Himself for me ? This shows how the papists ignore the Scriptures, particularly the doctrine of faith. If they had paid any attention at all to these words, that it was absolutely necessary for the Son of God to be given into death for me, they would never have invented so many hideous heresies.

I always say, there is no remedy against the sects, no power to resist them, except this article of Christian righteousness. If we lose this article we shall never be able to combat errors or sects. What business have they to make such a fuss about works or merits? If I, a condemned sinner, could have been purchased and redeemed by any other price, why should the Son of God have given Himself for me? Just because there was no other price in heaven and on earth big and good enough, was it necessary for the Son of God to be delivered for me. This He did out of His great love for me, for the Apostle says, "Who loved me."

Did the Law ever love me? Did the Law ever sacrifice itself for me? Did the Law ever die for me? On the contrary, it accuses me, it frightens me, it drives me crazy. Somebody else saved me from the Law, from sin and death unto eternal life. That Somebody is the Son of God, to whom be praise and glory forever.

Hence, Christ is no Moses, no tyrant, no lawgiver, but the Giver of grace, the Savior, full of mercy. In short, He is no less than infinite mercy and ineffable goodness, bountifully giving Himself for us. Visualize Christ in these His true colors. I do not say that it is easy. Even in the present diffusion of the Gospel light, I have much trouble to see Christ as Paul portrays Him. So deeply has the diseased opinion that Christ is a lawgiver sunk into my bones. You younger men are a good deal better off than we who are old. You have never become infected with the nefarious errors on which I suckled all my youth, until at the mention of the name of Christ I shivered with fear. You, I say, who are young may learn to know Christ in all His sweetness.

For Christ is Joy and Sweetness to a broken heart. Christ is a Lover of poor sinners, and such a Lover that He gave Himself for us. Now if this is true, and it is true, then are we never justified by our own righteousness.

Read the words "me" and "for me" with great emphasis. Print this "me" with capital letters in your heart, and do not ever doubt that you belong to the number of those who are meant by this "me." Christ did not only love Peter and Paul. The same love He felt for them He feels for us. If we cannot deny that we are sinners, we cannot deny that Christ died for our sins.

VERSE 21. I do not frustrate the grace of God.

Paul is now getting ready for the second argument of his Epistle, to the effect that to seek justification by works of the Law, is to reject the grace of God. I ask you, what sin can be more horrible than to reject the grace of God, and to refuse the righteousness of Christ? It is bad enough that we are wicked sinners and transgressors of all the commandments of God; on top of that to refuse the grace of God and the remission of sins offered unto us by Christ, is the worst sin of all, the sin of sins. That is the limit. There is no sin which Paul and the other apostles detested more than when a person despises the grace of God in Christ Jesus. Still there is no sin more common. That is why Paul can get so angry at the Antichrist, because he snubs Christ, rebuffs the grace of God, and refuses the merit of Christ. What else would you call it but spitting in Christ's face, pushing Christ to the side, usurping Christ's throne, and to say: "I am going to justify you people; I am going to save you." By what means? By masses, pilgrimages, pardons, merits, etc. For this is Antichrist's doctrine: Faith is no good, unless it is reinforced by works. By this abominable doctrine Antichrist has spoiled, darkened, and buried the benefit of Christ, and in place of the grace of Christ and His Kingdom, he has established the doctrine of works and the kingdom of ceremonies.

We despise the grace of God when we observe the Law for the purpose of being justified. The Law is good, holy, and profitable, but it does not justify. To keep the Law in order to be justified means to reject grace, to deny Christ, to despise His sacrifice, and to be lost.

VERSE 21. For if righteousness come by the law, then Christ is dead in vain.

Did Christ die, or did He not die? Was His death worth while, or was it not? If His death was worth while, it follows that righteousness does not come by the Law. Why was Christ born anyway? Why was He crucified? Why did He suffer? Why did He love me and give Himself for me? It was all done to no purpose if righteousness is to be had by the Law.

Or do you think that God spared not His Son, but delivered Him for us all, for the fun of it? Before I would admit anything like that, I would consign the holiness of the saints and of the angels to hell.

To reject the grace of God is a common sin, of which everybody is guilty who sees any righteousness in himself or in his deeds. And the Pope is the sole author of this iniquity. Not content to spoil the Gospel of Christ, he has filled the world with his cursed traditions, e.g., his bulls and indulgences.

We will always affirm with Paul that either Christ died in vain, or else the Law cannot justify us. But Christ did not suffer and die in vain. Hence, the Law does not justify.

If my salvation was so difficult to accomplish that it necessitated the death of Christ, then all my works, all the righteousness of the Law, are good for nothing. How can I buy for a penny what cost a million dollars?

The Law is a penny's worth when you compare it with Christ. Should I be so stupid as to reject the righteousness of Christ which cost me nothing, and slave like a fool to achieve the righteousness of the Law which God disdains?

Man's own righteousness is in the last analysis a despising and rejecting of the grace of God. No combination of words can do justice to such an outrage. It is an insult to say that any man died in vain. But to say that Christ died in vain is a deadly insult. To say that Christ died in vain is to make His resurrection, His victory, His glory, His kingdom, heaven, earth, God Himself, of no purpose and benefit whatever.

That is enough to set any person against the righteousness of the Law and all the trimmings of men's own righteousness, the orders of monks and friars, and their superstitions.

Who would not detest his own vows, his cowls, his shaven crown, his bearded traditions, yes, the very Law of Moses, when he hears that for such things he rejected the grace of God and the death of Christ. It seems that such a horrible wickedness could not enter a man's heart, that he should reject the grace of God, and despise the death of Christ. And yet this atrocity is all too common. Let us be warned. Everyone who seeks righteousness without Christ, either by works, merits, satisfactions, actions, or by the Law, rejects the grace of God, and despises the death of Christ.

GALATIANS 3:1-9

VERSE 1. O foolish Galatians.

The Apostle Paul manifests his apostolic care for the Galatians. Sometimes he entreats them, then again he reproaches them, in accordance with his own advice to Timothy: "Preach the word; be instant in season, out of season; reprove, rebuke, exhort."

In the midst of his discourse on Christian righteousness Paul breaks off, and turns to address the Galatians. "O foolish Galatians," he cries. "I have brought you the true Gospel, and you received it with eagerness and gratitude. Now all of a sudden you drop the Gospel. What has got into you?"

Paul reproves the Galatians rather sharply when he calls them "fools, bewitched, and disobedient." Whether he is indignant or sorry, I cannot say. He may be both. It is the duty of a Christian pastor to reprove the people committed to his charge. Of course, his anger must not flow from malice, but from affection and a real zeal for Christ.

There is no question that Paul is disappointed. It hurts him to think that his Galatians showed so little stability. We can hear him say: "I am sorry to hear of your troubles, and disappointed in you for the disgraceful part you played." I say rather much on this point to save Paul from the charge that he railed upon the churches, contrary to the spirit of the Gospel.

A certain distance and coolness can be noted in the title with which the Apostle addresses the Galatians. He does not now address them as his brethren, as he usually does. He addresses them as Galatians in order to remind them of their national trait to be foolish.

We have here an example of bad traits that often cling to individual Christians and entire congregations. Grace does not suddenly transform a Christian into a new and perfect creature. Dregs of the old and natural corruption remain. The Spirit of God cannot at once overcome human deficiency. Sanctification takes time.

Although the Galatians had been enlightened by the Holy Spirit through the preaching of faith, something of their national trait of foolishness plus their original depravity clung to them. Let no man think that once he has received faith, he can presently be converted into a faultless creature. The leavings of old vices will stick to him, be he ever so good a Christian.

VERSE 1. Who hath bewitched you, that ye should not obey the truth?

Paul calls the Galatians foolish and bewitched. In the fifth chapter he mentions sorcery among the works of the flesh, declaring that witchcraft and sorcery are real manifestations and legitimate activities of the devil. We are all exposed to the influence of the devil, because he is the prince and god of the world in which we live.

Satan is clever. He does not only bewitch men in a crude manner, but also in a more artful fashion. He bedevils the minds of men with hideous fallacies. Not only is he able to deceive the self-assured, but even those who profess the true Christian faith. There is not one among us who is not at times seduced by Satan into false beliefs.

This accounts for the many new battles we have to wage nowadays. But the attacks of the old Serpent are not without profit to us, for they confirm our doctrine and strengthen our faith in Christ. Many a time we were wrestled down in these conflicts with Satan, but Christ has always triumphed and always will triumph. Do not think that the Galatians were the only ones to be bewitched by the devil. Let us realize that we too may be seduced by Satan.

VERSE 1. Who hath bewitched you?

In this sentence Paul excuses the Galatians, while he blames the false apostles for the apostasy of the Galatians.

As if he were saying: "I know your defection was not willful. The devil sent the false apostles to you, and they tallied you into believing that you are justified by the Law. With this our epistle we endeavor to undo the damage which the false apostles have inflicted upon you."

Like Paul, we struggle with the Word of God against the fanatical Anabaptists of our day; and our efforts are not entirely in vain. The trouble is there are many who refuse to be instructed. They will not listen to reason; they will not listen to the Scriptures, because they are bewitched by the tricky devil who can make a lie look like the truth.

Since the devil has this uncanny ability to make us believe a lie until we would swear a thousand times it were the truth, we must not be proud, but walk in fear and humility, and call upon the Lord Jesus to save us from temptation.

Although I am a doctor of divinity, and have preached Christ and fought His battles for a long time, I know from personal experience how difficult it is to hold fast to the truth. I cannot always shake off Satan. I cannot always apprehend Christ as the Scriptures portray Him. Sometimes the devil distorts Christ to my vision. But thanks be to God, who keeps us in His Word, in faith, and in prayer.

The spiritual witchery of the devil creates in the heart a wrong idea of Christ. Those who share the opinion that a person is justified by the works of the Law, are simply bewitched. Their belief goes against faith and Christ.

VERSE 1. That ye should not obey the truth.

Paul incriminates the Galatians in worse failure. "You are so bewitched that you no longer obey the truth. I fear many of you have strayed so far that you will never return to the truth."

The apostasy of the Galatians is a fine indorsement of the Law, all right. You may preach the Law ever so fervently; if the preaching of the Gospel does not accompany it, the Law will never produce true conversion and heartfelt repentance. We do not mean to say that the preaching of the Law is without value, but it only serves to bring home to us the wrath of God. The Law bows a person down. It takes the Gospel and the preaching of faith in Christ to raise and save a person.

VERSE 1. Before whose eyes Jesus Christ hath been evidently set forth.

Paul's increasing severity becomes apparent as he reminds the Galatians that they disobeyed the truth in defiance of the vivid description he had given them of Christ. So vividly had he described Christ to them that they could almost see and handle Him. As if Paul were to say: "No artist with all his colors could have pictured Christ to you as vividly as I have pictured Him to you by my preaching. Yet you permitted yourselves to be seduced to the extent that you disobeyed the truth of Christ."

VERSE 1. Crucifed among you.

"You have not only rejected the grace of God, you have shamefully crucified Christ among you." Paul employs the same phraseology in Hebrews 6:6: "Seeing they crucify to themselves the Son of God afresh, and put him to an open shame."

It should make any person afraid to hear Paul say that those who seek to be justified by the Law, not only deny Christ, but also crucify Him anew. If those who seek to be justified by the Law and its works are crucifiers of Christ, what are they, I like to know, who seek salvation by the filthy rags of their own work-righteousness?

Can there be anything more horrible than the papacy, an alliance of people who crucify Christ in themselves, in the Church, and in the hearts of the believers?

Of all the diseased and vicious doctrines of the papacy the worst is this: "If you want to serve God you must earn your own remission of sins and everlasting life, and in addition help others to obtain salvation by giving them the benefit of your extra work-holiness." Monks, friars, and all the rest of them brag that besides the ordinary requirements common to all Christians, they do the works of supererogation, i.e., the performance of more than is required. This is certainly a fiendish illusion.

No wonder Paul employs such sharp language in his effort to recall the Galatians from the doctrine of the false apostles. He says to them: "Don't you realize what you have done? You have crucified Christ anew because you seek salvation by the Law."

True, Christ can no longer be crucified in person, but He is crucified in us when we reject grace, faith, free remission of sins and endeavor to be justified by our own works, or by the works of the Law.

The Apostle is incensed at the presumptuousness of any person who thinks he can perform the Law of God to his own salvation. He charges that person with the atrocity of crucifying anew the Son of God.

VERSE 2. This only would I learn of you, Received ye the Spirit by the works of the law, or by the hearing of faith?

There is a touch of irony in these words of the Apostle. "Come on now, my smart Galatians, you who all of a sudden have become doctors, while I seem to be your pupil: Received ye the Holy Ghost by the works of the Law, or by the preaching of the Gospel?" This question gave them something to think about, because their own experience contradicted them.

"You cannot say that you received the Holy Spirit by the Law. As long as you were servants of the Law, you never received the Holy Ghost. Nobody ever heard of the Holy Ghost being given to anybody, be he doctor or dunce, as a result of the preaching of the Law. In your own case, you have not only learned the Law by heart, you have labored with all your might to perform it. You most of all should have received the Holy Ghost by the Law, if that were possible. You cannot show me that this ever happened. But as soon as the Gospel came your way, you received the Holy Ghost by the simple hearing of faith, before you ever had a chance to do a single good deed." Luke verifies this statement of Paul in the Book of Acts: "While Peter yet spake these words, the Holy Ghost fell on all them which heard the word." (Acts 10:44.) "And as I began to speak, the Holy Ghost fell on them, as on us at the beginning." (Acts 11:15.)

Try to appreciate the force of Paul's argument which is so often repeated in the Book of Acts. That Book was written for the express purpose of verifying Paul's assertion, that the Holy Ghost comes upon men, not in response to the preaching of the Law, but in response to the preaching of the Gospel. When Peter preached Christ at the first Pentecost, the Holy Ghost fell upon the hearers, "and the same day there were added unto them about three thousand souls." Cornelius received the Holy Ghost while Peter was speaking of Christ. "The Holy Ghost fell on all of them which heard the word." These are actual experiences that cannot very well be denied. When Paul and Barnabas returned to Jerusalem and reported what they had been able to accomplish among the Gentiles, the whole Church was astonished, particularly when it heard that the uncircumcised Gentiles had received the Holy Ghost by the preaching of faith in Christ.

Now as God gave the Holy Ghost to the Gentiles without the Law by the simple preaching of the Gospel, so He gave the Holy Ghost also to the Jews, without the Law, through faith alone. If the righteousness of the Law were necessary unto salvation, the Holy Ghost would never have come to the Gentiles, because they did not bother about the Law. Hence the Law does not justify, but faith in Christ justifies.

How was it with Cornelius? Cornelius and his friends whom he had invited over to his house, do nothing but sit and listen. Peter is doing the talking. They just sit and do nothing. The Law is far removed from their thoughts. They burn no sacrifices. They are not at all interested in circumcision. All they do is to sit and listen to Peter. Suddenly the Holy Ghost enters their hearts. His presence is unmistakable, "for they spoke with tongues and magnified God."

Right here we have one more difference between the Law and the Gospel. The Law does not bring on the Holy Ghost. The Gospel, however, brings on the gift of the Holy Ghost, because it is the nature of the Gospel to convey good gifts. The Law and the Gospel are contrary ideas. They have contrary functions and purposes. To endow the Law with any capacity to produce righteousness is to plagiarize the Gospel. The Gospel brings donations. It pleads for open hands to take what is being offered. The Law has nothing to give. It demands, and its demands are impossible.

Our opponents come back at us with Cornelius. Cornelius, they point out, was "a devout man, and one that feared God with all his house, which gave much alms to the people and prayed God always." Because of these qualifications, he merited the forgiveness of sins, and the gift of the Holy Ghost. So reason our opponents.

I answer: Cornelius was a Gentile. You cannot deny it. As a Gentile he was uncircumcised. As a Gentile he did not observe the Law. He never gave the Law any thought. For all that, he was justified and received the Holy Ghost. How can the Law avail anything unto righteousness?

Our opponents are not satisfied. They reply: "Granted that Cornelius was a Gentile and did not receive the Holy Ghost by the Law, yet the text plainly states that he was a devout man who feared God, gave alms, and prayed. Don't you think he deserved the gift of the Holy Ghost?"

I answer: Cornelius had the faith of the fathers who were saved by faith in the Christ to come. If Cornelius had died before Christ, he would have been saved because he believed in the Christ to come. But because the Messiah had already come, Cornelius had to be apprized of the fact. Since Christ has come we cannot be saved by faith in the Christ to come, but we must believe that he has come. The object of Peter's visit was to acquaint Cornelius with the fact that Christ was no longer to be looked for, because He is here.

As to the contention of our opponents that Cornelius deserved grace and the gift of the Holy Ghost, because he was devout and just, we say that these attributes are the characteristics of a spiritual person who already has faith in Christ, and not the characteristics of a Gentile or of natural man. Luke first praises Cornelius for being a devout and God-fearing man, and then Luke mentions the good works, the alms and prayers of Cornelius. Our opponents ignore the sequence of Luke's words. They pounce on this one sentence, "which gave much alms to the people," because it serves their assertion that merit precedes grace. The fact is that Cornelius gave alms and prayed to God because he had faith. And because of his faith in the Christ to come, Peter was delegated to preach unto Cornelius faith in the Christ who had already come. This argument is convincing enough. Cornelius was justified without the Law, therefore the Law cannot justify.

Take the case of Naaman, the Syrian, who was a Gentile and did not belong to the race of Moses. Yet his flesh was cleansed, the God of Israel was revealed unto him, and he received the Holy Ghost. Naaman confessed his faith: "Behold, now I know that there is no God in all the earth, but in Israel." (II Kings 5:15.) Naaman does not do a thing. He does not busy himself with the Law. He was never circumcised. That does not mean that his faith was inactive. He said to the Prophet Elisha: "Thy servant will henceforth offer neither burnt offering nor sacrifice unto other gods, but unto the Lord. In this thing the Lord pardon thy servant, that when my master goeth into the house of Rimmon to worship there, and he leaneth on my hand, and I bow myself in the house of Rimmon: when I bow down myself in the house of Rimmon, the Lord pardon thy servant in this thing." What did the Prophet tell him?" Go in peace." The Jews do not like to hear the prophet say this. "What," they exclaim, "should this heathen be justified without the Law? Should he be made equal to us who are circumcised?"

Long before the time of Moses, God justified men without the Law. He justified many kings of Egypt and Babylonia. He justified Job. Nineveh, that great city, was justified and received the promise of God that He would not destroy the city. Why was Nineveh spared? Not because it fulfilled the Law, but because Nineveh believed the word of God. The Prophet Jonah writes: "So the people of Nineveh believed God, and proclaimed a fast, and put on sackcloth." They repented. Nowhere in the Book of Jonah do you read that the Ninevites received the Law of Moses, or that they were circumcised, or that they offered sacrifices.

All this happened long before Christ was born. If the Gentiles were justified without the Law and quietly received the Holy Spirit at a time when the Law was in full force, why should the Law count unto righteousness now, now that Christ has fulfilled the Law?

And yet many devote much time and labor to the Law, to the decrees of the fathers, and to the traditions of the Pope. Many of these specialists have incapacitated themselves for any kind of work, good or bad, by their rigorous attention to rules and laws. All the same, they could not obtain a quiet conscience and peace in Christ. But the moment the Gospel of Christ touches them, certainty comes to them, and joy, and a right judgment.

I have good reason for enlarging upon this point. The heart of man finds it difficult to believe that so great a treasure as the Holy Ghost is gotten by the mere hearing of faith. The hearer likes to reason like this: Forgiveness of sins, deliverance from death, the gift of the Holy Ghost, everlasting life are grand things. If you want to obtain these priceless benefits, you must engage in correspondingly great efforts. And the devil says, "Amen."

We must learn that forgiveness of sins, Christ, and the Holy Ghost, are freely granted unto us at the preaching of faith, in spite of our sinfulness. We are not to waste time thinking how unworthy we are of the blessings of God. We are to know that it pleased God freely to give us His unspeakable gifts. If He offers His gifts free of charge, why not take them? Why worry about our lack of worthiness? Why not accept gifts with joy and thanksgiving?

Right away foolish reason is once more offended. It scolds us. "When you say that a person can do nothing to obtain the grace of God, you foster carnal security. People become shiftless and will do no good at all. Better not preach this doctrine of faith. Rather urge the people to exert and to exercise themselves in good works, so that the Holy Ghost will feel like coming to them."

What did Jesus say to Martha when she was very "careful and troubled about many things" and could hardly stand to see her sister Mary sitting at the feet of Jesus, just listening? "Martha, Martha," Jesus said, "thou art careful and troubled about many things: but one thing is needful; and Mary hath chosen that good part, which shall not be taken away from her." A person becomes a Christian not by working, but by hearing. The first step to being a Christian is to hear the Gospel. When a person has accepted the Gospel, let him first give thanks unto God with a glad heart, and then let him get busy on the good works to strive for, works that really please God, and not man-made and self-chosen works.

Our opponents regard faith as an easy thing, but I know from personal experience how hard it is to believe. That the Holy Ghost is received by faith, is quickly said, but not so quickly done.

All believers experience this difficulty. They would gladly embrace the Word with a full faith, but the flesh deters them. You see, our reason always thinks it is too easy and cheap to have righteousness, the Holy Spirit, and life everlasting by the mere hearing of the Gospel.

VERSE 3. Are ye so foolish? having begun in the Spirit, are ye now made perfect by the flesh?

Paul now begins to warn the Galatians against a twofold danger. The first danger is: "Are ye so foolish, that after ye have begun in the Spirit, ye would now end in the flesh?"

"Flesh" stands for the righteousness of reason which seeks justification by the accomplishment of the Law. I am told that I began in the spirit under the papacy, but am ending up in the flesh because I got married. As though single life were a spiritual life, and married life a carnal life. They are silly. All the duties of a Christian husband, e.g., to love his wife, to bring up his children, to govern his family, etc., are the very fruits of the Spirit.

The righteousness of the Law which Paul also terms the righteousness of the flesh is so far from justifying a person that those who once had the Holy Spirit and lost Him, end up in the Law to their complete destruction.

VERSE 4. Have ye suffered so many things in vain?

The other danger against which the Apostle warns the Galatians is this: "Have ye suffered so many things in vain?" Paul wants to say: "Consider not only the good start you had and lost, but consider also the many things you have suffered for the sake of the Gospel and for the name of Christ. You have suffered the loss of your possessions, you have borne reproaches, you have passed through many dangers of body and life. You endured much for the name of Christ and you endured it faithfully. But now you have lost everything, the Gospel, faith, and the spiritual benefit of your sufferings for Christ's sake. What a miserable thing to endure so many amictions for nothing."

VERSE 4. If it be yet in vain.

The Apostle adds the afterthought: "If it be yet in vain. I do not despair of all hope for you. But if you continue to look to the Law for righteousness, I think you should be told that all your past true worship of God and all the afflictions that you have endured for Christ's sake are going to help you not at all. I do not mean to discourage you altogether. I do hope you will repent and amend."

VERSE 5. He therefore that ministereth to you the Spirit, and worketh miracles among you, doeth he it by the works of the law, or by the hearing of faith?

This argument based on the experience of the Galatians, pleased the Apostle so well that he returns to it after he had warned them against their twofold danger. "You have not only received the Spirit by the preaching of the Gospel, but by the same Gospel you were enabled to do things." "What things?" we ask. Miracles. At least the Galatians had manifested the striking fruits of faith which true disciples of the Gospel manifested in those days. On one occasion the Apostle wrote: "The kingdom of God is not in word, but in power." This "power" revealed itself not only in readiness of speech, but in demonstrations of the supernatural ability of the Holy Spirit.

When the Gospel is preached unto faith, hope, love, and patience, God gives His wonder-working Spirit. Paul reminds the Galatians of this. "God had not only brought you to faith by my preaching. He had also sanctified you to bring forth the fruits of faith. And one of the fruits of your faith was that you loved me so devotedly that you were willing to pluck out your eyes for me." To love a fellow-man so devotedly as to be ready to bestow upon him money, goods, eyes in order to secure his salvation, such love is the fruit of the Holy Spirit.

"These products of the Spirit you enjoyed before the false apostles misled you," the Apostle reminds the Galatians. "But you haven't manifested any of these fruits under the regime of the Law. How does it come that you do not grow the same fruits now? You no longer teach truly; you do not believe boldly; you do not live well; you do not work hard; you do not bear things patiently. Who has spoiled you that you no longer love me; that you are not now ready to pluck out your eyes for me? What has happened to cool your personal interest in me?"

The same thing happened to me. When I began to proclaim the Gospel, there were many, very many who were delighted with our doctrine and had a good opinion of us. And now? Now they have succeeded in making us so odious to those who formerly loved us that they now hate us like poison.

Paul argues: "Your experience ought to teach you that the fruits of love do not grow on the stump of the Law. You had not virtue prior to the preaching of the Gospel and you have no virtues now under the regime of the false apostles."

We, too, may say to those who misname themselves "evangelical" and flout their new-found liberty: Have you put down the tyranny of the Pope and obtained liberty in Christ through the Anabaptists and other fanatics? Or have you obtained your freedom from us who preach faith in Christ Jesus? If there is any honesty left in them they will have to confess that their freedom dates from the preaching of the Gospel.

VERSE 6. Even as Abraham believed God, and it was accounted to him for righteousness.

The Apostle next adduces the example of Abraham and reviews the testimony of the Scriptures concerning faith. The first passage is taken from Genesis 16:6: "And he believed in the Lord; and he counted it to him for righteousness." The Apostle makes the most of this passage. Abraham may have enjoyed a good standing with men for his upright life, but not with God. In the sight of God, Abraham was a condemned sinner. That he was justified before God was not due to his own exertions, but due to his faith. The Scriptures expressly state: "Abraham believed in the Lord; and he counted it to him for righteousness."

Paul places the emphasis upon the two words: Abraham believed. Faith in God constitutes the highest worship, the prime duty, the first obedience, and the foremost sacrifice. Without faith God forfeits His glory, wisdom, truth, and mercy in us. The first duty of man is to believe in God and to honor Him with his faith. Faith is truly the height of wisdom, the right kind of righteousness, the only real religion. This will give us an idea of the excellence of faith.

To believe in God as Abraham did is to be right with God because faith honors God. Faith says to God: "I believe what you say."

When we pay attention to reason, God seems to propose impossible matters in the Christian Creed. To reason it seems absurd that Christ should offer His body and blood in the Lord's Supper; that Baptism should be the washing of regeneration; that the dead shall rise; that Christ the Son of God was conceived in the womb of the Virgin Mary, etc. Reason shouts that all this is preposterous. Are you surprised that reason thinks little of faith? Reason thinks it ludicrous that faith should be the foremost service any person can render unto God.

Let your faith supplant reason. Abraham mastered reason by faith in the Word of God. Not as though reason ever yields meekly. It put up a fight against the faith of Abraham. Reason protested that it was absurd to think that Sarah who was ninety years old and barren by nature, should give birth to a son. But faith won the victory and routed reason, that ugly beast and enemy of God. Everyone who by faith slays reason, the world's biggest monster, renders God a real service, a better service than the religions of all races and all the drudgery of meritorious monks can render.

Men fast, pray, watch, suffer. They intend to appease the wrath of God and to deserve God's grace by their exertions. But there is no glory in it for God, because by their exertions these workers pronounce God an unmerciful slave driver, an unfaithful and angry Judge. They despise God, make a liar out of Him, snub Christ and all His benefits; in short they pull God from His throne and perch themselves on it.

Faith truly honors God. And because faith honors God, God counts faith for righteousness.

Christian righteousness is the confidence of the heart in God through Christ Jesus. Such confidence is accounted righteousness for Christ's sake. Two things make for Christian righteousness: Faith in Christ, which is a gift of God; and God's acceptance of this imperfect faith of ours for perfect righteousness. Because of my faith in Christ, God overlooks my distrust, the unwillingness of my spirit, my many other sins. Because the shadow of Christ's wing covers me I have no fear that God will cover all my sins and take my imperfections for perfect righteousness.

God "winks" at my sins and covers them up. God says: "Because you believe in My Son I will forgive your sins until death shall deliver you from the body of sin."

Learn to understand the constitution of your Christian righteousness. Faith is weak, but it means enough to God that He will not lay sin to our charge. He will not punish nor condemn us for it. He will forgive our sins as though they amount to nothing at all. He will do it not because we are worthy of such mercy. He will do it for Jesus' sake in whom we believe.

Paradoxically, a Christian is both right and wrong, holy and profane, an enemy of God and a child of God. These contradictions no person can harmonize who does not understand the true way of salvation. Under the papacy we were told to toil until the feeling of guilt had left us. But the authors of this deranged idea were frequently driven to despair in the hour of death. It would have happened to me, if Christ had not mercifully delivered me from this error.

We comfort the afflicted sinner in this manner: Brother, you can never be perfect in this life, but you can be holy. He will say: "How can I be holy when I feel my sins?" I answer: You feel sin? That is a good sign. To realize that one is ill is a step, and a very necessary step, toward recovery. "But how will I get rid of my sin?" he will ask. I answer: See the heaven-

ly Physician, Christ, who heals the broken-hearted. Do not consult that
Quackdoctor, Reason. Believe in Christ and your sins will be pardoned.
His righteousness will become your righteousness, and your sins will be-
come His sins.

On one occasion Jesus said to His disciples: "The Father loveth you."
Why? Not because the disciples were Pharisees, or circumcised, or particularly attentive to the Law. Jesus said: "The Father loveth you, because
ye have loved me, and have believed that I came out from God. It pleased
you to know that the Father sent me into the world. And because you
believed it the Father loves you." On another occasion Jesus called His
disciples evil and commanded them to ask for forgiveness.

A Christian is beloved of God and a sinner. How can these two contradictions be harmonized: I am a sinner and deserve God's wrath and punishment, and yet the Father loves me? Christ alone can harmonize these
contradictions. He is the Mediator.

Do you now see how faith justifies without works? Sin lingers in us,
and God hates sin. A transfusion of righteousness therefore becomes vi-
tally necessary. This transfusion of righteousness we obtain from Christ
because we believe in Him.

*VERSE 7. Know ye therefore that they which are of faith, the same are the
children of Abraham.*

This is the main point of Paul's argument against the Jews: The children of
Abraham are those who believe and not those who are born of Abraham's
flesh and blood. This point Paul drives home with all his might because
the Jews attached saving value to the genealogical fact: "We are the seed
and children of Abraham."

Let us begin with Abraham and learn how this friend of God was
justified and saved. Not because he left his country, his relatives, his father's house; not because he was circumcised; not because he stood ready
to sacrifice his own son Isaac in whom he had the promise of posterity.
Abraham was justified because he believed. Paul's argumentation runs
like this: "Since this is the unmistakable testimony of Holy Writ, why do
you take your stand upon circumcision and the Law? Was not Abraham,
your father, of whom you make so much, justified and saved without circumcision and the Law by faith alone?" Paul therefore concludes: "They
which are of faith, the same are the children of Abraham."

Abraham was the father of the faithful. In order to be a child of the
believing Abraham you must believe as he did. Otherwise you are merely the physical offspring of the procreating Abraham, i.e., you were conceived and born in sin unto wrath and condemnation.

Ishmael and Isaac were both the natural children of Abraham. By
rights Ishmael should have enjoyed the prerogatives of the firstborn, if
physical generation had any special value. Nevertheless he was left out
in the cold while Isaac was called. This goes to prove that the children of
faith are the real children of Abraham.

Some find fault with Paul for applying the term "faith" in Genesis 15:6 to Christ. They think Paul's use of the term too wide and general. They think its meaning should be restricted to the context. They claim Abraham's faith had no more in it than a belief in the promise of God that he should have seed.

We reply: Faith presupposes the assurance of God's mercy. This assurance takes in the confidence that our sins are forgiven for Christ's sake. Never will the conscience trust in God unless it can be sure of God's mercy and promises in Christ. Now all the promises of God lead back to the first promise concerning Christ: "And I will put enmity between thee and the woman, and between thy seed and her seed; it shall bruise thy head, and thou shalt bruise his heel." The faith of the fathers in the Old Testament era, and our faith in the New Testament are one and the same faith in Christ Jesus, although times and conditions may differ. Peter acknowledged this in the words: "Which neither our fathers nor we were able to bear? But we believe that through the grace of the Lord Jesus Christ we shall be saved, even as they." (Acts 15: 10, 11.) And Paul writes: "And did all drink the spiritual drink; for they drank of that spiritual Rock that followed them: and that Rock was Christ." (I Cor. 10 :4.) And Christ Himself declared: "Your father Abraham rejoiced to see my day: and he saw it and was glad." (John 8:56.) The faith of the fathers was directed at the Christ who was to come, while ours rests in the Christ who has come. Time does not change the object of true faith, or the Holy Spirit. There has always been and always will be one mind, one impression, one faith concerning Christ among true believers whether they live in times past, now, or in times to come. We too believe in the Christ to come as the fathers did in the Old Testament, for we look for Christ to come again on the last day to judge the quick and the dead.

VERSE 7. Know ye therefore that they which are of faith, the same are the children of Abraham.

Paul is saying: "You know from the example of Abraham and from the plain testimony of the Scriptures that they are the children of Abraham, who have faith in Christ, regardless of their nationality, regardless of the Law, regardless of works, regardless of their parentage. The promise was made unto Abraham, 'Thou shalt be a father of many nations'; again, 'And in thee shall all families of the earth be blessed.'" To prevent the Jews from misinterpreting the word "nations," the Scriptures are careful to say "many nations." The true children of Abraham are the believers in Christ from all nations.

VERSE 8. And the Scripture, foreseeing that God would justify the heathen through faith.

"Your boasting does not get you anywhere," says Paul to the Galatians, "because the Sacred Scriptures foresaw and foretold long before the Law was ever given, that the heathen should be justified by the blessed 'seed' of Abraham and not by the Law. This promise was made four hundred and thirty years before the Law was given. Because the Law was given so many years after Abraham, it could not abolish the promised blessing." This argument is strong because it is based on the exact factor of time. "Why should you boast of the Law, my Galatians, when the Law came four hundred and thirty years after the promise ?"

The false apostles glorified the Law and despised the promise made unto Abraham, although it antedated the Law by many years. It was after Abraham was accounted righteous because of his faith that the Scriptures first make mention of circumcision. "The Scriptures," says Paul, "meant to forestall your infatuation for the righteousness of the Law by installing the righteousness of faith before circumcision and the Law ever were ordained."

VERSE 8. Preached before the gospel unto Abraham, saying, In thee shall all nations be blessed.

The Jews misconstrue this passage. They want the term "to bless" to mean "to praise." They want the passage to read: In thee shall all the nations of the earth be praised. But this is a perversion of the words of Holy Writ. With the words "Abraham believed" Paul describes a spiritual Abraham, renewed by faith and regenerated by the Holy Ghost, that he should be the spiritual father of many nations. In that way all the Gentiles could be given to him for an inheritance.

The Scriptures ascribe no righteousness to Abraham except through faith. The Scriptures speak of Abraham as he stands before God, a man justified by faith. Because of his faith God extends to him the promise: "In thee shall all nations be blessed."

VERSE 9. So then they which be of faith are blessed with faithful Abraham.

The emphasis lies on the words "with faithful Abraham." Paul distinguishes between Abraham and Abraham. There is a working and there is a believing Abraham. With the working Abraham we have nothing to do. Let the Jews glory in the generating Abraham; we glory in the believing Abraham of whom the Scriptures say that he received the blessing of righteousness by faith, not only for himself but for all who believe as he did. The world was promised to Abraham because he believed. The whole world is blessed if it believes as Abraham believed.

The blessing is the promise of the Gospel. That all nations are to be blessed means that all nations are to hear the Gospel. All nations are to be declared righteous before God through faith in Christ Jesus. To bless simply means to spread abroad the knowledge of Christ's salvation. This is the office of the New Testament Church which distributes the promised blessing by preaching the Gospel, by administering the sacraments, by comforting the broken- hearted, in short, by dispensing the benefits of Christ.

The Jews exhibited a working Abraham. The Pope exhibits a working Christ, or an exemplary Christ. The Pope quotes Christ's saying recorded in John 13:15, "I have given you an example, that ye should do as I have done to you." We do not deny that Christians ought to imitate the example of Christ; but mere imitation will not satisfy God. And bear in mind that Paul is not now discussing the example of Christ, but the salvation of Christ.

That Abraham submitted to circumcision at the command of God, that he was endowed with excellent virtues, that he obeyed God in all things, was certainly admirable of him. To follow the example of Christ, to love one's neighbor, to do good to them that persecute you, to pray for one's enemies, patiently to bear the ingratitude of those who return evil for good, is certainly praiseworthy. But praiseworthy or not, such virtues do not acquit us before God. It takes more than that to make us righteous before God. We need Christ Himself, not His example, to save us. We need a redeeming, not an exemplary Christ, to save us. Paul is here speaking of the redeeming Christ and the believing Abraham, not of the model Christ or the sweating Abraham.

The believing Abraham is not to lie buried in the grave. He is to be dusted off and brought out before the world. He is to be praised to the sky for his faith. Heaven and earth ought to know about him and about his faith in Christ. The working Abraham ought to look pretty small next to the believing Abraham.

Paul's words contain the implication of contrast. When he quotes Scripture to the effect that all nations that share the faith of faithful Abraham are to be blessed, Paul means to imply the contrast that all nations are accursed without faith in Christ.

GALATIANS 3:10-19

VERSE 10. For as many as are of the works of the law are under the curse.

The curse of God is like a flood that swallows everything that is not of faith. To avoid the curse we must hold on to the promise of the blessing in Christ.

The reader is reminded that all this has no bearing upon civil laws, customs, or political matters. Civil laws and ordinances have their place and purpose. Let every government enact the best possible laws. But civil righteousness will never deliver a person from the condemnation of God's Law.

I have good reason for calling your attention to this. People easily mistake civil righteousness for spiritual righteousness. In civil life we must, of course, pay attention to laws and deeds, but in the spiritual life we must not think to be justified by laws and works, but always keep in mind the promise and blessing of Christ, our only Savior.

According to Paul everything that is not of faith is sin. When our opponents hear us repeat this statement of Paul, they make it appear as if we taught that governments should not be honored, as if we favored rebellion against the constituted authorities, as if we condemned all laws. Our opponents do us a great wrong, for we make a clear-cut distinction between civil and spiritual affairs.

Governmental laws and ordinances are blessings of God for this life only. As for everlasting life, temporal blessings are not good enough. Unbelievers enjoy more temporal blessings than the Christians. Civil or legal righteousness may be good enough for this life but not for the life hereafter. Otherwise the infidels would be nearer heaven than the Christians, for infidels often excel in civil righteousness.

VERSE 10. For it is written, Cursed is every one that continueth not in all things which are written in the book of the law to do them.

Paul goes on to prove from this quotation out of the Book of Deuteronomy that all men who are under the Law are under the sentence of sin, of the wrath of God, and of everlasting death. Paul produces his proof in a roundabout way. He turns the negative statement, "Cursed is every one that continueth not in all things which are written in the book of the law to do them," into a positive statement, "As many as are of the works of the law are under the curse." These two statements, one by Paul and the other by Moses, appear to conflict. Paul declares, "Whosoever shall do the works of the Law, is accursed." Moses declares, "Whosoever shall not do the works of the Law, is accursed." How can these two contradictory statements be reconciled? How can the one statement prove the other? No person can hope to understand Paul unless he understands the article of justification. These two statements are not at all inconsistent.

We must bear in mind that to do the works of the Law does not mean only to live up to the superficial requirements of the Law, but to obey the spirit of the Law to perfection. But where will you find the person who can do that? Let him step forward and we will praise him.

Our opponents have their answer ready-made. They quote Paul's own statement in Romans 2:13, "The doers of the law shall be justified." Very well. But let us first find out who the doers of the law are. They call a "doer" of the Law one who performs the Law in its literal sense. This is not to "do" the Law. This is to sin. When our opponents go about to perform the Law they sin against the first, the second, and the third commandments, in fact they sin against the whole Law. For God requires above all that we worship Him in spirit and in faith. In observing the Law for the purpose of obtaining righteousness without faith in Christ these law-workers go smack against the Law and against God. They deny the righteousness of God, His mercy, and His promises. They deny Christ and all His benefits.

In their ignorance of the true purpose of the Law the exponents of the Law abuse the Law, as Paul says, Romans 10:3, "For they, being ignorant of God's righteousness, and going about to establish their own righteousness, have not submitted themselves unto the righteousness of God."

In their folly our opponents rush into the Scriptures, pick out a sentence here and a sentence there about the Law and imagine they know all about it. Their work-righteousness is plain idolatry and blasphemy against God. No wonder they abide under the curse of God.

Because God saw that we could not fulfill the Law, He provided a way of salvation long before the Law was ever given, a salvation that He promised to Abraham, saying, "In thee shall all nations be blessed."

The very first thing for us to do is to believe in Christ. First, we must receive the Holy Spirit, who enlightens and sanctifies us so that we can begin to do the Law, i.e., to love God and our neighbor. Now, the Holy Ghost is not obtained by the Law, but by faith in Christ. In the last analysis, to do the Law means to believe in Jesus Christ. The tree comes first, and then come the fruits.

The scholastics admit that a mere external and superficial performance of the Law without sincerity and good will is plain hypocrisy. Judas acted like the other disciples. What was wrong with Judas? Mark what Rome answers, "Judas was a reprobate. His motives were perverse, therefore his works were hypocritical and no good." Well, well. Rome does admit, after all, that works in themselves do not justify unless they issue from a sincere heart. Why do our opponents not profess the same truth in spiritual matters? There, above all, faith must precede everything. The heart must be purified by faith before a person can lift a finger to please God.

There are two classes of doers of the Law, true doers and hypocritical doers. The true doers of the Law are those who are moved by faith in Christ to do the Law. The hypocritical doers of the Law are those who seek to obtain righteousness by a mechanical performance of good works while their hearts are far removed from God. They act like the foolish carpenter who starts with the roof when he builds a house. Instead of doing the Law, these law-conscious hypocrites break the Law. They break the very first commandment of God by denying His promise in Christ. They do not worship God in faith. They worship themselves.

No wonder Paul was able to foretell the abominations that Antichrist would bring into the Church. That Antichrists would come, Christ Himself prophesied, Matthew 24:5, "For many shall come in my name, saying, I am Christ; and shall deceive many." Whoever seeks righteousness by works denies God and makes himself God. He is an Antichrist because he ascribes to his own works the omnipotent capability of conquering sin, death, devil, hell, and the wrath of God. An Antichrist lays claim to the honor of Christ. He is an idolater of himself. The law- righteous person is the worst kind of infidel.

Those who intend to obtain righteousness by their own efforts do not say in so many words: "I am God; I am Christ." But it amounts to that. They usurp the divinity and office of Christ. The effect is the same as if they said, "I am Christ; I am a Savior. I save myself and others." This is the impression the monks give out.

The Pope is the Antichrist, because he is against Christ, because he takes liberties with the things of God, because he lords it over the temple of God.

I cannot tell you in words how criminal it is to seek righteousness before God without faith in Christ, by the works of the Law. It is the abomination standing in the holy place. It deposes the Creator and deifies the creature.

The real doers of the Law are the true believers. The Holy Spirit enables them to love God and their neighbor. But because we have only the first- fruits of the Spirit and not the tenth-fruits, we do not observe the Law perfectly. This imperfection of ours, however, is not imputed to us, for Christ's sake.

Hence, the statement of Moses, "Cursed is every one that continueth not in all things which are written in the book of the law to do them," is not contrary to Paul. Moses requires perfect doers of the Law. But where will you find them? Nowhere. Moses himself confessed that he was not a perfect doer of the Law. He said to the Lord: "Pardon our iniquity and our sin." Christ alone can make us innocent of any transgression. How so? First, by the forgiveness of our sins and the imputation of His righteousness. Secondly, by the gift of the Holy Ghost, who engenders new life and activity in us.

OBJECTIONS TO THE DOCTRINE OF FAITH DISPROVED

Here we shall take the time to enter upon the objections which our opponents raise against the doctrine of faith. There are many passages in the Bible that deal with works and the reward of works which our opponents cite against us in the belief that these will disprove the doctrine of faith which we teach.

The scholastics grant that according to the reasonable order of nature being precedes doing. They grant that any act is faulty unless it proceeds from a right motive. They grant that a person must be right before he can do right. Why don't they grant that the right inclination of the heart toward God through faith in Christ must precede works?

In the eleventh chapter of the Epistle to the Hebrews we find a catalogue of various works and deeds of the saints of the Bible. David, who killed a lion and a bear, and defeated Goliath, is mentioned. In the heroic deeds of David the scholastic can discover nothing more than outward achievement. But the deeds of David must be evaluated according to the personality of David. When we understand that David was a man of faith, whose heart trusted in the Lord, we shall understand why he could do such heroic deeds. David said: "The Lord that delivered me out of the paw of the lion, and out of the paw of the bear, he will deliver me out of the hand of this Philistine." Again: "Thou comest to me with a sword, and with a spear, and with a shield: but I come to thee in the name of the Lord of hosts, the God of the armies of Israel, whom thou hast defied. This day will the Lord deliver thee into mine hand; and I will smite thee, and take thine head from thee." (I Samuel 17:37, 45, 46.) Before David could achieve a single heroic deed he was already a man beloved of God, strong and constant in faith.

Of Abel it is said in the same Epistle: "By faith Abel offered unto God a more excellent sacrifice than Cain." When the scholastics come upon the parallel passage in Genesis 4:4 they get no further than the words: "And the Lord had respect unto Abel and to his offering." "Aha!" they cry. "See, God has respect to offerings. Works do justify." With mud in their eyes they cannot see that the text says in Genesis that the Lord had respect to the person of Abel first. Abel pleased the Lord because of his faith. Because the person of Abel pleased the Lord, the offering of Abel pleased the Lord also. The Epistle to the Hebrews expressly states: "By faith Abel offered unto God a more excellent sacrifice."

In our dealings with God the work is worth nothing without faith, for "without faith it is impossible to please him." (Hebrews 11:6.) The sacrifice of Abel was better than the sacrifice of Cain, because Abel had faith. As to Cain he had no faith or trust in God's grace, but strutted about in his own fancied worth. When God refused to recognize Cain's worth, Cain got angry at God and at Abel.

The Holy Spirit speaks of faith in different ways in the Sacred Scriptures. Sometimes He speaks of faith independently of other matters. When the Scriptures speak of faith in the absolute or abstract, faith refers to justification directly. But when the Scripture speaks of rewards and works it speaks of compound or relative faith. We will furnish some examples. Galatians 5:6, "Faith which worketh by love." Leviticus 18:5, "Which if a man do, he shall live in them." Matthew 19:17, "If thou wilt enter into life, keep the commandments." Psalm 37:27, "Depart from evil, and do good." In these and other passages where mention is made of doing, the Scriptures always speak of a faithful doing, a doing inspired by faith. "Do this and thou shalt live," means: First have faith in Christ, and Christ will enable you to do and to live.

In the Word of God all things that are attributed to works are attributable to faith. Faith is the divinity of works. Faith permeates all the deeds of the believer, as Christ's divinity permeated His humanity. Abraham was accounted righteous because faith pervaded his whole personality and his every action.

When you read how the fathers, prophets, and kings accomplished great deeds, remember to explain them as the Epistle to the Hebrews accounts for them: "Who through faith subdued kingdoms, wrought righteousness, obtained promises, stopped the mouths of lions." (Hebrews 11:33.) In this way will we correctly interpret all those passages that seem to support the righteousness of works. The Law is truly observed only through faith. Hence, every "holy," "moral" law-worker is accursed.

Supposing that this explanation will not satisfy the scholastics, supposing that they should completely wrap me up in their arguments (they cannot do it), I would rather be wrong and give all credit to Christ alone. Here is Christ. Paul, Christ's apostle, declares that "Christ hath redeemed us from the curse of the law, being made a curse for us." (Gal. 3:13.) I hear with my own ears that I cannot be saved except by the blood and death of Christ. I conclude, therefore, that it is up to Christ to overcome my sins, and not up to the Law, or my own efforts. If He is the price of my redemption, if He was made sin for my justification, I don't give a care if you quote me a thousand Scripture passages for the righteousness of works against the righteousness of faith. I have the Author and Lord of the Scriptures on my side. I would rather believe Him than all that riffraff of "pious" law- workers.

VERSE 11. But that no man is justified by the law in the sight of God, it is evident: for, The just shall live by faith.

The Apostle draws into his argument the testimony of the Prophet Habakkuk: "The just shall live by his faith." This passage carries much weight because it eliminates the Law and the deeds of the Law as factors in the process of our justification.

The scholastics misconstrue this passage by saying: "The just shall live by faith, if it is a working faith, or a faith formed and performed by charitable works." Their annotation is a forgery. To speak of formed or unformed faith, a sort of double faith, is contrary to the Scriptures. If charitable works can form and perfect faith I am forced to say eventually that charitable deeds constitute the essential factor in the Christian religion. Christ and His benefits would be lost to us.

VERSE 12. And the law is not of faith.

In direct opposition to the scholastics Paul declares: "The law is not of faith." What is this charity the scholastics talk so much about? Does not the Law command charity? The fact is the Law commands nothing but charity, as we may gather from the following Scripture passages: "Thou shalt love the Lord thy God with all thine heart, and with all thy soul, and with all thy might" (Deut. 6:5.) "Strewing mercy unto thousands of them that love me, and keep my commandments." (Exodus 20:6.) "On these two commandments hang all the law and the prophets." (Matt. 22:40.) If the law requires charity, charity is part of the Law and not of faith. Since Christ has displaced the Law which commands charity, it follows that charity has been abrogated with the Law as a factor in our justification, and only faith is left.

VERSE 12. But, The man that doeth them shall live in them.

Paul undertakes to explain the difference between the righteousness of the Law and the righteousness of faith. The righteousness of the Law is the fulfillment of the Law according to the passage: "The man that doeth them shall live in them." The righteousness of faith is to believe the Gospel according to the passage: "The just shall live by faith." The Law is a statement of debit, the Gospel a statement of credit. By this distinction Paul explains why charity which is the commandment of the Law cannot justify, because the Law contributes nothing to our justification.

Indeed, works do follow after faith, but faith is not therefore a meritorious work. Faith is a gift. The character and limitations of the Law must be rigidly maintained.

When we believe in Christ we live by faith. When we believe in the Law we may be active enough but we have no life. The function of the Law is not to give life; the function of the Law is to kill. True, the Law says: "The man that doeth them shall live in them." But where is the person who can do "them," i.e., love God with all his heart, soul, and mind, and his neighbor as himself?

Paul has nothing against those who are justified by faith and therefore are true doers of the Law. He opposes those who think they can fulfill the Law when in reality they can only sin against the Law by trying to obtain righteousness by the Law. The Law demands that we fear, love, and worship God with a true faith. The law-workers fail to do this. Instead, they invent new modes of worship and new kinds of works which God never commanded. They provoke His anger according to the passage: "But in vain they do worship me, teaching for doctrines the commandments of men." (Matthew 15:9.) Hence, the law-righteous workers are downright rebels against God, and idolaters who constantly sin against the first com-

mandment. In short, they are no good at-all though outwardly they seem
to be extremely solicitous of the honor of God.

We who are justified by faith as the saints of old, may be under the
Law, but we are not under the curse of the Law because sin is not imputed to us for Christ's sake. If the Law cannot be fulfilled by the believers,
if sin continues to cling to them despite their love for God, what can you
expect of people who are not yet justified by faith, who are still enemies
of God and His Word, like the unbelieving law-workers? It goes to show
how impossible it is for those who have not been justified by faith to fulfill
the Law.

> *VERSE 13. Christ hath redeemed us from the curse of the law, being made
> a curse for us: for it is written, Cursed is every one that hangeth on a tree.*

Jerome and his present-day followers rack their miserable brains over this
comforting passage in an effort to save Christ from the fancied insult of being called a curse. They say: "This quotation from Moses does not apply to
Christ. Paul is taking liberties with Moses by generalizing the statements
in Deuteronomy 21:23. Moses has 'he that is hanged.' Paul puts it 'every
one that hangeth.' On the other hand, Paul omits the words 'of God' in his
quotation from Moses: 'For he that is hanged is accursed of God.' Moses
speaks of a criminal who is worthy of death." "How," our opponents ask,
"can this passage be applied to the holy Christ as if He were accursed of
God and worthy to be hanged?" This piece of exegesis may impress the
naive as a zealous attempt to defend the honor and glory of Christ. Let us
see what Paul has in mind.

Paul does not say that Christ was made a curse for Himself. The accent
is on the two words "for us." Christ is personally innocent. Personally, He
did not deserve to be hanged for any crime of His own doing. But because
Christ took the place of others who were sinners, He was hanged like any
other transgressor. The Law of Moses leaves no loopholes. It says that a
transgressor should be hanged. Who are the other sinners? We are. The
sentence of death and everlasting damnation had long been pronounced
over us. But Christ took all our sins and died for them on the Cross. "He
was numbered with the transgressors; and he bare the sin of many, and
made intercession for the transgressors." (Isaiah 53:12.)

All the prophets of old said that Christ should be the greatest transgressor, murderer, adulterer, thief, blasphemer that ever was or ever could
be on earth. When He took the sins of the whole world upon Himself,
Christ was no longer an innocent person. He was a sinner burdened with
the sins of a Paul who was a blasphemer; burdened with the sins of a Peter
who denied Christ; burdened with the sins of a David who committed
adultery and murder, and gave the heathen occasion to laugh at the Lord.
In short, Christ was charged with the sins of all men, that He should pay
for them with His own blood. The curse struck Him. The Law found Him
among sinners. He was not only in the company of sinners. He had gone

so far as to invest Himself with the flesh and blood of sinners. So the Law judged and hanged Him for a sinner.

In separating Christ from us sinners and holding Him up as a holy exemplar, errorists rob us of our best comfort. They misrepresent Him as a threatening tyrant who is ready to slaughter us at the slightest provocation.

I am told that it is preposterous and wicked to call the Son of God a cursed sinner. I answer: If you deny that He is a condemned sinner, you are forced to deny that Christ died. It is not less preposterous to say, the Son of God died, than to say, the Son of God was a sinner.

John the Baptist called Him "the lamb of God, which taketh away the sin of the world." Being the unspotted Lamb of God, Christ was personally innocent. But because He took the sins of the world His sinlessness was defiled with the sinfulness of the world. Whatever sins I, you, all of us have committed or shall commit, they are Christ's sins as if He had committed them Himself. Our sins have to be Christ's sins or we shall perish forever.

Isaiah declares of Christ: "The Lord hath laid on him the iniquity of us all." We have no right to minimize the force of this declaration. God does not amuse Himself with words. What a relief for a Christian to know that Christ is covered all over with my sins, your sins, and the sins of the whole world.

The papists invented their own doctrine of faith. They say charity creates and adorns their faith. By stripping Christ of our sins, by making Him sinless, they cast our sins back at us, and make Christ absolutely worthless to us. What sort of charity is this? If that is a sample of their vaunted charity we want none of it.

Our merciful Father in heaven saw how the Law oppressed us and how impossible it was for us to get out from under the curse of the Law. He therefore sent His only Son into the world and said to Him: "You are now Peter, the liar; Paul, the persecutor; David, the adulterer; Adam, the disobedient; the thief on the cross. You, My Son, must pay the world's iniquity." The Law growls: "All right. If Your Son is taking the sin of the world, I see no sins anywhere else but in Him. He shall die on the Cross." And the Law kills Christ. But we go free.

The argument of the Apostle against the righteousness of the Law is impregnable. If Christ bears our sins, we do not bear them. But if Christ is innocent of our sins and does not bear them, we must bear them, and we shall die in our sins. "But thanks be to God, which giveth us the victory through our Lord Jesus Christ."

Let us see how Christ was able to gain the victory over our enemies. The sins of the whole world, past, present, and future, fastened themselves upon Christ and condemned Him. But because Christ is God He had an everlasting and unconquerable righteousness. These two, the sin of the world and the righteousness of God, met in a death struggle. Furiously the sin of the world assailed the righteousness of God. Righteousness is immortal and invincible. On the other hand, sin is a mighty tyrant who subdues all men. This tyrant pounces on Christ. But Christ's righteousness is unconquerable. The result is inevitable. Sin is defeated and righteousness triumphs and reigns forever.

In the same manner was death defeated. Death is emperor of the world. He strikes down kings, princes, all men. He has an idea to destroy all life. But Christ has immortal life, and life immortal gained the victory over death. Through Christ death has lost her sting. Christ is the Death of death.

The curse of God waged a similar battle with the eternal mercy of God in Christ. The curse meant to condemn God's mercy. But it could not do it because the mercy of God is everlasting. The curse had to give way. If the mercy of God in Christ had lost out, God Himself would have lost out, which, of course, is impossible.

"Christ," says Paul, "spoiled principalities and powers, He made a show of them openly, triumphing over them in it." (Col. 2:15.) They cannot harm those who hide in Christ. Sin, death, the wrath of God, hell, the devil are mortified in Christ. Where Christ is near the powers of evil must keep their distance. St. John says: "And this is the victory that overcometh the world, even our faith." (I John 5:4.)

You may now perceive why it is imperative to believe and confess the divinity of Christ. To overcome the sin of a whole world, and death, and the wrath of God was no work for any creature. The power of sin and death could be broken only by a greater power. God alone could abolish sin, destroy death, and take away the curse of the Law. God alone could bring righteousness, life, and mercy to light. In attributing these achievements to Christ the Scriptures pronounce Christ to be God forever. The article of justification is indeed fundamental. If we remain sound in this one article, we remain sound in all the other articles of the Christian faith. When we teach justification by faith in Christ we confess at the same time that Christ is God.

I cannot get over the blindness of the Pope's theologians. To imagine that the mighty forces of sin, death, and the curse can be vanquished by the righteousness of man's paltry works, by fasting, pilgrimages, masses, vows, and such gewgaws. These blind leaders of the blind turn the poor people over to the mercy of sin, death, and the devil. What chance has a defenseless human creature against these powers of darkness? They train sinners who are ten times worse than any thief, whore, murderer. The divine power of God alone can destroy sin and death, and create righteousness and life.

When we hear that Christ was made a curse for us, let us believe it with joy and assurance. By faith Christ changes places with us. He gets our sins, we get His holiness.

By faith alone can we become righteous, for faith invests us with the sinlessness of Christ. The more fully we believe this, the fuller will be our joy. If you believe that sin, death, and the curse are void, why, they are null, zero. Whenever sin and death make you nervous write it down as an illusion of the devil. There is no sin now, no curse, no death, no devil because Christ has done away with them. This fact is sure. There is nothing wrong with the fact. The defect lies in our lack of faith.

In the Apostolic Creed we confess: "I believe in the holy Christian Church." That means, I believe that there is no sin, no curse, no evil in the Church of God. Faith says: "I believe that." But if you want to believe your eyes you will find many shortcomings and offenses in the members of the holy Church. You see them succumb to temptation, you see them weak in faith, you see them giving way to anger, envy, and other evil dispositions. "How can the Church be holy?" you ask. It is with the Christian Church as it is with the individual Christian. If I examine myself I find enough unholiness to shock me. But when I look at Christ in me I find that I am altogether holy. And so it is with the Church.

Holy Writ does not say that Christ was under the curse. It says directly that Christ was made a curse. In II Corinthians 5:21 Paul writes: "For he (God) hath made him (Christ) to be sin for us, who knew no sin; that we might be made the righteousness of God in him." Although this and similar passages may be properly explained by saying that Christ was made a sacrifice for the curse and for sin, yet in my judgment it is better to leave these passages stand as they read: Christ was made sin itself; Christ was made the curse itself. When a sinner gets wise to himself he does not only feel miserable, he feels like misery personified; he does not only feel like a sinner, he feels like sin itself.

To finish with this verse: All evils would have overwhelmed us, as they shall overwhelm the unbelievers forever, if Christ had not become the great transgressor and guilty bearer of all our sins. The sins of the world got Him down for a moment. They came around Him like water. Of Christ, the Old Testament Prophet complained: "Thy fierce wrath goeth over me; thy terrors have cut me off." (Psalm 88 16.) By Christ's salvation we have been delivered from the terrors of God to a life of eternal felicity.

VERSE 14. That the blessing of Abraham might come, on the Gentiles through Jesus Christ.

Paul always keeps this text before him: "In thy seed shall all the nations of the earth be blessed." The blessing promised unto Abraham could come upon the Gentiles only by Christ, the seed of Abraham. To become a blessing unto all nations Christ had to be made a curse to take away the curse from the nations of the earth. The merit that we plead, and the work that we proffer is Christ who was made a curse for us.

Let us become expert in the art of transferring our sins, our death, and every evil from ourselves to Christ; and Christ's righteousness and blessing from Christ to ourselves.

VERSE 14. That we might receive the promise of the Spirit through faith.

"The promise of the Spirit" is Hebrew for "the promised Spirit." The Spirit spells freedom from the Law, sin, death, the curse, hell, and the judgment of God. No merits are mentioned in connection with this promise of the Spirit and all the blessings that go with Him. This Spirit of many blessings is received by faith alone. Faith alone builds on the promises of God, as Paul says in this verse.

Long ago the prophets visualized the happy changes Christ would effect in all things. Despite the fact that the Jews had the Law of God they never ceased to look longingly for Christ. After Moses no prophet or king added a single law to the Book. Any changes or additions were deferred to the time of Christ's coming. Moses told the people: "The Lord thy God will raise up unto thee a Prophet from the midst of thee, of thy brethren, like unto me; unto him ye shall hearken." (Deut. 18:15.)

God's people of old felt that the Law of Moses could not be improved upon until the Messiah would bring better things than the Law, i.e., grace and remission of sins.

> VERSE 15. *Brethren, I speak after the manner of men; Though it be but a man's covenant, yet if it be confirmed, no man disannulleth, or addeth thereto.*

After the preceding, well-taken argument, Paul offers another based on the similarity between a man's testament and God's testament. A man's testament seems too weak a premise for the Apostle to argue from in confirmation of so important a matter as justification. We ought to prove earthly things by heavenly things, and not heavenly things by earthly things. But where the earthly thing is an ordinance of God we may use it to prove divine matters. In Matthew 7:11 Christ Himself argued from earthly to heavenly things when He said: "If ye then, being evil, know how to give good gifts to your children; how much more shall your Father which is in heaven give good things to them that ask him?"

To come to Paul's argument. Civil law, which is God's ordinance, prohibits tampering with any testament of man. Any person's last will and testament must be respected. Paul asks: "Why is it that man's last will is scrupulously respected and not God's testament? You would not think of breaking faith with a man's testament. Why do you not keep faith with God's testament?"

The Apostle says that he is speaking after the manner of men. He means to say: "I will give you an illustration from the customs of men. If a man's last will is respected. and it is, how much more ought the testament of God be honored: 'In thy seed shall all the nations of the earth be blessed.' When Christ died, this testament was sealed by His blood. After His death the testament was opened, it was published to the nations. No man ought to alter God's testament as the false apostles do who substitute the Law and traditions of men for the testament of God."

As the false prophets tampered with God's testament in the days of Paul, so many do in our day. They will observe human laws punctiliously, but the laws of God they transgress without the flicker of an eyelid. But

the time will come when they will find out that it is no joke to pervert the
testament of God.

*VERSE 16. Now to Abraham and his seed were the promises made. He saith
not, And to seeds, as of many; but as of one, And to thy seed, which is Christ.*

The word testament is another name for the promise that God made unto
Abraham concerning Christ. A testament is not a law, but an inheritance.
Heirs do not look for laws and assessments when they open a last will;
they look for grants and favors. The testament which God made out to
Abraham did not contain laws. It contained promises of great spiritual
blessings.

The promises were made in view of Christ, in one seed, not in many
seeds. The Jews will not accept this interpretation. They insist that the
singular "seed" is put for the plural "seeds." We prefer the interpretation
of Paul, who makes a fine case for Christ and for us out of the singular
"seed," and is after all inspired to do so by the Holy Ghost.

*VERSE 17. And this I say, that the covenant, that was confirmed before
of God in Christ, the law which was four hundred and thirty years after,
cannot disannul, that it should make the promise of none effect.*

The Jews assert that God was not satisfied with His promises, but after
four hundred and thirty years He gave the Law. "God," they say, "must
have mistrusted His own promises, and considered them inadequate for
salvation. Therefore He added to His promises something better, the Law.
The Law," they say, "canceled the promises."

Paul answers: "The Law was given four hundred and thirty years
after the promise was made to Abraham. The Law could not cancel the
promise because the promise was the testament of God, confirmed by God
in Christ many years before the Law. What God has once promised He
does not take back. Every promise of God is a ratified promise."

Why was the Law added to the promise? Not to serve as a medium by
which the promise might be obtained. The Law was added for these reasons: That there might be in the world a special people, rigidly controlled
by the Law, a people out of which Christ should be born in due time;
and that men burdened by many laws might sigh and long for Him, their
Redeemer, the seed of Abraham. Even the ceremonies prescribed by the
Law foreshadowed Christ. Therefore the Law was never meant to cancel
the promise of God. The Law was meant to confirm the promise until the
time should come when God would open His testament in the Gospel of
Jesus Christ.

God did well in giving the promise so many years before the Law, that
it may never be said that righteousness is granted through the Law and
not through the promise. If God had meant for us to be justified by the
Law, He would have given the Law four hundred and thirty years before
the promise, at least He would have given the Law at the same time He
gave the promise. But He never breathed a word about the Law until four

hundred years after. The promise is therefore better than the Law. The Law does not cancel the promise, but faith in the promised Christ cancels the Law.

The Apostle is careful to mention the exact number of four hundred and thirty years. The wide divergence in the time between the promise and the Law helps to clinch Paul's argument that righteousness is not obtained by the Law.

Let me illustrate. A man of great wealth adopts a strange lad for his son. Remember, he does not owe the lad anything. In due time he appoints the lad heir to his entire fortune. Several years later the old man asks the lad to do something for him. And the young lad does it. Can the lad then go around and say that he deserved the inheritance by his obedience to the old man's request? How can anybody say that righteousness is obtained by obedience to the Law when the Law was given four hundred and thirty years after God's promise of the blessing?

One thing is certain, Abraham was never justified by the Law, for the simple reason that the Law was not in his day. If the Law was non-existent how could Abraham obtain righteousness by the Law? Abraham had nothing else to go by but the promise. This promise he believed and that was counted unto him for righteousness. If the father obtained righteousness through faith, the children get it the same way.

We use the argument of time also. We say our sins were taken away by the death of Christ fifteen hundred years ago, long before there were any religious orders, canons, or rules of penance, merits, etc. What did people do about their sins before these new inventions were hatched up?

Paul finds his arguments for the righteousness of faith everywhere. Even the element of time serves to build his case against the false apostles. Let us fortify our conscience with similar arguments. They help us in the trials of our faith. They turn our attention from the Law to the promises, from sin to righteousness; from death to life.

It is not for nothing that Paul bears down on this argument. He foresaw this confusion of the promise and the Law creeping into the Church. Accustom yourself to separate Law and Gospel even in regard to time. When the Law comes to pay your conscience a visit, say: "Mister Law, you come too soon. The four hundred and thirty years aren't up yet. When they are up, you come again. Won't you?"

VERSE 18. For if the inheritance be of the law, it is no more of promise.

In Romans 4:14, the Apostle writes: "For if they which are made of the law be heirs, faith is made void, and the promise made of none effect." It cannot be otherwise. That the Law is something entirely different from the promise is plain. The Law thunders: "Thou shalt, thou shalt not." The promise of the "seed" pleads: "Take this gift of God." If the inheritance of the gifts of God were obtained by the Law, God would be a liar. We would have the right to ask Him: "Why did you make this promise in the first place: 'In thy seed shall all the nations of the earth be blessed'? Why did you not say: 'In thy works thou shalt be blessed'?"

VERSE 18. But God gave it to Abraham by promise.

So much is certain, before the Law ever existed, God gave Abraham the inheritance or blessing by the promise. In other words, God granted unto Abraham remission of sins, righteousness, salvation, and everlasting life. And not only to Abraham but to all believers, because God said: "In thy seed shall all the nations of the earth be blessed." The blessing was given unconditionally. The Law had no chance to butt in because Moses was not yet born. "How then can you say that righteousness is obtained by the Law?"

The Apostle now goes to work to explain the province and purpose of the Law.

VERSE 19. Wherefore then serveth the law?

The question naturally arises: If the Law was not given for righteousness or salvation, why was it given? Why did God give the Law in the first place if it cannot justify a person?

The Jews believed if they kept the Law they would be saved. When they heard that the Gospel proclaimed a Christ who had come into the world to save sinners and not the righteous; when they heard that sinners were to enter the kingdom of heaven before the righteous, the Jews were very much put out. They murmured: "These last have wrought but one hour, and thou hast made them equal unto us, which have borne the burden and heat of the day." (Matthew 20:12.) They complained that the heathen who at one time had been worshipers of idols obtained grace without the drudgery of the Law that was theirs.

Today we hear the same complaints. "What was the use of our having lived in a cloister, twenty, thirty, forty years; what was the sense of having vowed chastity, poverty, obedience; what good are all the masses and canonical hours that we read; what profit is there in fasting, praying, etc., if any man or woman, any beggar or scour woman is to be made equal to us, or even be considered more acceptable unto God than we?"

Reason takes offense at the statement of Paul: "The law was added because of transgressions." People say that Paul abrogated the Law, that he is a radical, that he blasphemed God when he said that. People say: "We might as well live like wild people if the Law does not count. Let us abound in sin that grace may abound. Let us do evil that good may come of it."

What are we to do? Such scoffing distresses us, but we cannot stop it. Christ Himself was accused of being a blasphemer and rebel. Paul and all the other apostles were told the same things. Let the scoffers slander us, let them spare us not. But we must not on their account keep silent. We must speak frankly in order that afflicted consciences may find surcease. Neither are we to pay any attention to the foolish and ungodly people for abusing our doctrine. They are the kind that would scoff, Law or no Law.

Our first consideration must be the comfort of troubled consciences, that they may not perish with the multitudes.

When he saw that some were offended at his doctrine, while others found in it encouragement to live after the flesh, Paul comforted himself with the thought that it was his duty to preach the Gospel to the elect of God, and that for their sake he must endure all things. Like Paul we also do all these things for the sake of God's elect. As for the scoffers and skeptics, I am so disgusted with them that in all my life I would not open my mouth for them once. I wish that they were back there where they belong under the iron heel of the Pope.

People foolish but wise in their conceits jump to the conclusion: If the Law does not justify, it is good for nothing. How about that? Because money does not justify, would you say that money is good for nothing? Because the eyes do not justify, would you have them taken out? Because the Law does not justify it does not follow that the Law is without value. We must find and define the proper purpose of the Law. We do not off-hand condemn the Law because we say it does not justify.

We say with Paul that the Law is good if it is used properly. Within its proper sphere the Law is an excellent thing. But if we ascribe to the Law functions for which it was never intended, we pervert not only the Law but also the Gospel.

It is the universal impression that righteousness is obtained through the deeds of the Law. This impression is instinctive and therefore doubly dangerous. Gross sins and vices may be recognized or else repressed by the threat of punishment. But this sin, this opinion of man's own righteousness refuses to be classified as sin. It wants to be esteemed as high-class religion. Hence, it constitutes the mighty influence of the devil over the entire world. In order to point out the true office of the Law, and thus to stamp out that false impression of the righteousness of the Law, Paul answers the question: "Wherefore then serveth the Law?" with the words:

VERSE 19. It was added because of transgressions.

All things differ. Let everything serve its unique purpose. Let the sun shine by day, the moon and the stars by night. Let the sea furnish fish, the earth grain, the woods trees, etc. Let the Law also serve its unique purpose. It must not step out of character and take the place of anything else. What is the function of the Law? "Transgression," answers the Apostle.

THE TWOFOLD PURPOSE OF THE LAW

The Law has a twofold purpose. One purpose is civil. God has ordained civil laws to punish crime. Every law is given to restrain sin. Does it not then make men righteous? No. In refraining from murder, adultery, theft, or other sins, I do so under compulsion because I fear the jail, the noose, the electric chair. These restrain me as iron bars restrain a lion and a bear. Otherwise they would tear everything to pieces. Such forceful restraint cannot be regarded as righteousness, rather as an indication of unrighteousness. As a wild beast is tied to keep it from running amuck, so the Law bridles mad and furious man to keep him from running wild. The need for restraint shows plainly enough that those who need the Law are not righteous, but wicked men who are fit to be tied. No, the Law does not justify.

The first purpose of the Law, accordingly, is to restrain the wicked. The devil gets people into all kinds of scrapes. Therefore God instituted governments, parents, laws, restrictions, and civil ordinances. At least they help to tie the devil's hands so that he does not rage up and down the earth. This civil restraint by the Law is intended by God for the preservation of all things, particularly for the good of the Gospel that it should not be hindered too much by the tumult of the wicked. But Paul is not now treating of this civil use and function of the Law.

The second purpose of the Law is spiritual and divine. Paul describes this spiritual purpose of the Law in the words, "Because of transgressions," i.e., to reveal to a person his sin, blindness, misery, his ignorance, hatred, and contempt of God, his death, hell, and condemnation.

This is the principal purpose of the Law and its most valuable contribution. As long as a person is not a murderer, adulterer, thief, he would swear that he is righteous. How is God going to humble such a person except by the Law? The Law is the hammer of death, the thunder of hell, and the lightning of God's wrath to bring down the proud and shameless hypocrites. When the Law was instituted on Mount Sinai it was accompanied by lightning, by storms, by the sound of trumpets, to tear to pieces that monster called self-righteousness. As long as a person thinks he is right he is going to be incomprehensibly proud and presumptuous. He is going to hate God, despise His grace and mercy, and ignore the promises in Christ. The Gospel of the free forgiveness of sins through Christ will never appeal to the self-righteous.

This monster of self-righteousness, this stiff-necked beast, needs a big axe. And that is what the Law is, a big axe. Accordingly, the proper use and function of the Law is to threaten until the conscience is scared stiff.

The awful spectacle at Mount Sinai portrayed the proper use of the Law. When the children of Israel came out of Egypt a feeling of singular holiness possessed them. They boasted: "We are the people of God. All that the Lord hath spoken we will do." (Ex. 19:8) This feeling of holiness was heightened when Moses ordered them to wash their clothes, to refrain from their wives, and to prepare themselves all around. The third day came and Moses led the people out of their tents to the foot of the mountain into the presence of the Lord. What happened? When the children of Israel saw the whole mountain burning and smoking, the black clouds rent by fierce lightning flashing up and down in the inky darkness, when they heard the sound of the trumpet blowing louder and longer, shattered by the roll of thunder, they were so frightened that they begged Moses: "Speak thou with us, and we will hear: but let not God speak with us, lest we die." (Ex. 20:19.) I ask you, what good did their scrubbing, their snow-white clothes, and their continence do them? No good at all. Not a single one could stand in the presence of the glorious Lord. Stricken by the terror of God, they fled back into their tents, as if the devil were after them.

The Law is meant to produce the same effect today which it produced at Mount Sinai long ago. I want to encourage all who fear God, especially those who intend to become ministers of the Gospel, to learn from the Apostle the proper use of the Law. I fear that after our time the right handling of the Law will become a lost art. Even now, although we continually explain the separate functions of the Law and the Gospel, we have those among us who do not understand how the Law should be used. What will it be like when we are dead and gone?

We want it understood that we do not reject the Law as our opponents claim. On the contrary, we uphold the Law. We say the Law is good if it is used for the purposes for which it was designed, to check civil transgression, and to magnify spiritual transgressions. The Law is also a light like the Gospel. But instead of revealing the grace of God, righteousness, and life, the Law brings sin, death, and the wrath of God to light. This is the business of the Law, and here the business of the Law ends, and should go no further.

The business of the Gospel, on the other hand, is to quicken, to comfort, to raise the fallen. The Gospel carries the news that God for Christ's sake is merciful to the most unworthy sinners, if they will only believe that Christ by His death has delivered them from sin and everlasting death unto grace, forgiveness, and everlasting life. By keeping in mind the difference between the Law and the Gospel we let each perform its special task. Of this difference between the Law and the Gospel nothing can be discovered in the writings of the monks or scholastics, nor for that matter in the writings of the ancient fathers. Augustine understood the difference somewhat. Jerome and others knew nothing of it. The silence in the Church concerning the difference between the Law and the Gospel has resulted in untold harm. Unless a sharp distinction is maintained between the purpose and function of the Law and the Gospel, the Christian doctrine cannot be kept free from error.

VERSE 19. It was added because of transgressions.

In other words, that transgressions might be recognized as such and thus increased. When sin, death, and the wrath of God are revealed to a person by the Law, he grows impatient, complains against God, and rebels. Before that he was a very holy man; he worshipped and praised God; he bowed his knees before God and gave thanks, like the Pharisee. But now that sin and death are revealed to him by the Law he wishes there were no God. The Law inspires hatred of God. Thus sin is not only revealed by the Law; sin is actually increased and magnified by the Law.

The Law is a mirror to show a person what he is like, a sinner who is guilty of death, and worthy of everlasting punishment. What is this bruising and beating by the hand of the Law to accomplish? This, that we may find the way to grace. The Law is an usher to lead the way to grace. God is the God of the humble, the miserable, the afflicted. It is His nature to exalt the humble, to comfort the sorrowing, to heal the broken-hearted, to justify the sinners, and to save the condemned. The fatuous idea that a person can be holy by himself denies God the pleasure of saving sinners. God must therefore first take the sledge-hammer of the Law in His fists and smash the beast of self-righteousness and its brood of self-confidence, self-wisdom, self-righteousness, and self-help. When the conscience has been thoroughly frightened by the Law it welcomes the Gospel of grace with its message of a Savior who came into the world, not to break the bruised reed, nor to quench the smoking flax, but to preach glad tidings to the poor, to heal the broken-hearted, and to grant forgiveness of sins to all the captives.

Man's folly, however, is so prodigious that instead of embracing the message of grace with its guarantee of the forgiveness of sin for Christ's sake, man finds himself more laws to satisfy his conscience. "If I live," says he, "I will mend my life. I will do this, I will do that." Man, if you don't do the very opposite, if you don't send Moses with the Law back to Mount Sinai and take the hand of Christ, pierced for your sins, you will never be saved.

When the Law drives you to the point of despair, let it drive you a little farther, let it drive you straight into the arms of Jesus who says: "Come unto me, all ye that labour and are heavy laden, and I will give you rest."

VERSE 19. Till the seed should come to whom the promise was made.

The Law is not to have its say indefinitely. We must know how long the Law is to put in its licks. If it hammers away too long, no person would and could be saved. The Law has a boundary beyond which it must not go. How long ought the Law to hold sway? "Till the seed should come to whom the promise was made."

That may be taken literally to mean until the time of the Gospel. "From the days of John the Baptist," says Jesus, "until now the kingdom of heaven suffereth violence, and the violent take it by force. For all the prophets and the law prophesied until John." (Matthew 11:12, 13.) When Christ came the Law and the ceremonies of Moses ceased.

Spiritually, it means that the Law is not to operate on a person after he has been humbled and frightened by the exposure of his sins and the wrath of God. We must then say to the Law: "Mister Law, lay off him. He has had enough. You scared him good and proper." Now it is the Gospel's turn. Now let Christ with His gracious lips talk to him of better things, grace, peace, forgiveness of sins, and eternal life.

VERSE 19. And it was ordained by angels in the hand of a mediator.

The Apostle digresses a little from his immediate theme. Something occurred to him and he throws it in by the way. It occurred to him that the

Law differs from the Gospel in another respect, in respect to authorship. The Law was delivered by the angels, but the Gospel by the Lord Himself. Hence, the Gospel is superior to the Law, as the word of a lord is superior to the word of his servant.

The Law was handed down by a being even inferior to the angels, by a middleman named Moses. Paul wants us to understand that Christ is the mediator of a better testament than mediator Moses of the Law. Moses led the people out of their tents to meet God. But they ran away. That is how good a mediator Moses was.

Paul says: "How can the Law justify when that whole sanctified people of Israel and even mediator Moses trembled at the voice of God? What kind of righteousness do you call that when people run away from it and hate it the worst way? If the Law could justify, people would love the Law. But look at the children of Israel running away from it."

The flight of the children of Israel from Mount Sinai indicates how people feel about the Law. They don't like it. If this were the only argument to prove that salvation is not by the Law, this one Bible history would do the work. What kind of righteousness is this law-righteousness when at the commencement exercises of the Law Moses and the scrubbed people run away from it so fast that an iron mountain, the Red Sea even, could not have stopped them until they were back in Egypt once again? If they could not hear the Law, how could they ever hope to perform the Law?

If all the world had stood at the mountain, all the world would have hated the Law and fled from it as the children of Israel did. The whole world is an enemy of the Law. How, then, can anyone be justified by the Law when everybody hates the Law and its divine author?

All this goes to show how little the scholastics know about the Law. They do not consider its spiritual effect and purpose, which is not to justify or to pacify afflicted consciences, but to increase sin, to terrify the conscience, and to produce wrath. In their ignorance the papists spout about man's good will and right judgment, and man's capacity to perform the Law of God. Ask the people of Israel who were present at the presentation of the Law on Mount Sinai whether what the scholastics say is true. Ask David, who often complains in the Psalms that he was cast away from God and in hell, that he was frantic about his sin, and sick at the thought of the wrath and judgment of God. No, the Law does not justify.

GALATIANS 3:20-29

VERSE 20. Now a mediator is not a mediator of one.

Here the Apostle briefly compares the two mediators: Moses and Christ. "A mediator," says Paul, "is not a mediator of one." He is necessarily a mediator of two: The offender and the offended. Moses was such a mediator between the Law and the people who were offended at the Law. They were offended at the Law because they did not understand its purpose. That was the veil which Moses put over his face. The people were also offended at the Law because they could not look at the bare face of Moses. It shone with the glory of God. When Moses addressed the people he had to cover his face with that veil of his. They could not listen to their mediator Moses without another mediator, the veil. The Law had to change its face and voice. In other words, the Law had to be made tolerable to the people.

Thus covered, the Law no longer spoke to the people in its undisguised majesty. It became more tolerable to the conscience. This explains why men fail to understand the Law properly, with the result that they become secure and presumptuous hypocrites. One of two things has to be done: Either the Law must be covered with a veil and then it loses its full effectiveness, or it must be unveiled and then the full blast of its force kills. Man cannot stand the Law without a veil over it. Hence, we are forced either to look beyond the Law to Christ, or we go through life as shameless hypocrites and secure sinners.

Paul says: "A mediator is not a mediator of one." Moses could not be a mediator of God only, for God needs no mediator. Again, Moses could not be a mediator of the people only. He was a mediator between God and the people. It is the office of a mediator to conciliate the party that is offended and to placate the party that is the offender. However, Moses' mediation consisted only in changing the tone of the Law to make it more tolerable to the people. Moses was merely a mediator of the veil. He could not supply the ability to perform the Law.

What do you suppose would have happened if the Law had been given without a mediator and the people had been denied the services of a go- between? The people would have perished, or in case they had escaped they would have required the services of another mediator to preserve them alive and to keep the Law in force. Moses came along and he was made the mediator. He covered his face with a veil. But that is as much as he could do. He could not deliver men's consciences from the terror of the Law. The sinner needs a better mediator.

That better mediator is Jesus Christ. He does not change the voice of the Law, nor does He hide the Law with a veil. He takes the full blast of the wrath of the Law and fulfills its demands most meticulously.

Of this better Mediator Paul says: "A mediator is not a mediator of one." We are the offending party; God is the party offended. The offense is of such a nature that God cannot pardon it. Neither can we render adequate satisfaction for our offenses. There is discord between God and us. Could not God revoke His Law? No. How about running away from God? It cannot be done. It took Christ to come between us and God and to reconcile God to us. How did Christ do it? "Blotting out the handwriting of ordinances that was against us, which was contrary to us, and took it out of the way, nailing it to his cross." (Col. 2:14.)

This one word, "mediator," is proof enough that the Law cannot justify. Otherwise we should not need a mediator.

In Christian theology the Law does not justify. In fact it has the contrary effect. The Law alarms us, it magnifies our sins until we begin to hate the Law and its divine Author. Would you call this being justified by the Law?

Can you imagine a more arrant outrage than to hate God and to abhor His Law? What an excellent Law it is. Listen: "I am the Lord thy God, which have brought thee out of the land of Egypt, out of the house of bondage. Thou shalt have no other gods...showing mercy unto thousands... honor thy father and thy mother; that thy days may be long upon the land..." (Ex. 20:2, 3, 6, 12.) Are these not excellent laws, perfect wisdom? "Let not God speak with us, lest we die," cried the children of Israel. Is it not amazing that a person should refuse to hear things that are good for him? Any person would be glad to hear, I should think, that he has a gracious God who shows mercy unto thousands. Is it not amazing that people hate the Law that promotes their safety and welfare, e.g., "Thou shalt not kill; thou shalt not commit adultery; thou shalt not steal"?

The Law can do nothing for us except to arouse the conscience. Before the Law comes to me I feel no sin. But when the Law comes, sin, death, and hell are revealed to me. You would not call this being made righteous. You would call it being condemned to death and hell-fire.

VERSE 20. But God is one.

God does not offend anybody, therefore He needs no mediator. But we offend God, therefore we need a mediator. And we need a better mediator than Moses. We need Christ.

VERSE 21. Is the law then against the promises of God?

Before he digressed Paul stated that the Law does not justify. Shall we then discard the Law? No, no. It supplies a certain need. It supplies men with a needed realization of their sinfulness. Now arises another question:

If the Law does no more than to reveal sin, does it not oppose the promises of God? The Jews believed that by the restraint and discipline of the Law the promises of God would be hastened, in fact earned by them.

Paul answers: "Not so. On the contrary, if we pay too much attention to the Law the promises of God will be slowed up. How can God fulfill His promises to a people that hates the Law?"

VERSE 21. God forbid.

God never said to Abraham: "In thee shall all the nations of the earth be blessed because thou hast kept the Law." When Abraham was still uncircumcised and without the Law or any law, indeed, when he was still an idol worshiper, God said to him: "Get thee out of thy country, etc.; I am thy shield, etc.; In thy seed shall all the nations of the earth be blessed." These are unconditional promises which God freely made to Abraham without respect to works.

This is aimed especially at the Jews who think that the promises of God are impeded by their sins. Paul says: "The Lord is not slack concerning His promises because of our sins, or hastens His promises because of any merit on our part." God's promises are not influenced by our attitudes. They rest in His goodness and mercy.

Just because the Law increases sin, it does not therefore obstruct the promises of God. The Law confirms the promises, in that it prepares a person to look for the fulfillment of the promises of God in Christ.

The proverb has it that Hunger is the best cook. The Law makes afflicted consciences hungry for Christ. Christ tastes good to them. Hungry hearts appreciate Christ. Thirsty souls are what Christ wants. He invites them: "Come unto me, all ye that labour and are heavy laden, and I will give you rest." Christ's benefits are so precious that He will dispense them only to those who need them and really desire them.

VERSE 21. For if there had been a law given which could have given life, verily righteousness should have been by the law.

The Law cannot give life. It kills. The Law does not justify a person before God; it increases sin. The Law does not secure righteousness; it hinders righteousness. The Apostle declares emphatically that the Law of itself cannot save.

Despite the intelligibility of Paul's statement, our enemies fail to grasp it. Otherwise they would not emphasize free will, natural strength, the works of supererogation, etc. To escape the charge of forgery they always have their convenient annotation handy, that Paul is referring only to the ceremonial and not to the moral law. But Paul includes all laws. He expressly says: "If there had been a law given."

There is no law by which righteousness may be obtained, not a single one. Why not?

VERSE 22. But the Scripture hath concluded all under sin.

Where? First in the promises concerning Christ in Genesis 3:15 and in Genesis 22:18, which speak of the seed of the woman and the seed of Abraham. The fact that these promises were made unto the fathers concerning Christ implies that the fathers were subject to the curse of sin and eternal death. Otherwise why the need of promises?

Next, Holy Writ "concludes" all under sin in this passage from Paul: "For as many as are of the works of the law are under the curse." Again, in the passage which the Apostle quotes from Deuteronomy 27:26, "Cursed is every one that continueth not in all things which are written in the book of the law to do them." This passage clearly submits all men to the curse, not only those who sin openly against the Law, but also those who sincerely endeavor to perform the Law, inclusive of monks, friars, hermits, etc.

The conclusion is inevitable: Faith alone justified without works. If the Law itself cannot justify, much less can imperfect performance of the Law or the works of the Law, justify.

VERSE 22. That the promise by faith of Jesus Christ might be given to them that believe.

The Apostle stated before that "the Scripture hath concluded all under sin." Forever? No, only until the promise should be fulfilled. The promise, you will recall, is the inheritance itself or the blessing promised to Abraham, deliverance from the Law, sin, death, and the devil, and the free gift of grace, righteousness, salvation, and eternal life. This promise, says Paul, is not obtained by any merit, by any law, or by any work. This promise is given. To whom? To those who believe. In whom? In Jesus Christ.

VERSE 23. But before faith came.

The Apostle proceeds to explain the service which the Law is to render. Previously Paul had said that the Law was given to reveal the wrath and death of God upon all sinners. Although the Law kills, God brings good out of evil. He uses the Law to bring life. God saw that the universal illusion of self-righteousness could not be put down in any other way but by the Law. The Law dispels all self-illusions. It puts the fear of God in a man. Without this fear there can be no thirst for God's mercy. God accordingly uses the Law for a hammer to break up the illusion of self-righteousness, that we should despair of our own strength and efforts at self-justification.

VERSE 23. But before faith came, we were kept under the law, shut up unto the faith which should afterwards be revealed.

The Law is a prison to those who have not as yet obtained grace. No prisoner enjoys the confinement. He hates it. If he could he would smash the prison and find his freedom at all cost. As long as he stays in prison he refrains from evil deeds. Not because he wants to, but because he has to.

The bars and the chains restrain him. He does not regret the crime that put him in jail. On the contrary, he is mighty sore that he cannot rob and kill as before. If he could escape he would go right back to robbing and killing.

The Law enforces good behavior, at least outwardly. We obey the Law because if we don't we will be punished. Our obedience is inspired by fear. We obey under duress and we do it resentfully. Now what kind of righteousness is this when we refrain from evil out of fear of punishment? Hence, the righteousness of the Law is at bottom nothing but love of sin and hatred of righteousness.

All the same, the Law accomplishes this much, that it will outwardly at least and to a certain extent repress vice and crime.

But the Law is also a spiritual prison, a veritable hell. When the Law begins to threaten a person with death and the eternal wrath of God, a man just cannot find any comfort at all. He cannot shake off at will the nightmare of terror which the Law stirs up in his conscience. Of this terror of the Law the Psalms furnish many glimpses.

The Law is a civil and a spiritual prison. And such it should be. For that the Law is intended. Only the confinement in the prison of the Law must not be unduly prolonged. It must come to an end. The freedom of faith must succeed the imprisonment of the Law.

Happy the person who knows how to utilize the Law so that it serves the purposes of grace and of faith. Unbelievers are ignorant of this happy knowledge. When Cain was first shut up in the prison of the Law he felt no pang at the fratricide he had committed. He thought he could pass it off as an incident with a shrug of the shoulder. "Am I my brother's keeper?" he answered God flippantly. But when he heard the ominous words, "What hast thou done? the voice of thy brother's blood crieth unto me from the ground," Cain began to feel his imprisonment. Did he know how to get out of prison? No. He failed to call the Gospel to his aid. He said: "My punishment is greater than I can bear." He could only think of the prison. He forgot that he was brought face to face with his crime so that he should hurry to God for mercy and for pardon. Cain remained in the prison of the Law and despaired.

As a stone prison proves a physical handicap, so the spiritual prison of the Law proves a chamber of torture. But this it should only be until faith be revealed. The silly conscience must be educated to this. Talk to your conscience. Say: "Sister, you are now in jail all right. But you don't have to stay there forever. It is written that we are 'shut up unto faith which should afterwards be revealed.' Christ will lead you to freedom. Do not despair like Cain, Saul, or Judas. They might have gone free if they had called Christ to their aid. Just take it easy, Sister Conscience. It's good for you to be locked up for a while. It will teach you to appreciate Christ."

How anybody can say that he by nature loves the Law is beyond me. The Law is a prison to be feared and hated. Any unconverted person who says he loves the Law is a liar. He does not know what he is talking about. We love the Law about as well as a murderer loves his gloomy cell, his straight-jacket, and the iron bars in front of him. How then can the Law justify us?

VERSE 23. Shut up unto the faith which should afterwards be revealed.

We know that Paul has reference to the time of Christ's coming. It was then that faith and the object of faith were fully revealed. But we may apply the historical fact to our inner life. When Christ came He abolished the Law and brought liberty and life to light. This He continues to do in the hearts of the believers. The Christian has a body in whose members, as Paul says, sin dwells and wars. I take sin to mean not only the deed but root, tree, fruit, and all. A Christian may perhaps not fall into the gross sins of murder, adultery, theft, but he is not free from impatience, complaints, hatreds, and blasphemy of God. As carnal lust is strong in a young man, in a man of full age the desire for glory, and in an old man covetousness, so impatience, doubt, and hatred of God often prevail in the hearts of sincere Christians. Examples of these sins may be garnered from the Psalms, Job, Jeremiah, and all the Sacred Scriptures.

Accordingly each Christian continues to experience in his heart times of the Law and times of the Gospel. The times of the Law are discernible by heaviness of heart, by a lively sense of sin, and a feeling of despair brought on by the Law. These periods of the Law will come again and again as long as we live. To mention my own case. There are many times when I find fault with God and am impatient with Him. The wrath and the judgment of God displease me, my wrath and impatience displease Him. Then is the season of the Law, when "the flesh lusteth against the Spirit, and the Spirit against the flesh."

The time of grace returns when the heart is enlivened by the promise of God's mercy. It soliloquizes: "Why art thou cast down, O my soul? and why art thou disquieted within me? Can you see nothing but law, sin, death, and hell? Is there no grace, no forgiveness, no joy, peace, life, heaven, no Christ and God? Trouble me no more, my soul. Hope in God who has not spared His own dear Son but has given Him into death for thy sins." When the Law carries things too far, say: "Mister Law, you are not the whole show. There are other and better things than you. They tell me to trust in the Lord."

There is a time for the Law and a time for grace. Let us study to be good timekeepers. It is not easy. Law and grace may be miles apart in essence, but in the heart, they are pretty close together. In the heart fear and trust, sin and grace, Law and Gospel cross paths continually.

Whether reason hears that justification before God is obtained by grace alone, it draws the inference that the Law is without value. The doctrine of the Law must therefore be studied carefully lest we either reject the Law altogether, or are tempted to attribute to the Law a capacity to save.

There are three ways in which the Law may be abused. First, by the self-righteous hypocrites who fancy that they can be justified by the Law. Secondly, by those who claim that Christian liberty exempts a Christian from the observance of the Law. "These," says Peter, "use their liberty for a cloak of maliciousness," and bring the name and the Gospel of Christ into ill repute. Thirdly, the Law is abused by those who do not understand that the Law is meant to drive us to Christ. When the Law is properly used its value cannot be too highly appraised. It will take me to Christ every time.

This simile of the schoolmaster is striking. Schoolmasters are indispensable. But show me a pupil who loves his schoolmaster. How little love is lost upon them the Jews showed by their attitude toward Moses. They would have been glad to stone Moses to death. (Ex. 17:4.) You cannot expect anything else. How can a pupil love a teacher who frustrates his desires? And if the pupil disobeys, the schoolmaster whips him, and the pupil has to like it and even kiss the rod with which he was beaten. Do you think the schoolboy feels good about it? As soon as the teacher turns his back, the pupil breaks the rod and throws it into the fire. And if he were stronger than the teacher he would not take the beatings, but beat up the teacher. All the same, teachers are indispensable, otherwise the children would grow up without discipline, instruction, and training.

But how long are the scolding and the whippings of the schoolmaster to continue? Only for a time, until the boy has been trained to be a worthy heir of his father. No father wants his son to be whipped all the time. The discipline is to last until the boy has been trained to be his father's worthy successor.

The Law is such a schoolmaster. Not for always, but until we have been brought to Christ. The Law is not just another schoolmaster. The Law is a specialist to bring us to Christ. What would you think of a schoolmaster who could only torment and beat a child? Yet of such schoolmasters there were plenty in former times, regular bruisers. The Law is not that kind of a schoolmaster. It is not to torment us always. With its lashings it is only too anxious to drive us to Christ. The Law is like the good schoolmaster who trains his children to find pleasure in doing things they formerly detested.

VERSE 24. That we might be justified by faith.

The Law is not to teach us another Law. When a person feels the full force of the Law he is likely to think: I have transgressed all the commandments of God; I am guilty of eternal death. If God will spare me I will change and live right from now on. This natural but entirely wrong reaction to the Law has bred the many ceremonies and works devised to earn grace and remission of sins.

The Law means to enlarge my sins, to make me small, so that I may be justified by faith in Christ. Faith is neither law nor word; but confidence in Christ "who is the end of the law." How so is Christ the end of the Law? Not in this way that He replaced the old Law with new laws. Nor is Christ the end of the Law in a way that makes Him a hard judge who has to be bribed by works as the papists teach. Christ is the end or finish of the Law to all who believe in Him. The Law can no longer accuse or condemn them.

But what does the Law accomplish for those who have been justified by Christ? Paul answers this question next.

VERSE 25. But after that faith is come, we are no longer under a schoolmaster.

The Apostle declares that we are free from the Law. Christ fulfilled the Law for us. We may live in joy and safety under Christ. The trouble is, our flesh will not let us believe in Christ with all our heart. The fault lies not with Christ, but with us. Sin clings to us as long as we live and spoils our happiness in Christ. Hence, we are only partly free from the Law. "With the mind I myself serve the law of God; but with the flesh the law of sin." (Romans 7:25.)

As far as the conscience is concerned it may cheerfully ignore the Law. But because sin continues to dwell in the flesh, the Law waits around to molest our conscience. More and more, however, Christ increases our faith and in the measure in which our faith is increased, sin, Law, and flesh subside.

If anybody objects to the Gospel and the sacraments on the ground that Christ has taken away our sins once and for always, you will know what to answer. You will answer: Indeed, Christ has taken away my sins. But my flesh, the world, and the devil interfere with my faith. The little light of faith in my heart does not shine all over me at once. It is a gradual diffusion. In the meanwhile I console myself with the thought that eventually my flesh will be made perfect in the resurrection.

VERSE 26. For we are all the children of God by faith in Christ Jesus.

Paul as a true apostle of faith always has the word "faith" on the tip of his tongue. By faith, says he, we are the children of God. The Law cannot beget children of God. It cannot regenerate us. It can only remind us of the old birth by which we were born into the kingdom of the devil. The best the Law can do for us is to prepare us for a new birth through faith in Christ Jesus. Faith in Christ regenerates us into the children of God. St. John bears witness to this in his Gospel: "As many as received him, to them gave he power to become the sons of God, even to them that believe on his name." (John 1:12.) What tongue of man or angel can adequately extol the mercy of God toward us miserable sinners in that He adopted us for His own children and fellow-heirs with His Son by the simple means of faith in Christ Jesus!

VERSE 27. For as many of you as have been baptized into Christ have put on Christ.

To "put on Christ" may be understood in two ways, according to the Law and according to the Gospel. According to the Law as in Romans 13:14, "Put ye on the Lord Jesus Christ," which means to follow the example of Christ.

To put on Christ according to the Gospel means to clothe oneself with the righteousness, wisdom, power, life, and Spirit of Christ. By nature we are clad in the garb of Adam. This garb Paul likes to call "the old man." Before we can become the children of God this old man must be put off, as Paul says, Ephesians 4:29. The garment of Adam must come off like soiled clothes. Of course, it is not as simple as changing one's clothes. But God makes it simple. He clothes us with the righteousness of Christ by means of Baptism, as the Apostle says in this verse: "As many of you as have been baptized into Christ have put on Christ." With this change of garments a new birth, a new life stirs in us. New affections toward God spring up in the heart. New determinations affect our will. All this is to put on Christ according to the Gospel. Needless to say, when we have put on the robe of the righteousness of Christ we must not forget to put on also the mantle of the imitation of Christ.

VERSE 28. There is neither Jew nor Greek, there is neither bond nor free, there is neither male nor female; for ye are all one in Christ Jesus.

The list might be extended indefinitely: There is neither preacher nor hearer, neither teacher nor scholar, neither master nor servant, etc. In the matter of salvation, rank, learning, righteousness, influence count for nothing.

With this statement Paul deals a death blow to the Law. When a person has put on Christ nothing else matters. Whether a person is a Jew, a punctilious and circumcised observer of the Law of Moses, or whether a person is a noble and wise Greek does not matter. Circumstances, personal worth, character, achievements have no bearing upon justification. Before God they count for nothing. What counts is that we put on Christ.

Whether a servant performs his duties well; whether those who are in authority govern wisely; whether a man marries, provides for his family, and is an honest citizen; whether a woman is chaste, obedient to her husband, and a good mother: all these advantages do not qualify a person for salvation. These virtues are commendable, of course; but they do not count points for justification. All the best laws, ceremonies, religions, and deeds of the world cannot take away sin guilt, cannot dispatch death, cannot purchase life.

There is much disparity among men in the world, but there is no such disparity before God. "For all have sinned, and come short of the glory of God." (Romans 3:23.) Let the Jews, let the Greeks, let the whole world keep silent in the presence of God. Those who are justified are justified by Christ. Without faith in Christ the Jew with his laws, the monk with his holy orders, the Greek with his wisdom, the servant with his obedience, shall perish forever.

Verse 28. For ye are all one in Christ Jesus.

There is much imparity among men in the world. And it is a good thing. If the woman would change places with the man, if the son would change places with the father, the servant with the master, nothing but confusion would result. In Christ, however, all are equal. We all have one and the same Gospel, "one faith, one baptism, one God and Father of all," one Christ and Savior of all. The Christ of Peter, Paul, and all the saints is our Christ. Paul can always be depended on to add the conditional clause, "In Christ Jesus." If we lose sight of Christ, we lose out.

Verse 29. And if ye be Christ's, then are ye Abraham's seed, and heirs according to the promise.

"If ye be Christ's" means, if you believe in Christ. If you believe in Christ, then are you the children of Abraham indeed. Through our faith in Christ Abraham gains paternity over us and over the nations of the earth according to the promise: "In thy seed shall all the nations of the earth be blessed." Through faith we belong to Christ and Christ to us.

GALATIANS 4:1-9

VERSE 1. Now I say, That the heir, as long as he is a child, differeth nothing from a servant, though he be Lord of all;

VERSE 2. But is under tutors and governors until the time appointed of the father.

The Apostle had apparently finished his discourse on justification when this illustration of the youthful heir occurred to him. He throws it in for good measure. He knows that plain people are sooner impressed by an apt illustration than by learned discussion.

"I want to give you another illustration from everyday life," he writes to the Galatians. "As long as an heir is under age he is treated very much like a servant. He is not permitted to order his own affairs. He is kept under constant surveillance. Such discipline is good for him, otherwise he would waste his inheritance in no time. This discipline, however, is not to last forever. It is to last only until 'the time appointed of the father.'"

VERSE 3. Even so we, when we were children, were in bondage under the elements of the world.

As children of the Law we were treated like servants and prisoners. We were oppressed and condemned by the Law. But the tyranny of the Law is not to last forever. It is to last only until "the time appointed of the father," until Christ came and redeemed us.

VERSE 3. Under the elements of the world.

By the elements of the world the Apostle does not understand the physical elements, as some have thought. In calling the Law "the elements of the world" Paul means to say that the Law is something material, mundane, earthly. It may restrain evil, but it does not deliver from sin. The Law does not justify; it does not bring a person to heaven. I do not obtain eternal life because I do not kill, commit adultery, steal, etc. Such mere outward decency does not constitute Christianity. The heathen observe the same restraints to avoid punishment or to secure the advantages of a good reputation. In the last analysis such restraint is simple hypocrisy. When the Law exercises its higher function it accuses and condemns the conscience. All these effects of the Law cannot be called divine or heavenly. These effects are elements of the world.

In calling the Law the elements of the world Paul refers to the whole Law, principally to the ceremonial law which dealt with external matters, as meat, drink, dress, places, times, feasts, cleansings, sacrifices, etc. These are mundane matters which cannot save the sinner. Ceremonial laws are like the statutes of governments dealing with purely civil matters, as commerce, inheritance, etc. As for the pope's church laws forbidding marriage and meats, Paul calls them elsewhere the doctrines of devils. You would not call such laws elements of heaven.

The Law of Moses deals with mundane matters. It holds the mirror to the evil which is in the world. By revealing the evil that is in us it creates a longing in the heart for the better things of God. The Law forces us into the arms of Christ, "who is the end of the law for righteousness to every one that believeth." (Romans 1:4.) Christ relieves the conscience of the Law. In so far as the Law impels us to Christ it renders excellent service.

I do not mean to give the impression that the Law should be despised. Neither does Paul intend to leave that impression. The Law ought to be honored. But when it is a matter of justification before God, Paul had to speak disparagingly of the Law, because the Law has nothing to do with justification. If it thrusts its nose into the business of justification we must talk harshly to the Law to keep it in its place. The conscience ought not to be on speaking terms with the Law. The conscience ought to know only Christ. To say this is easy, but in times of trial, when the conscience writhes in the presence of God, it is not so easy to do. As such times we are to believe in Christ as if there were no Law or sin anywhere, but only Christ. We ought to say to the Law: "Mister Law, I do not get you. You stutter so much. I don't think that you have anything to say to me."

When it is not a question of salvation or justification with us, we are to think highly of the Law and call it "holy, just, and good." (Romans 7:12) The Law is of no comfort to a stricken conscience. Therefore it should not be allowed to rule in our conscience, particularly in view of the fact that Christ paid so great a price to deliver the conscience from the tyranny of the Law. Let us understand that the Law and Christ are impossible bedfellows. The Law must leave the bed of the conscience, which is so narrow that it cannot hold two, as Isaiah says, chapter 28, verse 20.

Only Paul among the apostles calls the Law "the elements of the world, weak and beggarly elements, the strength of sin, the letter that killeth," etc. The other apostles do not speak so slightingly of the Law. Those who want to be first-class scholars in the school of Christ want to pick up the language of Paul. Christ called him a chosen vessel and equipped with a facility of expression far above that of the other apostles, that he as the chosen vessel should establish the doctrine of justification in clear-cut words.

VERSES 4, 5. But when the fullness of the time was come, God sent forth his Son, made of a woman, made under the law, to redeem them that were under the law.

"The fullness of the time" means when the time of the Law was fulfilled and Christ was revealed. Note how Paul explains Christ. "Christ," says he, "is the Son of God and the son of a woman. He submitted Himself under the Law to redeem us who were under the Law." In these words the Apostle explains the person and office of Christ. His person is divine and human. "God sent forth His Son, made of a woman." Christ therefore is true God and true man. Christ's office the Apostle describes in the words: "Made under the law, to redeem them that were under the law."

Paul calls the Virgin Mary a woman. This has been frequently deplored even by some of the ancient fathers who felt that Paul should have written "virgin" instead of woman. But Paul is now treating of faith and Christian righteousness, of the person and office of Christ, not of the virginity of Mary. The inestimable mercy of God is sufficiently set forth by the fact that His Son was born of a woman. The more general term "woman" indicates that Christ was born a true man. Paul does not say that Christ was born of man and woman, but only of woman. That he has a virgin in mind is obvious.

This passage furthermore declares that Christ's purpose in coming was the abolition of the Law, not with the intention of laying down new laws, but "to redeem them that were under the law." Christ himself declared: "I judge no man." (John 8:15.) Again, "I came not to judge the world, but to save the world." (John 12:47.) In other words: "I came not to bring more laws, or to judge men according to the existing Law. I have a higher and better office. I came to judge and to condemn the Law, so that it may no more judge and condemn the world."

How did Christ manage to redeem us? "He was made under the law." When Christ came He found us all in prison. What did He do about it? Although He was the Lord of the Law, He voluntarily placed Himself under the Law and permitted it to exercise dominion over Him, indeed to accuse and to condemn Him. When the Law takes us into judgment it has a perfect right to do so. "For we are by nature the children of wrath, even as others." (Eph. 2:3.) Christ, however, "did no sin, neither was guile found in his mouth." (I Pet. 2:22.) Hence the Law had no jurisdiction over Him. Yet the Law treated this innocent, just, and blessed Lamb of God as cruelly as it treated us. It accused Him of blasphemy and treason. It made Him guilty of the sins of the whole world. It overwhelmed him with such anguish of soul that His sweat was as blood. The Law condemned Him to the shameful death on the Cross.

It is truly amazing that the Law had the effrontery to turn upon its divine Author, and that without a show of right. For its insolence the Law in turn was arraigned before the judgment seat of God and condemned. Christ might have overcome the Law by an exercise of His omnipotent authority over the Law. Instead, He humbled Himself under the Law for and together with them that were under the Law. He gave the Law license to accuse and condemn Him. His present mastery over the Law was obtained by virtue of His Sonship and His substitutionary victory.

Thus Christ banished the Law from the conscience. It dare no longer banish us from God. For that matter,—the Law continues to reveal sin. It still raises its voice in condemnation. But the conscience finds quick relief in the words of the Apostle: "Christ has redeemed us from the law." The conscience can now hold its head high and say to the Law: "You are not so holy yourself. You crucified the Son of God. That was an awful thing for you to do. You have lost your influence forever."

The words, "Christ was made under the law," are worth all the attention we can bestow on them. They declare that the Son of God did not only fulfill one or two easy requirements of the Law, but that He endured all the tortures of the Law. The Law brought all its fright to bear upon Christ until He experienced anguish and terror such as nobody else ever experienced. His bloody sweat. His need of angelic comfort, His tremulous prayer in the garden, His lamentation on the Cross, "My God, my God, why hast thou forsaken me?" bear eloquent witness to the sting of the Law. He suffered "to redeem them that were under the law."

The Roman conception of Christ as a mere lawgiver more stringent than Moses, is quite contrary to Paul's teaching. Christ, according to Paul, was not an agent of the Law but a patient of the Law. He was not a law-giver, but a law-taker.

True enough, Christ also taught and expounded the Law. But it was incidental. It was a sideline with Him. He did not come into the world for the purpose of teaching the Law, as little as it was the purpose of His coming to perform miracles. Teaching the Law and performing miracles did not constitute His unique mission to the world. The prophets also taught the Law and performed miracles. In fact, according to the promise of Christ, the apostles performed greater miracles than Christ Himself. (John 14:12.) The true purpose of Christ's coming was the abolition of the Law, of sin, and of death.

If we think of Christ as Paul here depicts Him, we shall never go wrong. We shall never be in danger of misconstruing the meaning of the Law. We shall understand that the Law does not justify. We shall understand why a Christian observes laws: For the peace of the world, out of gratitude to God, and for a good example that others may be attracted to the Gospel.

VERSE 5. That we might receive the adoption of sons.

Paul still has for his text Genesis 22:18, "In thy seed shall all the nations of the earth be blessed." In the course of his Epistle he calls this promise of the blessing righteousness, life, deliverance from the Law, the testament, etc. Now he also calls the promise of blessing "the adoption of sons," the inheritance of everlasting life.

What ever induced God to adopt us for His children and heirs? What claim can men who are subservient to sin, subject to the curse of the Law, and worthy of everlasting death, have on God and eternal life? That God adopted us is due to the merit of Jesus Christ, the Son of God, who humbled Himself under the Law and redeemed us law-ridden sinners.

VERSE 6. And because ye are sons, God hath sent forth the Spirit of his Son into your hearts.

In the early Church the Holy Spirit was sent forth in visible form. He descended upon Christ in the form of a dove (Matt. 3:16), and in the likeness of fire upon the apostles and other believers. (Acts 2:3.) This visible outpouring of the Holy Spirit was necessary to the establishment of the early Church, as were also the miracles that accompanied the gift of the Holy Ghost. Paul explained the purpose of these miraculous gifts of the Spirit in I Corinthians 14:22, "Tongues are for a sign, not to them that believe, but to them that believe not." Once the Church had been established and properly advertised by these miracles, the visible appearance of the Holy Ghost ceased.

Next, the Holy Ghost is sent forth into the hearts of the believers, as here stated, "God sent the Spirit of his Son into your hearts." This sending is accomplished by the preaching of the Gospel through which the Holy Spirit inspires us with fervor and light, with new judgment, new desires, and new motives. This happy innovation is not a derivative of reason or personal development, but solely the gift and operation of the Holy Ghost.

This renewal by the Holy Spirit may not be conspicuous to the world, but it is patent to us by our better judgment, our improved speech, and our unashamed confession of Christ. Formerly we did not confess Christ to be our only merit, as we do now in the light of the Gospel. Why, then, should we feel bad if the world looks upon us as ravagers of religion and insurgents against constituted authority? We confess Christ and our conscience approves of it.

Then, too, we live in the fear of God. If we sin, we sin not on purpose, but unwittingly, and we are sorry for it. Sin sticks in our flesh, and the flesh gets us into sin even after we have been imbued by the Holy Ghost. Outwardly there is no great difference between a Christian and any honest man. The activities of a Christian are not sensational. He performs his duty according to his vocation. He takes good care of his family, and is kind and helpful to others. Such homely, everyday performances are not much admired. But the setting-up exercises of the monks draw great applause. Holy works, you know. Only the acts of a Christian are truly good and acceptable to God, because they are done in faith, with a cheerful heart, out of gratitude to Christ.

We ought to have no misgivings about whether the Holy Ghost dwells in us. We are "the temple of the Holy Ghost." (I Cor. 3:16.) When we have a love for the Word of God, and gladly hear, talk, write, and think of Christ, we are to know that this inclination toward Christ is the gift and work of the Holy Ghost. Where you come across contempt for the Word of God, there is the devil. We meet with such contempt for the Word of God mostly among the common people. They act as though the Word of God does not concern them. Wherever you find a love for the Word, thank God for the Holy Spirit who infuses this love into the hearts of men. We never come by this love naturally, neither can it be enforced by laws. It is the gift of the Holy Spirit.

The Roman theologians teach that no man can know for a certainty whether he stands in the favor of God or not. This teaching forms one of the chief articles of their faith. With this teaching they tormented men's consciences, excommunicated Christ from the Church, and limited the operations of the Holy Ghost.

St. Augustine observed that "every man is certain of his faith, if he has faith." This the Romanists deny. "God forbid," they exclaim piously, "that I should ever be so arrogant as to think that I stand in grace, that I am holy, or that I have the Holy Ghost." We ought to feel sure that we stand in the grace of God, not in view of our own worthiness, but through the good services of Christ. As certain as we are that Christ pleases God, so sure ought we to be that we also please God, because Christ is in us. And although we daily offend God by our sins, yet as often as we sin, God's mercy bends over us. Therefore sin cannot get us to doubt the grace of God. Our certainty is of Christ, that mighty Hero who overcame the Law, sin, death, and all evils. So long as He sits at the right hand of God to intercede for us, we have nothing to fear from the anger of God.

This inner assurance of the grace of God is accompanied by outward indications such as gladly to hear, preach, praise, and to confess Christ, to do one's duty in the station in which God has placed us, to aid the needy, and to comfort the sorrowing. These are the affidavits of the Holy Spirit testifying to our favorable standing with God.

If we could be fully persuaded that we are in the good grace of God, that our sins are forgiven, that we have the Spirit of Christ, that we are the beloved children of God, we would be ever so happy and grateful to God. But because we often feel fear and doubt we cannot come to that happy certainty.

Train your conscience to believe that God approves of you. Fight it out with doubt. Gain assurance through the Word of God. Say: "I am all right with God. I have the Holy Ghost. Christ, in whom I do believe, makes me worthy. I gladly hear, read, sing, and write of Him. I would like nothing better than that Christ's Gospel be known throughout the world and that many, many be brought to faith in Him."

VERSE 6. *Crying, Abba, Father.*

Paul might have written, "God sent forth the Spirit of his Son into your hearts, calling Abba, Father." Instead, he wrote, "Crying, Abba, Father." In the eighth chapter of the Epistle to the Romans the Apostle describes this crying of the Spirit as "groanings which cannot be uttered." He writes in the 26th verse: "Likewise the Spirit also helpeth our infirmities: for we know not what we should pray for as we ought: but the Spirit itself maketh intercession for us with groanings which cannot be uttered."

The fact that the Spirit of Christ in our hearts cries unto God and makes intercession for us with groanings should reassure us greatly. However, there are many factors that prevent such full reassurance on our part. We are born in sin. To doubt the good will of God is an inborn suspicion of God with all of us. Besides, the devil, our adversary, goeth about seeking to devour us by roaring: "God is angry at you and is going to destroy you forever." In all these difficulties we have only one support, the Gospel of Christ. To hold on to it, that is the trick. Christ cannot be perceived with the senses. We cannot see Him. The heart does not feel His helpful presence. Especially in times of trials a Christian feels the power of sin, the infirmity of his flesh, the goading darts of the devil, the agues of death, the scowl and judgment of God. All these things cry out against us. The Law scolds us, sin screams at us, death thunders at us, the devil roars at us. In the midst of the clamor the Spirit of Christ cries in our hearts: "Abba, Father." And this little cry of the Spirit transcends the hullabaloo of the Law, sin, death, and the devil, and finds a hearing with God.

The Spirit cries in us because of our weakness. Because of our infirmity the Holy Ghost is sent forth into our hearts to pray for us according to the will of God and to assure us of the grace of God.

Let the Law, sin, and the devil cry out against us until their outcry fills heaven and earth. The Spirit of God outcries them all. Our feeble groans, "Abba, Father," will be heard of God sooner than the combined racket of hell, sin, and the Law.

We do not think of our groanings as a crying. It is so faint we do not know we are groaning. "But he," says Paul, "that searcheth the hearts knoweth what is the mind of the Spirit." (Romans 8:27.) To this Searcher of hearts our feeble groaning, as it seems to us, is a loud shout for help in comparison with which the howls of hell, the din of the devil, the yells of the Law, the shouts of sin are like so many whispers.

In the fourteenth chapter of Exodus the Lord addresses Moses at the Red Sea: "Wherefore criest thou unto me?" Moses had not cried unto the Lord. He trembled so he could hardly talk. His faith was at low ebb. He saw the people of Israel wedged between the Sea and the approaching armies of Pharaoh. How were they to escape? Moses did not know what to say. How then could God say that Moses was crying to Him? God heard the groaning heart of Moses and the groans to Him sounded like loud shouts for help. God is quick to catch the sigh of the heart.

Some have claimed that the saints are without infirmities. But Paul says: "The Spirit helpeth our infirmities, and maketh intercession for us with groanings which cannot be uttered." We need the help of the Holy Spirit because we are weak and infirm. And the Holy Spirit never disappoints us. Confronted by the armies of Pharaoh, retreat cut off by the waters of the Red Sea, Moses was in a bad spot. He felt himself to blame.

The devil accused him: "These people will all perish, for they cannot escape. And you are to blame because you led the people out of Egypt. You started all this." And then the people started in on Moses. "Because there were no graves in Egypt, hast thou taken us away to die in the wilderness? For it had been better for us to serve the Egyptians, than that we should die in the wilderness." (Ex. 14:11, 12.) But the Holy Ghost was in Moses and made intercession for him with unutterable groanings, sighings unto the Lord: "O Lord, at Thy commandment have I led forth this people. So help me now."

The Spirit intercedes for us not in many words or long prayers, but with groanings, with little sounds like "Abba." Small as this word is, it says ever so much. It says: "My Father, I am in great trouble and you seem so far away. But I know I am your child, because you are my Father for Christ's sake. I am loved by you because of the Beloved." This one little word "Abba" surpasses the eloquence of a Demosthenes and a Cicero.

I have spent much time on this verse in order to combat the cruel teaching of the Roman church, that a person ought to be kept in a state of uncertainty concerning his status with God. The monasteries recruit the youth on the plea that their "holy" orders will assuredly recruit them for heaven. But once inside the monastery the recruits are told to doubt the promises of God.

In support of their error the papists quote the saying of Solomon: "The righteous, and the wise, and their works, are in the hand of God: no man knoweth either love or hatred by all that is before them." (Eccles. 9:1.) They take this hatred to mean the wrath of God to come. Others take it to mean God's present anger. None of them seem to understand this passage from Solomon. On every page the Scriptures urge us to believe that God is merciful, loving, and patient; that He is faithful and true, and that He keeps His promises. All the promises of God were fulfilled in the gift of His only- begotten Son, that "whosoever believeth in him should not perish, but have everlasting life." The Gospel is reassurance for sinners. Yet this one saying from Solomon, misinterpreted at that, is made to count for more than all the many promises of all the Scriptures.

If our opponents are so uncertain about their status with God, and even go so far as to say that the conscience ought to be kept in a state of doubt, why is it that they persecute us as vile heretics? When it comes to persecuting us they do not seem to be in doubt and uncertainty one minute.

Let us not fail to thank God for delivering us from the doctrine of doubt. The Gospel commands us to look away from our own good works to the promises of God in Christ, the Mediator. The pope commands us to look away from the promises of God in Christ to our own merit. No wonder they are the eternal prey of doubt and despair. We depend upon God for salvation. No wonder that our doctrine is certified, because it does not rest in our own strength, our own conscience, our own feelings, our own person, our own works. It is built on a better foundation. It is built on the promises and truth of God.

Besides, the passage from Solomon does not treat of the hatred and love of God towards men. It merely rebukes the ingratitude of men. The more deserving a person is, the less he is appreciated. Often those who should be his best friends, are his worst enemies. Those who least deserve the praise of the world, get most. David was a holy man and a good king. Nevertheless he was chased from his own country. The prophets, Christ, the apostles, were slain. Solomon in this passage does not speak of the love and hatred of God, but of love and hatred among men. As though Solomon wanted to say: "There are many good and wise men whom God uses for the advancement of mankind. Seldom, if ever, are their efforts crowned with gratitude. They are usually repaid with hatred and ingratitude."

We are being treated that way. We thought we would find favor with men for bringing them the Gospel of peace, life, and eternal salvation. Instead of favor, we found fury. At first, yes, many were delighted with our doctrine and received it gladly. We counted them as our friends and brethren, and were happy to think that they would help us in sowing the seed of the Gospel. But they revealed themselves as false brethren and deadly enemies of the Gospel. If you experience the ingratitude of men, don't let it get you down. Say with Christ: "They hated me without cause." And, "For my love they are my adversaries; but I give myself unto prayer." (Ps. 109:4.)

Let us never doubt the mercy of God in Christ Jesus, but make up our minds that God is pleased with us, that He looks after us, and that we have the Holy Spirit who prays for us.

VERSE 7. Wherefore thou art no more a servant, but a son.

This sentence clinches Paul's argument. He says: "With the Holy Spirit in our hearts crying, 'Abba, Father,' there can be no doubt that God has adopted us for His children and that our subjection to the Law has come to an end." We are now the free children of God. We may now say to the Law: "Mister Law, you have lost your throne to Christ. I am free now and a son of God. You cannot curse me any more." Do not permit the Law to lie in your conscience. Your conscience belongs to Christ. Let Christ be in it and not the Law.

As the children of God we are the heirs of His eternal heaven. What a wonderful gift heaven is, man's heart cannot conceive, much less describe. Until we enter upon our heavenly inheritance we are only to have our little faith to go by. To man's reason our faith looks rather forlorn. But because our faith rests on the promises of the infinite God, His promises are also infinite, so much so that nothing can accuse or condemn us.

VERSE 7. And if a son, then an heir of God through Christ.

A son is an heir, not by virtue of high accomplishments, but by virtue of his birth. He is a mere recipient. His birth makes him an heir, not his labors. In exactly the same way we obtain the eternal gifts of righteousness, resurrection, and everlasting life. We obtain them not as agents, but as beneficiaries. We are the children and heirs of God through faith in Christ. We have Christ to thank for everything.

We are not the heirs of some rich and mighty man, but heirs of God, the almighty Creator of all things. If a person could fully appreciate what it means to be a son and heir of God, he would rate the might and wealth of nations small change in comparison with his heavenly inheritance. What is the world to him who has heaven? No wonder Paul greatly desired to depart and to be with Christ. Nothing would be more welcome to us than early death, knowing that it would spell the end of all our miseries and the beginning of all our happiness. Yes, if a person could perfectly believe this he would not long remain alive. The anticipation of his joy would kill him.

But the law of the members strives against the law of the mind, and makes perfect joy and faith impossible. We need the continued help and comfort of the Holy Spirit. We need His prayers. Paul himself cried out: "O wretched man that I am! Who shall deliver me from the body of this death?" The body of this death spoiled the joy of his spirit. He did not always entertain the sweet and glad expectation of his heavenly inheritance. He often felt miserable.

This goes to show how hard it is to believe. Faith is feeble, because the flesh wars against the spirit. If we could have perfect faith, our loathing for this life in the world would be complete. We would not be so careful about this life. We would not be so attached to the world and the things of the world. We would not feel so good when we have them; we would not feel so bad when we lose them. We would be far more humble and patient and kind. But our faith is weak, because our spirit is weak. In this life we can have only the first- fruits of the Spirit, as Paul says.

VERSE 7. Through Christ.

The Apostle always has Christ on the tip of his tongue. He foresaw that nothing would be less known in the world some day than the Gospel of Christ. Therefore he talks of Christ continually. As often as he speaks of righteousness, grace, the promise, the adoption, and the inheritance of heaven, he adds the words, "In Christ," or "Through Christ," to show that these blessings are not to be had by the Law, or the deeds of the Law, much less by our own exertions, or by the observance of human traditions, but only by and through and in Christ.

VERSES 8, 9. Howbeit then, when ye knew not God, ye did service unto
them which by nature are no gods. But now, after that ye have known God,
or rather are known of God, how turn ye again to the weak and beggarly
elements, whereunto ye desire again to be in bondage?

This concludes Paul's discourse on justification. From now to the end of
the Epistle the Apostle writes mostly of Christian conduct. But before he
follows up his doctrinal discourse with practical precepts he once more
reproves the Galatians. He is deeply displeased with them for relinquish-
ing their divine doctrine. He tells them: "You have taken on teachers who
intend to recommit you to the Law. By my doctrine I called you out of
the darkness of ignorance into the wonderful light of the knowledge of
God. I led you out of bondage into the freedom of the sons of God, not by
the prescription of laws, but by the gift of heavenly and eternal blessings
through Christ Jesus. How could you so soon forsake the light and return
to darkness? How could you so quickly stray from grace into the Law,
from freedom into bondage?"

The example of the Galatians, of Anabaptists, and other sectarians
in our day bears testimony to the ease with which faith may be lost. We
take great pains in setting forth the doctrine of faith by preaching and by
writing. We are careful to apply the Gospel and the Law in their proper
turn. Yet we make little headway because the devil seduces people into
misbelief by taking Christ out of their sight and focusing their eyes upon
the Law.

But why does Paul accuse the Galatians of reverting to the weak and
beggarly elements of the Law when they never had the Law? Why does
he not say to them: "At one time you Galatians did not know God. You
then served idols that were no gods. But now that you have come to know
the true God, why do you go back to the worship of idols?" Paul seems to
identify their defection from the Gospel to the Law with their former idolatry. Indeed he does. Whoever gives up the article of justification does not
know the true God. It is one and the same thing whether a person reverts
to the Law or to the worship of idols. When the article of justification is
lost, nothing remains except error, hypocrisy, godlessness, and idolatry.

God will and can be known in no other way than in and through
Christ according to the statement of John 1:18, "The only begotten Son,
which is in the bosom of the Father, he hath declared him." Christ is the
only means whereby we can know God and His will. In Christ we perceive that God is not a cruel judge, but a most loving and merciful Father
who to bless and to save us "spared not his own Son, but gave him up for
us all." This is truly to know God.

Those who do not know God in Christ arrive at this erroneous conclusion: "I will serve God in such and such a way. I will join this or that order.
I will be active in this or that charitable endeavor. God will sanction my
good intentions and reward me with everlasting life. For is He not a merciful and generous Father who gives good things even to the unworthy and
ungrateful? How much more will He grant unto me everlasting life as a

due payment in return for my many good deeds and merits." This is the religion of reason. This is the natural religion of the world. "The natural man receiveth not the things of the Spirit of God. (I Cor. 2:14.) "There is none that understandeth, there is none that seeketh after God." (Romans 3:11.) Hence, there is really no difference between a Jew, a Mohammedan, and any other old or new heretic. There may be a difference of persons, places, rites, religions, ceremonies, but as far as their fundamental beliefs are concerned they are all alike.

Is it therefore not extreme folly for Rome and the Mohammedans to fight each other about religion? How about the monks? Why should one monk want to be accounted more holy than another monk because of some silly ceremony, when all the time their basic beliefs are as much alike as one egg is like the other? They all imagine, if we do this or that work, God will have mercy on us; if not, God will be angry.

God never promised to save anybody for his religious observance of ceremonies and ordinances. Those who rely upon such things do serve a god, but it is their own invention of a god, and not the true God. The true God has this to say: No religion pleases Me whereby the Father is not glorified through His Son Jesus. All who give their faith to this Son of Mine, to them I am God and Father. I accept, justify, and save them. All others abide under My curse because they worship creatures instead of Me.

Without the doctrine of justification there can be only ignorance of God. Those who refuse to be justified by Christ are idolaters. They remain under the Law, sin, death, and the power of the devil. Everything they do is wrong.

Nowadays there are many such idolaters who want to be counted among the true confessors of the Gospel. They may even teach that men are delivered from their sins by the death of Christ. But because they attach more importance to charity than to faith in Christ they dishonor Him and pervert His Word. They do not serve the true God, but an idol of their own invention. The true God has never yet smiled upon a person for his charity or virtues, but only for the sake of Christ's merits.

The objection is frequently raised that the Bible commands that we should love God with all our heart. True enough. But because God commands it, it does not follow that we do it. If we could love God with all our heart we should undoubtedly be justified by our obedience, for it is written, "Which if a man do, he shall live in them." (Lev. 18:5.) But now comes the Gospel and says: "Because you do not do these things, you cannot live in them." The words, "Thou shalt love the Lord, thy God," require perfect obedience, perfect fear, perfect trust, and perfect love. But where are the people who can render perfection? Hence, this commandment, instead of justifying men, only accuses and condemns them. "Christ is the end of the law for righteousness to every one that believeth" (Romans 10:1.)

How may these two contradictory statements of the Apostle, "Ye knew not God," and "Ye worshipped God," be reconciled? I answer: By nature all men know that there is a God, "because that which may be known of God is manifest in them, for God hath showed it unto them. For the invisible things of him from the creation of the world are clearly seen." (Romans 1:19, 20.) Furthermore, the different religions to be found among all nations at all times bear witness to the fact that all men have a certain intuitive knowledge of God.

If all men know God how can Paul say that the Galatians did not know God prior to the hearing of the Gospel? I answer: There is a twofold knowledge of God, general and particular. All men have the general and instinctive recognition that there is a God who created heaven and earth, who is just and holy, and who punishes the wicked. How God feels about us, what His intentions are, what He will do for us, or how He will save us, that men cannot know instinctively. It must be revealed to them. I may know a person by sight, and still not know him, because I do not know how he feels about me. Men know instinctively that there is a God. But what His will is toward them, they do not know. It is written: "There is none that understandeth God." (Romans 3:11.) Again, "No man hath seen God." (John 1:18.) Now, what good does it do you if you know that there is a God, if you do not know how He feels about you, or what He wants of you? People have done a good deal of guessing. The Jew imagines he is doing the will of God if he concentrates on the Law of Moses. The Mohammedan thinks his Koran is the will of God. The monk fancies he is doing the will of God if he performs his vows. But they deceive themselves and become "vain in their imaginations," as Paul says, Romans 1:21. Instead of worshipping the true God, they worship the vain imaginations of their foolish hearts.

What Paul means by saying to the Galatians, "When ye knew not God," is simply this: "There was a time when you did not know the will of God in Christ, but you worshipped gods of your own invention, thinking that you had to perform this or that labor."

Whether you understand the "elements of the world" to mean the Law of Moses, or the religions of the heathen nations, it makes no difference. Those who lapse from the Gospel to the Law are no better off than those who lapse from grace into idolatry. Without Christ all religion is idolatry. Without Christ men will entertain false ideas about God, call their ideas what you like, the laws of Moses, the ordinances of the Pope, the Koran of the Mohammedans, or what have you.

VERSE 9. But now, after that ye have known God.

"Is it not amazing," cries Paul, "that you Galatians who knew God intimately by the hearing of the Gospel, should all of a sudden revert from the true knowledge of His will in which I thought you were confirmed, to the weak and beggarly elements of the Law which can only enslave you again?"

VERSE 9. Or rather are known of God.

The Apostle turns the foregoing sentence around. He fears the Galatians have lost God altogether. "Alas," he cries, "have you come to this, that you no longer know God? What else am I to think? Nevertheless, God knows you." Our knowledge of God is rather passive than active. God knows us better than we know God. "Ye are known of God" means that God brings His Gospel to our attention, and endows us with faith and the Holy Spirit. Even in these words the Apostle denies the possibility of our knowing God by the performance of the Law. "No man knoweth who the Father is, but the Son, and he to whom the Son will reveal him." (Luke 10:22.) "By his knowledge shall my righteous servant justify many; for he shall bear their iniquities." (Isaiah 53:11.)

The Apostle frankly expresses his surprise to the Galatians that they who had known God intimately through the Gospel, should so easily be persuaded by the false apostles to return to the weak and beggarly elements of the Law. I would not be surprised to see my church perverted by some fanatic through one or two sermons. We are no better than the apostles who had to witness the subversion of the churches which they had planted with their own hands. Nevertheless, Christ will reign to the end of the world, and that miraculously, as He did during the Dark Ages.

Paul seems to think rather ill of the Law. He calls it the elements of the world, the weak and beggarly elements of the world. Was it not irreverent for him to speak that way about the holy Law of God? The Law ought to prepare the way of Christ into the hearts of men. That is the true purpose and function of the Law. But if the Law presumes to usurp the place and function of the Gospel, it is no longer the holy Law of God, but a pseudo-Gospel.

If you care to amplify this matter you may add the observation that the Law is a weak and beggarly element because it makes people weak and beggarly. The Law has no power and affluence to make men strong and rich before God. To seek to be justified by the Law amounts to the same thing as if a person who is already weak and feeble should try to find strength in weakness, or as if a person with the dropsy should seek a cure by exposing himself to the pestilence, or as if a leper should go to a leper, and a beggar to a beggar to find health and wealth.

Those who seek to be justified by the Law grow weaker and more destitute right along. They are weak and bankrupt to begin with. They are by nature the children of wrath. Yet for salvation they grasp at the straw of the Law. The Law can only aggravate their weakness and poverty. The Law makes them ten times weaker and poorer than they were before.

I and many others have experienced the truth of this. I have known monks who zealously labored to please God for salvation, but the more they labored the more impatient, miserable, uncertain, and fearful they became. What else can you expect? You cannot grow strong through weakness and rich through poverty. People who prefer the Law to the Gospel are like Aesop's dog who let go of the meat to snatch at the shadow of the water. There is no satisfaction in the Law. What satisfaction can there be in collecting laws with which to torment oneself and others? One law breeds ten more until their number is legion.

Who would have thought it possible that the Galatians, taught as they were by that efficient apostle and teacher, Paul, could so quickly be led astray by the false apostles? To fall away from the Gospel is an easy matter because few people appreciate what an excellent treasure the knowledge of Christ really is. People are not sufficiently exercised in their faith by afflictions. They do not wrestle against sin. They live in security without conflict. Because they have never been tried in the furnace of affliction they are not properly equipped with the armor of God and know not how to use the sword of the Spirit. As long as they are being shepherded by faithful pastors, all is well. But when their faithful shepherds are gone and wolves disguised as sheep break into the fold, back they go to the weak and beggarly elements of the Law.

Whoever goes back to the Law loses the knowledge of the truth, fails in the recognition of his sinfulness, does not know God, nor the devil, nor himself, and does not understand the meaning and purpose of the Law. Without the knowledge of Christ a man will always argue that the Law is necessary for salvation, that it will strengthen the weak and enrich the poor. Wherever this opinion holds sway the promises of God are denied, Christ is demoted, hypocrisy and idolatry are established.

VERSE 9. *Whereunto ye desire again to be in bondage.*

The Apostle pointedly asks the Galatians whether they desire to be in bondage again to the Law. The Law is weak and poor, the sinner is weak and poor — two feeble beggars trying to help each other. They cannot do it. They only wear each other out. But through Christ a weak and poor sinner is revived and enriched unto eternal life.

Galatians 4:10-31

VERSE 10. Ye observe days, and months, and times, and years.

The Apostle Paul knew what the false apostles were teaching the Galatians: The observance of days, and months, and times, and years. The Jews had been obliged to keep holy the Sabbath Day, the new moons, the feast of the passover, the feast of tabernacles, and other feasts. The false apostles constrained the Galatians to observe these Jewish feasts under threat of damnation. Paul hastens to tell the Galatians that they were exchanging their Christian liberty for the weak and beggarly elements of the world.

VERSE 11. I am afraid of you, lest I have bestowed upon you labor in vain.

It grieves the Apostle to think that he might have preached the Gospel to the Galatians in vain. But this statement expresses more than grief. Behind his apparent disappointment at their failure lurks the sharp reprimand that they had forsaken Christ and that they were proving themselves to be obstinate unbelievers. But he does not openly condemn them for fear that oversharp criticism might alienate them altogether. He therefore changes the tone of his voice and speaks kindly to them.

VERSE 12. Be as I am; for I am as ye are.

Up to this point Paul has been occupied with the doctrinal aspect of the apostasy of the Galatians. He did not conceal his disappointment at their lack of stability. He had rebuked them. He had called them fools, crucifiers of Christ, etc. Now that the more important part of his Epistle has been finished, he realizes that he has handled the Galatians too roughly. Anxious lest he should do more harm than good, he is careful to let them see that his criticism proceeds from affection and a true apostolic concern for their welfare. He is eager to mitigate his sharp words with gentle sentiments in order to win them again.

Like Paul, all pastors and ministers ought to have much sympathy for their poor straying sheep, and instruct them in the spirit of meekness. They cannot be straightened out in any other way. Oversharp criticism provokes anger and despair, but no repentance. And here let us note, by the way, that true doctrine always produces concord. When men embrace errors, the tie of Christian love is broken.

At the beginning of the Reformation we were honored as the true ministers of Christ. Suddenly certain false brethren began to hate us. We had given them no offense, no occasion to hate us. They knew then as they know now that ours is the singular desire to publish the Gospel of Christ everywhere. What changed their attitude toward us? False doctrine. Seduced into error by the false apostles, the Galatians refused to acknowledge St. Paul as their pastor. The name and doctrine of Paul became obnoxious to them. I fear this Epistle recalled very few from their error.

Paul knew that the false apostles would misconstrue his censure of the Galatians to their own advantage and say: "So this is your Paul whom you praise so much. What sweet names he is calling you in his letter. When he was with you he acted like a father, but now he acts like a dictator." Paul knew what to expect of the false apostles and therefore he is worried. He does not know what to say. It is hard for a man to defend his cause at a distance, especially when he has reason to think that he personally has fallen into disfavor.

VERSE 12. Be as I am; for I am as ye are.

In beseeching the Galatians to be as he is, Paul expresses the hope that they might hold the same affection for him that he holds for them. "Perhaps I have been a little hard with you. Forgive it. Do not judge my heart according to my words."

We request the same consideration for ourselves. Our way of writing is incisive and straightforward. But there is no bitterness in our heart. We seek the honor of Christ and the welfare of men. We do not hate the Pope as to wish him ill. We do not desire the death of our false brethren. We desire that they may turn from their evil ways to Christ and be saved with us. A teacher chastises the pupil to reform him. The rod hurts, but correction is necessary. A father punishes his son because he loves his son. If he did not love the lad he would not punish him but let him have his own way in everything until he comes to harm. Paul beseeches the Galatians to look upon his correction as a sign that he really cared for them. "Now no chastening for the present seemeth to be joyous, but grievous; nevertheless, afterward it yieldeth the peaceable fruit of righteousness unto them which are exercised thereby." (Heb. 12:11.)

Although Paul seeks to soften the effect of his reproachful words, he does not take them back. When a physician administers a bitter potion to a patient, he does it to cure the patient. The fact that the medicine is bitter is no fault of the physician. The malady calls for a bitter medicine. Paul wants the Galatians to judge his words according to the situation that made them necessary.

VERSE 12. Brethren, I beseech you... Ye have not injured me at all.

Would you call it beseeching the Galatians to call them "bewitched," "disobedient," "crucifiers of Christ"? The Apostle calls it an earnest beseeching. And so it is. When a father corrects his son it means as if he were saying, "My son, I beseech you, be a good boy."

VERSE 12. Ye have not injured me at all.

"I am not angry with you," says Paul. "Why should I be angry with you, since you have done me no injury at all?"

To this the Galatians reply: "Why, then, do you say that we are perverted, that we have forsaken the true doctrine, that we are foolish, bewitched, etc., if you are not angry? We must have offended you somehow."

Paul answers: "You Galatians have not injured me. You have injured yourselves. I chide you not because I wish you ill. I have no reason to wish you ill. God is my witness, you have done me no wrong. On the contrary, you have been very good to me. The reason I write to you is because I love you."

The bitter potion must be sweetened with honey and sugar to make it palatable. When parents have punished their children they give them apples, pears, and other good things to show them that they mean well.

VERSES 13, 14. Ye know how through infirmity of the flesh I preached the gospel unto you at the first. And my temptation which was in my flesh ye despised not, nor rejected; but received me as an angel of God, even as Christ Jesus.

"You Galatians were very good to me. When I began to preach the Gospel to you in the infirmity of my flesh and in great temptation you were not at all offended. On the contrary, you were so loving, so kind, so friendly towards me, you received me like an angel, like Jesus Himself."

Indeed, the Galatians are to be commended for receiving the Gospel from a man as unimposing and afflicted all around as Paul was. Wherever he preached the Gospel, Jews and Gentiles raved against him. All the influential and religious people of his day denounced him. But the Galatians did not mind it. That was greatly to their honor. And Paul does not neglect to praise them for it. This praise Paul bestows on none of the other churches to which he wrote.

St. Jerome and others of the ancient fathers allege this infirmity of Paul's to have been some physical defect, or concupiscence. Jerome and the other diagnosticians lived at a time when the Church enjoyed peace and prosperity, when the bishops increased in wealth and standing, when pastors and bishops no longer sat over the Word of God. No wonder they failed to understand Paul.

When Paul speaks of the infirmity of his flesh he does not mean some physical defect or carnal lust, but the sufferings and afflictions which he endured in his body. What these infirmities were he himself explains in II Corinthians 12:9, 10: "Most gladly therefore will I rather glory in my infirmities, that the power of Christ may rest upon me. Therefore I take pleasure in infirmities, in reproaches, in necessities, in persecutions, in distresses for Christ's sake: for when I am weak, then am I strong." And in the eleventh chapter of the same Epistle the Apostle writes: "In labors more abundant, in stripes above measure, in prisons more frequent, in deaths oft. Of the Jews five times received I forty stripes save one. Thrice was I beaten with rods, once was I stoned, thrice I suffered shipwreck," etc. (II Cor. 11:23-25.) By the infirmity of his flesh Paul meant these afflictions and not some chronic disease. He reminds the Galatians how he was always in peril at the hands of the Jews, Gentiles, and false brethren, how he suffered hunger and want.

Now, the afflictions of the believers always offend people. Paul knew it and therefore has high praise for the Galatians because they over looked his afflictions and received him like an angel. Christ forewarned the faithful against the offense of the Cross, saying: "Blessed is he, whosoever shall not be offended in me." (Matt. 11:6.) Surely it is no easy thing to confess Him Lord of all and Savior of the world who was a reproach of men, and despised of the people, and the laughing stock of the world. (Ps. 22:7.) I say, to value this poor Christ, so spitefully scorned, spit upon, scourged, and crucified, more than the riches of the richest, the strength of the strongest, the wisdom of the wisest, is something. It is worth being called blessed.

Paul not only had outward afflictions but also inner, spiritual afflictions. He refers to these in II Corinthians 7:6, "Without were fightings, within were fears." In his letter to the Philippians Paul makes mention of the restoration of Epaphroditus as a special act of mercy on the part of God, "lest I should have sorrow upon sorrow."

Considering the many afflictions of Paul, we are not surprised to hear him loudly praising the Galatians for not being offended at him as others were. The world thinks us mad because we go about to comfort, to help, to save others while we ourselves are in distress. People tell us: "Physician, heal thyself." (Luke 4:23.)

The Apostle tells the Galatians that he will keep their kindness in perpetual remembrance. Indirectly, he also reminds them how much they had loved him before the invasion of the false apostles, and gives them a hint that they should return to their first love for him.

VERSE 15. *Where is then the blessedness ye spake of?*

"How much happier you used to be. And how you Galatians used to tell me that you were blessed. And how much did I not praise and commend you formerly." Paul reminds them of former and better times in an effort to mitigate his sharp reproaches, lest the false apostles should slander him and misconstrue his letter to his disadvantage and to their own advantage. Such snakes in the grass are equal to anything. They will pervert words spoken from a sincere heart and twist them to mean just the opposite of what they were intended to convey. They are like spiders that suck venom out of sweet and fragrant flowers. The poison is not in the flowers, but it is the nature of the spider to turn what is good and wholesome into poison.

VERSE 15. For I bear you record, that, if it had been possible, ye would have plucked out your own eyes, and have given them to me.

The Apostle continues his praise of the Galatians. "You did not only treat me very courteously. If it had been necessary you would have plucked out your eyes and sacrificed your lives for me." And in very fact the Galatians sacrificed their lives for Paul. By receiving and maintaining Paul they called upon their own heads the hatred and malice of all the Jews and Gentiles.

Nowadays the name of Luther carries the same stigma. Whoever praises Luther is a worse sinner than an idolater, perjurer, or thief.

VERSE 16. Am I therefore become your enemy, because I tell you the truth?

Paul's reason for praising the Galatians is to avoid giving them the impression as if he were their enemy because he had reprimanded them.

A true friend will admonish his erring brother, and if the erring brother has any sense at all he will thank his friend. In the world truth produces hatred. Whoever speaks the truth is counted an enemy. But among friends it is not so, much less among Christians. The Apostle wants his Galatians to know that just because he had told them the truth they are not to think that he dislikes them. "I told you the truth because I love you."

VERSE 17. They zealously affect you, but not well.

Paul takes the false apostles to task for their flattery. Satan's satellites soft-soap the people. Paul calls it "by good words and fair speeches to deceive the hearts of the simple." (Romans 16:18.)

They tell me that by my stubbornness in this doctrine of the Sacrament I am destroying the harmony of the church. They say it would be better if we would make some slight concession rather than cause such commotion and controversy in the Church regarding an article which is not even one of the fundamental doctrines. My reply is, cursed be any love or harmony which demands for its preservation that we place the Word of God in jeopardy!

VERSE 17. Yea, they would exclude you, that ye might affect them.

"Do you Galatians know why the false apostles are so zealous about you? They expect you to reciprocate. And that would leave me out. If their zeal were right they would not mind your loving me. But they hate my doctrine and want to stamp it out. In order to bring this to pass they go about to alienate your hearts from me and to make me obnoxious to you." In this way Paul brings the false apostles into suspicion. He questions their motives. He maintains that their zeal is mere pretense to deceive the Galatians. Our Savior Christ also warned us, saying: "Beware of false prophets, which come to you in sheep's clothing." (Matt. 7:15.)

Paul was considerably disturbed by the commissions and changes that followed in the wake of his preaching. He was accused of being "a pestilent fellow, a mover of sedition among all the Jews throughout the world." (Acts 24:5.) In Philippi the townspeople cried that he troubled their city and taught customs which were not lawful for them to receive. (Acts 16:20, 21.)

All troubles, calamities, famines, wars were laid to the charge of the Gospel of the apostles. However, the apostles were not deterred by such calumnies from preaching the Gospel. They knew that they "ought to obey God rather than men," and that it was better for the world to be upset than to be ignorant of Christ.

Do you think for a moment that these reactions did not worry the apostles? They were not made of iron. They foresaw the revolutionary character of the Gospel. They also foresaw the dissensions that would creep into the Church. It was bad news for Paul when he heard that the Corinthians were denying the resurrection of the dead, that the churches he had planted were experiencing all kinds of difficulties, and that the Gospel was being supplanted by false doctrines.

But Paul also knew that the Gospel was not to blame. He did not resign his office because he knew that the Gospel he preached was the power of God unto salvation to every one that believes.

The same criticism which was leveled at the apostles is leveled at us. The doctrine of the Gospel, we are told, is the cause of all the present unrest in the world. There is no wrong that is not laid to our charge. But why? We do not spread wicked lies. We preach the glad tidings of Christ. Our opponents will bear us out when we say that we never fail to urge respect for the constituted authorities, because that is the will of God.

All of these vilifications cannot discourage us. We know that there is nothing the devil hates worse than the Gospel. It is one of his little tricks to blame the Gospel for every evil in the world. Formerly, when the traditions of the fathers were taught in the Church, the devil was not excited as he is now. It goes to show that our doctrine is of God, else "behemoth would lie under shady trees, in the covert of the reed, and fens." The fact that he is again walking about as a roaring lion to stir up riots and disorders is a sure sign that he has begun to feel the effect of our preaching.

VERSE 18. But it is good to be zealously affected always in a good thing, and not only when I am present with you.

"When I was present with you, you loved me, although I preached the Gospel to you in the infirmity of my flesh. The fact that I am now absent from you ought not to change your attitude towards me. Although I am absent in the flesh, I am with you in spirit and in my doctrine which you ought to retain by all means because through it you received the Holy Spirit."

VERSE 19. My little children, of whom I travail in birth again until Christ be formed in you.

With every single word the Apostle seeks to regain the confidence of the Galatians. He now calls them lovingly his little children. He adds the simile: "Of whom I travail in birth again." As parents reproduce their physical characteristics in their children, so the apostles reproduced their faith in the hearts of the hearers, until Christ was formed in them. A person has the form of Christ when he believes in Christ to the exclusion of everything else. This faith in Christ is engendered by the Gospel as the Apostle declares in I Corinthians 4:15: "In Christ Jesus I have begotten you through the Gospel"; and in II Corinthians 3:3, "Ye are the epistle of Christ ministered by us, written not with ink, but with the Spirit of the living God." The Word of God falling from the lips of the apostle or minister enters into the heart of the hearer. The Holy Ghost impregnates the Word so that it brings forth the fruit of faith. In this manner every Christian pastor is a spiritual father who forms Christ in the hearts of his hearers.

At the same time Paul indicts the false apostles. He says: "I have begotten you Galatians through the Gospel, giving you the form of Christ. But these false apostles are giving you a new form, the form of Moses." Note the Apostle does not say, "Of whom I travail in birth again until I be formed in you," but "until Christ be formed in you." The false apostles had torn the form of Christ out of the hearts of the Galatians and substituted their own form. Paul endeavors to reform them, or rather reform Christ in them.

VERSE 20. I desire to be present with you now, and to change my voice.

A common saying has it that a letter is a dead messenger. Something is lacking in all writing. You can never be sure how the written page will affect the reader, because his mood, his circumstances, his affections are so changeable. It is different with the spoken word. If it is harsh and ill-timed it can always be remodeled. No wonder the Apostle expresses the wish that he could speak to the Galatians in person. He could change his voice according to their attitude. If he saw that they were repentant he could soften the tone of his voice. If he saw that they were stubborn he could speak to them more earnestly. This way he did not know how to deal with them by letter. If his Epistle is too severe it will do more damage than good. If it is too gentle, it will not correct conditions. But if he could be with them in person he could change his voice as the occasion demanded.

VERSE 20. For I stand in doubt of you.

"I do not know how to take you. I do not know how to approach you by letter." In order to make sure that he leaves no stone unturned in his effort to recall them to the Gospel of Christ, he chides, entreats, praises, and blames the Galatians, trying every way to hit the right note and tone of voice.

VERSE 21. Tell me, ye that desire to be under the law, do ye not hear the law?

Here Paul would have closed his Epistle because he did not know what else to say. He wishes he could see the Galatians in person and straighten out their difficulties. But he is not sure whether the Galatians have fully understood the difference between the Gospel and the Law. To make sure, he introduces another illustration. He knows people like illustrations and stories. He knows that Christ Himself made ample use of parables.

Paul is an expert at allegories. They are dangerous things. Unless a person has a thorough knowledge of Christian doctrine he had better leave allegories alone.

The allegory which Paul is about to bring is taken from the Book of Genesis which he calls the Law. True, that book contains no mention of the Law. Paul simply follows the custom of the Jews who included the first book of Moses in the collective term, "Law." Jesus even included the Psalms.

VERSES 22, 23. For it is written, that Abraham had two sons, the one by a bondmaid, the other by a freewoman. But he who was of the bondwoman was born after the flesh; but he of the freewoman was by promise.

This is Paul's allegory. Abraham had two sons: Ishmael by Hagar, and Isaac by Sarah. They were both the true sons of Abraham, with this difference, that Ishmael was born after the flesh, i.e., without the commandment and promise of God, while Isaac was born according to the promise.

With the permission of Sarah, Abraham took Hagar, Sarah's bondwoman, to wife. Sarah knew that God had promised to make her husband Abraham the father of a nation, and she hoped that she would be the mother of this promised nation. But with the passage of the years her hope died out. In order that the promise of God should not be annulled by her barrenness this holy woman resigned her right and honor to her maid. This was no easy thing for her to do. She abased herself. She thought: "God is no liar. What He has promised He will perform. But perhaps God does not want me to be the mother of Abraham's posterity. Perhaps He prefers Hagar for the honor."

Ishmael was thus born without a special word or promise of God, at the mere request of Sarah. God did not command Abraham to take Hagar, nor did God promise to bless the coalition. It is evident that Ishmael was the son of Abraham after the flesh, and not after the promise.

In the ninth chapter of the Epistle to the Romans St. Paul advances the same argument which he amplifies into an allegory in writing to the Galatians. There he argues that all the children of Abraham are not the children of God. For Abraham had two kinds of children, children born of the promise, like Isaac, and other children born without the promise, as Ishmael. With this argument Paul squelched the proud Jews who gloried that they were the children of God because they were the seed and the children of Abraham. Paul makes it clear enough that it takes more than an Abrahamic pedigree to be a child of God. To be a child of God requires faith in Christ.

VERSE 24. Which things are an allegory.

Allegories are not very convincing, but like pictures they visualize a matter. If Paul had not brought in advance indisputable arguments for the righteousness of faith over against the righteousness of works this allegory would do little good. Having first fortified his case with invincible arguments, he can afford to inject this allegory to add impressiveness and beauty to his presentation.

VERSES 24, 25. For these are the two covenants; the one from the mount Sinai, which gendereth to bondage, which is Agar. For this Agar is mount Sinai in Arabia.

In this allegory Abraham represents God. Abraham had two sons, born respectively of Hagar and Sarah. The two women represent the two Testaments. The Old Testament is Mount Sinai, the bondwoman, Hagar. The Arabians call Mount Sinai Agar. It may be that the similarity of these two names gave Paul his idea for this allegory. As Hagar bore Abraham a son who was not an heir but a servant, so Sinai, the Law, the allegorical Hagar, bore God a carnal and servile people of the Law without promise. The Law has a promise but it is a conditional promise, depending upon whether people fulfill the Law.

The Jews regarded the conditional promises of the Law as if they were unconditional. When the prophets foretold the destruction of Jerusalem, the Jews stoned them as blasphemers of God. They never gave it any thought that there was a condition attached to the Law which reads: "If you keep the commandments it shall be well with thee."

VERSE 25. And answereth to Jerusalem which now is, and is in bondage with her children.

A little while ago Paul called Mount Sinai, Hagar. He would now gladly make Jerusalem the Sarah of the New Testament, but he cannot. The earthly Jerusalem is not Sarah, but a part of Hagar. Hagar lives there in the home of the Law, the Temple, the priesthood, the ceremonies, and whatever else was ordained in the Law at Mount Sinai.

I would have been tempted to call Jerusalem, Sarah, or the New Testament. I would have been pleased with this turn of the allegory. It goes to show that not everybody has the gift of allegory. Would you not think it perfectly proper to call Sinai Hagar and Jerusalem Sarah? True, Paul does call Sarah Jerusalem. But he has the spiritual and heavenly Jerusalem in mind, not the earthly Jerusalem. Sarah represents that spiritual Jerusalem where there is no Law but only the promise, and where the inhabitants are free.

To show that the Law has been quite abolished, the earthly Jerusalem was completely destroyed with all her ornaments, temples, and ceremonies.

VERSE 26. But Jerusalem which is above is free, which is the mother of us all.

The earthly Jerusalem with its ordinances and laws represents Hagar and her offspring. They are slaves to the Law, sin and death. But the heavenly Jerusalem is Sarah, the free woman. This heavenly Jerusalem is the Church, that is to say the number of all believers throughout the world, having one and the same Gospel, one and the same faith in Christ, one and the same Holy Ghost, and the same sacraments.

Do not mistake this one word "above" to refer to the triumphant Church in heaven, but to the militant Church on earth. In Philippians 3:20, the Apostle uses the phrase: "Our conversation is in heaven," not locally in heaven, but in spirit. When a believer accepts the heavenly gifts of the Gospel he is in heaven. So also in Ephesians 1:3, "Who hath blessed us with all spiritual blessings in heavenly places in Christ." Jerusalem here means the universal Christian Church on earth.

Sarah, the Church, as the bride of Christ bears free children who are not subject to the Law.

VERSE 27. For it is written, Rejoice, thou barren that bearest not; break forth and cry, thou that travailest not: for the desolate hath many more children than she which hath an husband.

Paul quotes the allegorical prophecy of Isaiah to the effect that the mother of many children must die desolately, while the barren woman shall have an abundance of children. (Isaiah 54:1.) He applies this prophecy to Hagar and Sarah, to the Law and the Gospel. The Law as the husband of the fruitful woman procreates many children. For men of all ages have had the idea that they are right when they follow after the Law and outwardly perform its requirements.

Although the Law has many children, they are not free. They are slaves. As servants they cannot have a share in the inheritance, but are driven from the house as Ishmael was cast out of the house of Abraham. In fact the servants of the Law are even now barred from the kingdom of light and liberty, for "he that believeth not, is condemned already." (John 3:18.) As the servants of the Law they remain under the curse of the Law, under sin and death, under the power of the devil, and under the wrath and judgment of God.

On the other hand, Sarah, the free Church, seems barren. The Gospel of the Cross which the Church proclaims does not have the appeal that the Law has for men, and therefore it does not find many adherents. The Church does not look prosperous. Unbelievers have always predicted the death of the Church. The Jews were quite certain that the Church would not long endure. They said to Paul: "As concerning this sect, we know that everywhere it is spoken against." (Acts 28:22.) No matter how barren and forsaken, how weak and desolate the Church may seem, she alone is really fruitful before God. By the Gospel she procreates an infinite number of children that are free heirs of everlasting life.

The Law, "the old husband," is really dead. But not all people know it, or want to know it. They labor and bear the burden and the heat of the day, and bring forth many children, children that are bastards like themselves, children born to be put out of the house like Ishmael to perish forever. Accursed be that doctrine, life, and religion which endeavors to obtain righteousness before God by the Law and its creeds.

The scholastics think that the judicial and ceremonial laws of Moses were abolished by the coming of Christ, but not the moral law. They are blind. When Paul declares that we are delivered from the curse of the Law he means the whole Law, particularly the moral law which more than the other laws accuses, curses, and condemns the conscience. The Ten Commandments have no right to condemn that conscience in which Jesus dwells, for Jesus has taken from the Ten Commandments the right and power to curse us.

Not as if the conscience is now insensitive to the terrors of the Law, but the Law cannot drive the conscience to despair. "There is now no condemnation to them which are in Christ Jesus." (Romans 8:1.) "If the Son shall make you free, ye shall be free indeed." (John 8:36.)

You will complain: "But I am not doing anything." That is right. You cannot do a thing to be delivered from the tyranny of the Law. But listen to the glad tidings which the Holy Ghost brings to you in the words of the prophet: "Rejoice, thou barren." As Christ is greater than the Law, so much more excellent is the righteousness of Christ than the righteousness of the Law.

In one more respect the Law has been abolished. The civil laws of Moses do not concern us, and should not be put back in force. That does not mean that we are exempt from obedience to the civil laws under which we live. On the contrary, the Gospel commands Christians to obey government "not only for wrath, but also for conscience sake." (Romans 13:5.)

Neither do the ordinances of Moses or those of the Pope concern us. But because life cannot go on without some ordinances, the Gospel permits regulations to be made in the Church in regard to special days, times, places, etc., in order that the people may know upon what day, at what hour, and in what place to assemble for the Word of God. Such directions are desirable that "all things be done decently and in order." (I Cor. 14:40.) These directions may be changed or omitted altogether, as long as no offense is given to the weak.

Paul, however, refers particularly to the abolition of the moral law. If faith alone in Christ justifies, then the whole Law is abolished without exception. And this the Apostle proves by the testimony of Isaiah, who bids the barren to rejoice because she will have many children, whereas she that has a husband and many children will be forsaken.

Isaiah calls the Church barren because her children are born without effort by the Word of faith through the Spirit of God. It is a matter of birth, not of exertion. The believer too works, but not in an effort to become a son and an heir of God. He is that before he goes to work. He is born a son and an heir. He works for the glory of God and the welfare of his fellowmen.

VERSE 28. *Now we, brethren, as Isaac was, are the children of promise.*

The Jews claimed to be the children of God because they were the children of Abraham. Jesus answered them, John 8:39, 40, "If ye were Abraham's children, ye would do the works of Abraham. But now ye seek to kill me, a man that hath told you the truth." And in verse 42: "If God were your Father, ye would love me." In other words: "You are not the children of God. If you were, you would know and love me. Brothers born and living together in the same house recognize each other. You do not recognize me. You are of your father, the devil."

We are not like these Jews, the children of the bondwoman, the Law, who were cast out of the house by Jesus. We are children of the promise like Isaac, born of grace and faith unto an everlasting inheritance.

VERSE 29. *But as that he that was born after the flesh persecuted him that was born after the Spirit, even so it is now.*

This is a cheering thought. We who are born of the Gospel, and live in Christ, and rejoice in our inheritance, have Ishmael for our enemy. The children of the Law will always persecute the children of the Gospel. This is our daily experience. Our opponents tell us that everything was at peace before the Gospel was revived by us. Since then the whole world has been upset. People blame us and the Gospel for everything, for the disobedience of subjects to their rulers, for wars, plagues, and famines, for revolutions, and every other evil that can be imagined. No wonder our opponents think they are doing God a favor by hating and persecuting us. Ishmael will persecute Isaac.

We invite our opponents to tell us what good things attended the preaching of the Gospel by the apostles. Did not the destruction of Jerusalem follow on the heels of the Gospel? And how about the overthrow of the Roman Empire? Did not the whole world seethe with unrest as the Gospel was preached in the whole world? We do not say that the Gospel instigated these upheavals. The iniquity of man did it.

Our opponents blame our doctrine for the present turmoil. But ours is a doctrine of grace and peace. It does not stir up trouble. Trouble starts when the people, the nations and their rulers of the earth rage and take counsel together against the Lord, and against His anointed. (Psalm 2.) But all their counsels shall be brought to naught. "He that sitteth in the heavens shall laugh: the Lord shall have them in derision." (Psalm 2:4.) Let them cry out against us as much as they like. We know that they are the cause of all their own troubles.

As long as we preach Christ and confess Him to be our Savior, we must be content to be called vicious trouble makers. "These that have turned the world upside down are come hither also; and these all do contrary to the decrees of Caesar," so said the Jews of Paul and Silas. (Acts 17:6, 7.) Of Paul they said: "We have found this man a pestilent fellow, and a mover of sedition among all the Jews throughout the world, and a ringleader of the sect of the Nazarenes." The Gentiles uttered similar complaints: "These men do exceedingly trouble our city."

This man Luther is also accused of being a pestilent fellow who troubles the papacy and the Roman empire. If I would keep silent, all would be well, and the Pope would no more persecute me. The moment I open my mouth the Pope begins to fume and to rage. It seems we must choose between Christ and the Pope. Let the Pope perish.

Christ foresaw the reaction of the world to the Gospel. He said: "I am come to send fire on the earth, and what will I, if it be already kindled?" (Luke 12:49.)

Do not take the statement of our opponents seriously, that no good can come of the preaching of the Gospel. What do they know? They would not recognize the fruits of the Gospel if they saw them.

At any rate, our opponents cannot accuse us of adultery, murder, theft, and such crimes. The worst they can say about us is that we have the Gospel. What is wrong with the Gospel? We teach that Christ, the Son of God, has redeemed us from sin and everlasting death. This is not our doctrine. It belongs to Christ. If there is anything wrong with it, it is not our fault. If they want to condemn Christ for being our Savior and Redeemer, that is their lookout. We are mere onlookers, watching to see who will win the victory, Christ or His opponents.

On one occasion Jesus remarked: "If ye were of the world, the world would love his own, but because ye are not of the world, but I have chosen you out of the world, therefore the world hateth you." (John 15:19.) In other words: "I am the cause of all your troubles. I am the one for whose sake you are killed. If you did not confess my name, the world would not hate you. The servant is not greater than his lord. If they have persecuted me, they will also persecute you."

Christ takes all the blame. He says: "You have not incurred the hatred and persecutions of the world. I have. But be of good cheer; I have overcome the world."

VERSE 30. Nevertheless what saith the Scripture? Cast out the bondwoman and her son: for the son of the bondwoman shall not be heir with the son of the free woman.

Sarah's demand that the bondwoman and her son be cast out of the house was undoubtedly a blow to Abraham. He felt sorry for his son Ishmael. The Scripture explicitly states Abraham's grief in the words: "And the thing was very grievous in Abraham's sight, because of his son." (Gen. 21:11.) But God approved Sarah's action and said to Abraham: "Let it not be grievous in thy sight because of the lad, and because of thy bondwoman; in all that Sarah hath said unto thee, hearken unto her voice; for in Isaac shall thy seed be called." (Gen. 21:12.)

The Holy Ghost contemptuously calls the admirers of the Law the children of the bondwoman. "If you do not know your mother, I will tell you what kind of a woman she is. She is a slave. And you are slaves. You are slaves of the Law and therefore slaves of sin, death, and everlasting damnation. You are not fit to be heirs. You are put out of the house."

This is the sentence which God pronounces upon the Ishmaelites, the papists, and all others who trust in their own merits, and persecute the Church of Christ. Because they are slaves and persecutors of the children of the free woman, they shall be cast out of the house of God forever. They shall have no inheritance with the children of the promise. This sentence stands forever.

This sentence affects not only those popes, cardinals bishops, and monks who were notoriously wicked and made their bellies their Gods. It strikes, also, those who lived in all sincerity to please God and to merit the forgiveness of their sins through a life of self-denial. Even these will be cast out, because they are children of the bondwoman.

Our opponents do not defend their own moral delinquency. The better ones deplore and abhor it. But they defend and uphold their doctrine of works which is of the devil. Our quarrel is not with those who live in manifest sins. Our quarrel is with those among them who think they live like angels, claiming that they do not only perform the Ten Commandments of God, but also the sayings of Christ, and many good works that God does not expect of them. We quarrel with them because they refuse to have Jesus' merit count alone for righteousness.

St. Bernard was one of the best of the medieval saints. He lived a chaste and holy life. But when it came to dying he did not trust in his chaste life for salvation. He prayed: "I have lived a wicked life. But Thou, Lord Jesus, hast a heaven to give unto me. First, because Thou art the Son of God. Secondly, because Thou hast purchased heaven for me by Thy suffering and death. Thou givest heaven to me, not because I earned it, but because Thou hast earned it for me." If any of the Romanists are saved it is because they forget their good deeds and merits and feel like Paul: "Not having mine own righteousness which is of the law, but that which is through the faith of Christ." (Phil. 3:9.)

VERSE 31. So then, brethren, we are not children of the bondwoman, but of the free.

With this sentence the Apostle Paul concludes his allegory of the barren Church. This sentence forms a clear rejection of the righteousness of the Law and a confirmation of the doctrine of justification. In the next chapter Paul lays special stress upon the freedom which the children of the free woman enjoy. He treats of Christian liberty, the knowledge of which is very necessary. The liberty which Christ purchased for us is a bulwark to us in our battle against spiritual tyranny. Therefore we must carefully study this doctrine of Christian liberty, not only for the confirmation of the doctrine of justification, but also for the comfort and encouragement of those who are weak in faith.

GALATIANS 5:1-13

In this chapter the Apostle Paul presents the doctrine of Christian liberty in a final effort to persuade the Galatians to give up the nefarious doctrine of the false apostles. To accomplish his purpose he adduces threats and promises, trying in every way possible to keep them in the liberty which Christ purchased for them.

VERSE 1. Stand fast therefore in the liberty wherewith Christ hath made us free.

"Be steadfast, not careless. Lie not down and sleep, but stand up. Be watchful. Hold fast the liberty wherewith Christ hath made you free." Those who loll cannot keep this liberty. Satan hates the light of the Gospel. When it begins to shine a little he fights against it with might and main.

What liberty does Paul mean? Not civil liberty (for which we have the government to thank), but the liberty which Christ has procured for us.

At one time the emperor was compelled to grant to the bishop of Rome certain immunities and privileges. This is civil liberty. That liberty exempts the clergy from certain public charges. Then there is also another kind of "liberty," when people obey neither the laws of God nor the laws of men, but do as they please. This carnal liberty the people want in our day. We are not now speaking of this liberty. Neither are we speaking of civil liberty.

Paul is speaking of a far better liberty, the liberty "wherewith Christ hath made us free," not from material bonds, not from the Babylonian captivity, not from the tyranny of the Turks, but from the eternal wrath of God.

Where is this liberty?

In the conscience.

Our conscience is free and quiet because it no longer has to fear the wrath of God. This is real liberty, compared with which every other kind of liberty is not worth mentioning. Who can adequately express the boon that comes to a person when he has the heart-assurance that God will nevermore be angry with him, but will forever be merciful to him for Christ's sake? This is indeed a marvelous liberty, to have the sovereign God for our Friend and Father who will defend, maintain, and save us in this life and in the life to come.

As an outgrowth of this liberty, we are at the same time free from the Law, sin, death, the power of the devil, hell, etc. Since the wrath of God has been assuaged by Christ no Law, sin, or death may now accuse and condemn us. These foes of ours will continue to frighten us, but not too much. The worth of our Christian liberty cannot be exaggerated.

Our conscience must he trained to fall back on the freedom purchased for us by Christ. Though the fears of the Law, the terrors of sin, the horror of death assail us occasionally, we know that these feelings shall not endure, because the prophet quotes God as saying: "In a little wrath I hid my face from thee for a moment: but with everlasting kindness will I have mercy on thee." (Isa. 54:8.)

We shall appreciate this liberty all the more when we bear in mind that it was Jesus Christ, the Son of God, who purchased it with His own blood. Hence, Christ's liberty is given us not by the Law, or for our own righteousness, but freely for Christ's sake. In the eighth chapter of the Gospel of St. John, Jesus declares: "If the Son shall make you free, ye shall be free indeed." He only stands between us and the evils which trouble and afflict us and which He has overcome for us.

Reason cannot properly evaluate this gift. Who can fully appreciate the blessing of the forgiveness of sins and of everlasting life? Our opponents claim that they also possess this liberty. But they do not. When they are put to the test all their self-confidence slips from them. What else can they expect when they trust in works and not in the Word of God?

Our liberty is founded on Christ Himself, who sits at the right hand of God and intercedes for us. Therefore our liberty is sure and valid as long as we believe in Christ. As long as we cling to Him with a steadfast faith we possess His priceless gifts. But if we are careless and indifferent we shall lose them. It is not without good reason that Paul urges us to watch and to stand fast. He knew that the devil delights in taking this liberty away from us.

VERSE 1. And be not entangled again with the yoke of bondage.

Because reason prefers the righteousness of the Law to the righteousness of faith, Paul calls the Law a yoke, a yoke of bondage. Peter also calls it a yoke. "Why tempt ye God, to put a yoke upon the neck of the disciples which neither our fathers nor we were able to bear?" (Acts 15:10.)

In this passage Paul again disparages the pernicious notion that the Law is able to make men righteous before God, a notion deeply rooted in man's reason. All mankind is so wrapped up in this idea that it is hard to drag it out of people. Paul compares those who seek to be justified by the Law to oxen that are hitched to the yoke. Like oxen that toil in the yoke all day, and in the evening are turned out to graze along the dusty road, and at last are marked for slaughter when they no longer can draw the burden, so those who seek to be justified by the Law are "entangled with the yoke of bondage," and when they have grown old and broken-down in the service of the Law they have earned for their perpetual reward God's wrath and everlasting torment.

We are not now treating of an unimportant matter. It is a matter that involves everlasting liberty or everlasting slavery. For as a liberation from God's wrath through the kind office of Christ is not a passing boon, but a permanent blessing, so also the yoke of the Law is not a temporary but an everlasting affliction.

Rightly are the doers of the Law called devil's martyrs. They take more pains to earn hell than the martyrs of Christ to obtain heaven. Theirs is a double misfortune. First they torture themselves on earth with self-inflicted penances and finally when they die they gain the reward of eternal damnation.

VERSE 2. *Behold, I Paul say unto you, that if ye be circumcised, Christ shall profit you nothing.*

Paul is incensed at the thought of the tyranny of the Law. His antagonism to the Law is a personal matter with him. "Behold, I, Paul," he says, "I who have received the Gospel not from men, but by the revelation of Jesus Christ: I who have been commissioned from above to preach the Gospel to you: I Paul say to you, If you submit to circumcision Christ will profit you nothing." Paul emphatically declares that for the Galatians to be circumcised would mean for them to lose the benefits of Christ's suffering and death. This passage may well serve as a criterion for all the religions. To teach that besides faith in Christ other devices like works, or the observance of rules, traditions, or ceremonies are necessary for the attainment of righteousness and everlasting life, is to make Christ and His salvation of no benefit to anybody.

This passage is an indictment of the whole papacy. All priests, monks, and nuns—and I am now speaking of the best of them—who repose their hope for salvation in their own works, and not in Christ, whom they imagine to he an angry judge, hear this sentence pronounced against them that Christ shall profit them nothing. If one can earn the forgiveness of sins and everlasting life through one's own efforts to what purpose was Christ born? What was the purpose of His suffering and death, His resurrection, His victory over sin, death, and the devil, if men may overcome these evils by their own endeavor? Tongue cannot express, nor heart conceive what a terrible thing it is to make Christ worthless.

The person who is not moved by these considerations to leave the Law and the confidence in his own righteousness for the liberty in Christ, has a heart that is harder than stone and iron.

Paul does not condemn circumcision in itself. Circumcision is not injurious to the person who does not ascribe any particular importance to it. Neither are works injurious provided a person does not attach any saving value to them. The Apostle does not say that works are objectionable, but to build one's hopes for righteousness on works is disastrous, for that makes Christ good for nothing.

Let us bear this in mind when the devil accuses our conscience. When that dragon accuses us of having done no good at all, but only evil, say to him: "You trouble me with the remembrance of my past sins; you remind me that I have done no good. But this does not bother me, because if I were to trust in my own good deeds, or despair because I have done no good deeds, Christ would profit me neither way. I am not going to make him unprofitable to me. This I would do, if I should presume to purchase for myself the favor of God and everlasting life by my good deeds, or if I should despair of my salvation because of my sins."

VERSE 3. For I testify again to every man that is circumcised, that he is a debtor to do the whole law.

The first fault with circumcision is that it makes Christ unprofitable. The second fault is that it obligates those who are circumcised to observe the whole Law. Paul is so very much in earnest about this matter that he confirms it with an oath. "I testify," he says, "I swear by the living God." Paul's statement may be explained negatively to mean: "I testify to every man who is being circumcised that he cannot perform the Law in any point. In the very act of circumcision he is not being circumcised, and in the very act of fulfilling the Law he fulfills it not." This seems to be the simple meaning of Paul's statement. Later on in the sixth chapter he explicitly states, "They themselves which are circumcised keep not the law. The fact that you are circumcised does not mean you are righteous and free from the Law. The truth is that by circumcision you have become debtors and servants of the Law. The more you endeavor to perform the Law, the more you will become tangled up in the yoke of the Law."

The truth of this I have experienced in myself and in others. I have seen many work themselves down to the bones in their hungry effort to obtain peace of conscience. But the harder they tried the more they worried. Especially in the presence of death they were so uneasy that I have seen murderers die with better grace and courage.

This holds true also in regard to the church regulations. When I was a monk I tried ever so hard to live up to the strict rules of my order. I used to make a list of my sins, and I was always on the way to confession, and whatever penances were enjoined upon me I performed religiously. In spite of it all, my conscience was always in a fever of doubt. The more I sought to help my poor stricken conscience the worse it got. The more I paid attention to the regulations the more I transgressed them.

Hence those that seek to be justified by the Law are much further away from the righteousness of life than the publicans, sinners, and harlots. They know better than to trust in their own works. They know that they cannot ever hope to obtain forgiveness by their sins.

Paul's statement in this verse may be taken to mean that those who submit to circumcision are thereby submitting to the whole Law. To obey Moses in one point requires obedience to him in all points. It does no good to say that only circumcision is necessary, and not the rest of Moses' laws. The same reasons that obligate a person to accept circumcision also obligate a person to accept the whole Law. Thus to acknowledge the Law is tantamount to declaring that Christ is not yet come. And if Christ is not yet come, then all the Jewish ceremonies and laws concerning meats, places, and times are still in force, and Christ must be awaited as one who is still to come. The whole Scripture, however, testifies that Christ has come, that by His death He has abolished the Law, and that He has fulfilled all things which the prophets have foretold about Him.

Some would like to subjugate us to certain parts of the Mosaic Law. But this is not to be permitted under any circumstances. If we permit Moses to rule over us in one thing, we must obey him in all things.

VERSE 4. Christ is become of no effect unto you, whosoever of you are justified by the law; ye are fallen from grace.

Paul in this verse discloses that he is not speaking so much of circumcision as the trust which men repose in the outward act. We can hear him say: "I do not condemn the Law in itself; what I condemn is that men seek to be justified by the Law, as if Christ were still to come, or as if He alone were unable to justify sinners. It is this that I condemn, because it makes Christ of no effect. It makes you void of Christ so that Christ is not in you, nor can you be partakers of the knowledge, the spirit, the fellowship, the liberty, the life, or the achievements of Christ. You are completely separated from Him, so much so that He has nothing to do with you any more, or for that matter you with Him." Can anything worse be said against the Law? If you think Christ and the Law can dwell together in your heart, you may be sure that Christ dwells not in your heart. For if Christ is in your heart He neither condemns you, nor does He ever bid you to trust in your own good works. If you know Christ at all, you know that good works do not serve unto righteousness, nor evil works unto condemnation. I do not want to withhold from good works their due praise, nor do I wish to encourage evil works. But when it comes to justification, I say, we must concentrate upon Christ alone, or else we make Him non-effective. You must choose between Christ and the righteousness of the Law. If you choose Christ you are righteous before God. If you stick to the Law, Christ is of no use to you.

VERSE 4. Ye are fallen from grace.

That means you are no longer in the kingdom or condition of grace. When a person on board ship falls into the sea and is drowned it makes no difference from which end or side of the ship he falls into the water. Those who fall from grace perish no matter how they go about it. Those who seek to be justified by the Law are fallen from grace and are in grave danger of eternal death. If this holds true in the case of those who seek to be justified by the moral Law, what will become of those, I should like to know, who endeavor to be justified by their own regulations and vows? They will fall to the very bottom of hell. "Oh, no," they say, "we will fly straight into heaven. If you live according to the rules of Saint Francis, Saint Dominick, Saint Benedict, you will obtain the peace and mercy of God. If you perform the vows of chastity, obedience, etc., you will be rewarded with everlasting life." Let these playthings of the devil go to the place where they came from and listen to what Paul has to say in this verse in accordance with Christ's own teaching: "He that believeth in the Son of God, hath everlasting life; but he that believeth not in the Son shall not see life, but the wrath of God abideth in him."

The words, "Ye are fallen from grace," must not be taken lightly. They are important. To fall from grace means to lose the atonement, the forgiveness of sins, the righteousness, liberty, and life which Jesus has merited for us by His death and resurrection. To lose the grace of God means to gain the wrath and judgment of God, death, the bondage of the devil, and everlasting condemnation.

VERSE 6. *For we through the Spirit wait for the hope of righteousness by faith.*

Paul concludes the whole matter with the above statement. "You want to be justified by the Law, by circumcision, and by works. We cannot see it. To be justified by such means would make Christ of no value to us. We would be obliged to perform the whole law. We rather through the Spirit wait for the hope of righteousness." The Apostle is not satisfied to say "justified by faith." He adds hope to faith.

Holy Writ speaks of hope in two ways: as the object of the emotion, and hope as the emotion itself. In the first chapter of the Epistle to the Colossians we have an instance of its first use: "For the hope which is laid up for you in heaven," i.e., the thing hoped for. In the sense of emotion we quote the passage from the eighth chapter of the Epistle to the Romans: "For we are saved by hope." As Paul uses the term "hope" here in writing to the Galatians, we may take it in either of its two meanings. We may understand Paul to say, "We wait in spirit, through faith, for the righteousness that we hope for, which in due time will be revealed to us." Or we may understand Paul to say: "We wait in Spirit, by faith for righteousness with great hope and desire." True, we are righteous, but our righteousness is not yet revealed; as long as we live here sin stays with us, not to forget the law in our members striving against the law of our mind. When sin rages in our body and we through the Spirit wrestle against it, then we have cause for hope. We are not yet perfectly righteous. Perfect righteousness is still to be attained. Hence we hope for it.

This is sweet comfort for us. And we are to make use of it in comforting the afflicted. We are to say to them: "Brother, you would like to feel God's favor as you feel your sin. But you are asking too much. Your righteousness rests on something much better than feelings. Wait and hope until it will be revealed to you in the Lord's own time. Don't go by your feelings, but go by the doctrine of faith, which pledges Christ to you."

The question occurs to us, What difference is there between faith and hope? We find it difficult to see any difference. Faith and hope are so closely linked that they cannot be separated. Still there is a difference between them.

First, hope and faith differ in regard to their sources. Faith originates in the understanding, while hope rises in the will.

Secondly, they differ in regard to their functions. Faith says what is to be done. Faith teaches, describes, directs. Hope exhorts the mind to be strong and courageous.

Thirdly, they differ in regard to their objectives. Faith concentrates on the truth. Hope looks to the goodness of God.

Fourthly, they differ in sequence. Faith is the beginning of life before tribulation. (Hebrews 11.) Hope comes later and is born of tribulation. (Romans 5.)

Fifthly, they differ in regard to their effects. Faith is a judge. It judges errors. Hope is a soldier. It fights against tribulations, the Cross, despondency, despair, and waits for better things to come in the midst of evil.

Without hope faith cannot endure. On the other hand, hope without faith is blind rashness and arrogance because it lacks knowledge. Before anything else a Christian must have the insight of faith, so that the intellect may know its directions in the day of trouble and the heart may hope for better things. By faith we begin, by hope we continue.

This passage contains excellent doctrine and much comfort. It declares that we are justified not by works, sacrifices, or ceremonies, but by Christ alone. The world may judge certain things to be ever so good; without Christ they are all wrong. Circumcision and the law and good works are carnal. "We," says Paul, "are above such things. We possess Christ by faith and in the midst of our afflictions we hopefully wait for the consummation of our righteousness."

You may say, "The trouble is I don't feel as if I am righteous." You must not feel, but believe. Unless you believe that you are righteous, you do Christ a great wrong, for He has cleansed you by the washing of regeneration, He died for you so that through Him you may obtain righteousness and everlasting life.

VERSE 6. For in Jesus Christ neither circumcision availeth any thing, nor uncircumcision, but faith which worketh by love.

Faith must of course be sincere. It must be a faith that performs good works through love. If faith lacks love it is not true faith. Thus the Apostle bars the way of hypocrites to the kingdom of Christ on all sides. He declares on the one hand, "In Christ Jesus circumcision availeth nothing," i.e., works avail nothing, but faith alone, and that without any merit whatever, avails before God. On the other hand, the Apostle declares that without fruits faith serves no purpose. To think, "If faith justifies without works, let us work nothing," is to despise the grace of God. Idle faith is not justifying faith. In this terse manner Paul presents the whole life of a Christian. Inwardly it consists in faith towards God, outwardly in love towards our fellow-men.

VERSE 7. Ye did run well; who did hinder you that ye should not obey the truth?

This is plain speaking. Paul asserts that he teaches the same truth now which he has always taught, and that the Galatians ran well as long as they obeyed the truth. But now, misled by the false apostles, they no longer run. He compares the Christian life to a race. When everything runs along smoothly the Hebrews spoke of it as a race. "Ye did run well," means that everything went along smoothly and happily with the Galatians. They lived a Christian life and were on the right way to everlasting life. The words, "Ye did run well," are encouraging indeed. Often our lives seem to creep rather than to run. But if we abide in the true doctrine and walk in the spirit, we have nothing to worry about. God judges our lives differently. What may seem to us a life slow in Christian development may seem to God a life of rapid progression in grace.

VERSE 7. Who did hinder you that ye should not obey the truth?

The Galatians were hindered in the Christian life when they turned from faith and grace to the Law. Covertly the Apostle blames the false apostles for impeding the Christian progress of the Galatians. The false apostles persuaded the Galatians to believe that they were in error and that they had made little or no progress under the influence of Paul. Under the baneful influence of the false apostles the Galatians thought they were well off and advancing rapidly in Christian knowledge and living.

VERSE 8. This persuasion cometh not of him that calleth you.

Paul explains how those who had been deceived by false teachers may be restored to spiritual health. The false apostles were amiable fellows. Apparently they surpassed Paul in learning and godliness. The Galatians were easily deceived by outward appearances. They supposed they were being taught by Christ Himself. Paul proved to them that their new doctrine was not of Christ, but of the devil. In this way he succeeded in regaining many. We also are able to win back many from the errors into which they were seduced by showing that their beliefs are imaginary, wicked, and contrary to the Word of God.

The devil is a cunning persuader. He knows how to enlarge the smallest sin into a mountain until we think we have committed the worst crime ever committed on earth. Such stricken consciences must be comforted and set straight as Paul corrected the Galatians by showing them that their opinion is not of Christ because it runs counter to the Gospel, which describes Christ as a meek and merciful Savior.

Satan will circumvent the Gospel and explain Christ in this his own diabolical way: "Indeed Christ is meek, gentle, and merciful, but only to those who are holy and righteous. If you are a sinner you stand no chance. Did not Christ say that unbelievers are already damned? And did not Christ perform many good deeds, and suffer many evils patiently, bidding us to follow His example? You do not mean to say that your life is in accord with Christ's precepts or example? You are a sinner. You are no good at all."

Satan is to be answered in this way: The Scriptures present Christ in a twofold aspect. First, as a gift. "He of God is made unto us wisdom, and righteousness, and sanctification and redemption." (I Cor. 1:30.) Hence my many and grievous sins are nullified if I believe in Him. Secondly, the Scriptures present Christ for our example. As an exemplar He is to be placed before me only at certain times. In times of joy and gladness that I may have Him as a mirror to reflect upon my shortcomings. But in the day of trouble I will have Christ only as a gift. I will not listen to anything else, except that Christ died for my sins.

To those that are cast down on account of their sins Christ must be introduced as a Savior and Gift, and not as an example. But to sinners who live in a false assurance, Christ must be introduced as an example. The hard sayings of Scripture and the awful judgments of God upon sin must be impressed upon them. Defy Satan in times of despair. Say: "O cursed Satan, you choose a nice time to talk to me about doing and working when you know very well that I am in trouble over my sins. I will not listen to you. I will listen to Christ, who says that He came into the world to save sinners. This is the true Christ and there is none other. I can find plenty of examples for a holy life in Abraham, Isaiah, John the Baptist, Paul, and other saints. But they cannot forgive my sins. They cannot save me. They cannot procure for me everlasting life. Therefore I will not have you for my teacher, O Satan."

VERSE 9. A little leaven leaveneth the whole lump.

Paul's concern for them meant nothing to some of the Galatians. Many had disowned him as their teacher and gone over to the false apostles. No doubt the false apostles took every occasion to defame Paul as a stubborn and contemptuous fellow who thought nothing of disrupting the unity of the churches for no other reason than his selfish pride and jealousy.

Others of the Galatians perhaps saw no harm in deviating a trifle from the doctrine of justification and faith. When they noticed that Paul made so much ado about a matter that seemed of no particular importance to them they raised their eyebrows and thought within themselves: "What if we did deviate a little from the doctrine of Paul? What if we are a little to blame? He ought to overlook the whole matter, and not make such an issue out of it, lest the unity of the churches be disturbed." To this Paul replies: "A little leaven leaveneth the whole lump."

Our opponents record the same complaints about us. They put us down as contentious, ill-tempered faultfinders. But these are the crafty passes of the devil, with which he seeks to overthrow our faith. We answer with Paul: "A little leaven leaveneth the whole lump."

Small faults grow into big faults. To tolerate a trifling error inevitably leads to crass heresy. The doctrine of the Bible is not ours to take or to allow liberties with. We have no right to change even a tittle of it. When it comes to life we are ready to do, to suffer, to forgive anything our opponents demand as long as faith and doctrine remain pure and uncorrupt. The Apostle James says, "For whosoever shall keep the whole law and yet offend in one point, he is guilty of all." This passage supports us over against our critics who claim that we disregard all charity to the great injury of the churches. We protest we desire nothing more than peace with all men. If they would only permit us to keep our doctrine of faith! The pure doctrine takes precedence before charity, apostles, or an angel from heaven.

Let others praise charity and concord to the skies; we magnify the authority of the Word and faith. Charity may be neglected at times without peril, but not the Word and faith. Charity suffers all things, it gives in. Faith suffers nothing; it never yields. Charity is often deceived but is never put out because it lies nothing to lose; it continues to do well even to the ungrateful. When it comes to faith and salvation in the midst of lies and errors that parade as truth and deceive many, charity has no voice or vote. Let us not be influenced by the popular cry for charity and unity. If we do not love God and His Word what difference does it make if we love anything at all?

Paul, therefore, admonishes both teachers and hearers not to esteem lightly the doctrine of faith as if it were a toy with which to amuse oneself in idle hours.

Verse 10. I have confidence in you through the Lord.

"I have taught, admonished, and reproved you enough. I hope the best for you."

The question occurs to us whether Paul did well to trust the Galatians. Does not Holy Writ forbid us to trust in men? Faith trusts in God and is never wrong. Charity trusts in men and is often wrong. This charitable trust in man is necessary to life. Without it life would be impossible in the world. What kind of life would ours be if nobody could trust anybody else? True Christians are more ready to believe in men than the children of this world. Such charitable confidence is the fruit of the Spirit. Paul had such trust in the Galatians although they had forsaken his doctrine. He trusts them "through the Lord," insofar as they were in Christ and Christ in them. Once they had forsaken Christ altogether, the Apostle will trust the Galatians no longer.

Verse 10. That ye will be none otherwise minded.

"Not minded otherwise than I have taught you. In other words, I have confidence that you will accept no doctrine that is contrary to the one you have learned from me."

Verse 10. But be that troubleth you shall bear his judgment, whosoever he be.

Paul assumes the role of a judge and condemns the false apostles as troublers of the Galatians. He wants to frighten the Galatians with his severe judgments of the false apostles into avoiding false doctrine like a contagious disease. We can hear him say to the Galatians: "Why do you give these pestilent fellows a hearing in the first place? They only trouble you. The doctrine they bring causes your conscience only trouble."

The clause, "whosoever he be," seems to indicate that the false apostles in outward appearance at least were very good and devout men. It may be that among them was some outstanding disciple of the apostles, a man of fame and authority. The Apostle must have been faced by this very situation, otherwise his vehemence would have been uncalled for. No doubt many of the Galatians were taken back with the vehemency of the Apostle. They perhaps thought: why should he be so stubborn in such small matters? Why is he so quick to pronounce damnation upon his brethren in the ministry?

I cannot say it often enough, that we must carefully differentiate between doctrine and life. Doctrine is a piece of heaven, life is a piece of earth. Life is sin, error, uncleanness, misery, and charity must forbear, believe, hope, and suffer all things. Forgiveness of sins must be continuous so that sin and error may not be defended and sustained. But with doctrine there must be no error, no need of pardon. There can be no comparison between doctrine and life. The least little point of doctrine is of greater importance than heaven and earth. Therefore we cannot allow the least jot of doctrine to be corrupted. We may overlook the offenses and errors of life, for we daily sin much. Even the saints sin, as they themselves confess in the Lord's Prayer and in the Creed. But our doctrine, God be praised, is pure, because all the articles of our faith are grounded on the Holy Scriptures.

Verse 11. And I, brethren, if I yet preach circumcision, why do I yet suffer persecution? then is the offense of the cross ceased.

In his great desire to recall the Galatians, Paul draws himself into the argument. He says: "Because I refuse to recognize circumcision as a factor in our salvation, I have brought upon myself the hatred and persecution of my whole nation. If I were to acknowledge circumcision the Jews would cease to persecute me; in fact they would love and praise me. But because I preach the Gospel of Christ and the righteousness of faith I must suffer persecution. The false apostles know how to avoid the Cross and the deadly hatred of the Jewish nation. They preach circumcision and thus retain the favor of the Jews. If they had their way they would ignore all differences in doctrine and preserve unity at all cost. But their unionistic dreams cannot be realized without loss to the pure doctrine of the Cross. It would be too bad if the offense of the Cross were to cease." To the Corinthians he expressed the same conviction: "Christ sent me...to preach the gospel: not with wisdom of words, lest the cross of Christ should be made of none effect." (I Cor. 1:17.)

Here someone may be tempted to call the Christians crazy. Deliberately to court danger by preaching and confessing the truth, and thus to bring upon ourselves the hatred and enmity of the whole world, is this not madness? But Paul does not mind the enmity of the world. It made him all the bolder to confess Christ. The enmity of the world in his estimation augurs well for the success and growth of the Church, which fares best in times of persecution. When the offense of the Cross ceases, when the rage of the enemies of the Cross abates, when everything is quiet, it is a sign that the devil is the door-keeper of the Church and that the pure doctrine of God's Word has been lost.

Saint Bernard observed that the Church is in best shape when Satan assaults it on every side by trickery and violence; and in worst shape when it is at peace. In support of his statement he quotes the passage from the song of Hezekiah: "Behold, for peace I had great bitterness." Paul looks with suspicion upon any doctrine that does not provoke antagonism.

Persecution always follows on the heels of the Word of God as the Psalmist experienced. "I believe, therefore have I spoken: I was greatly afflicted." (Ps. 116:10.) The Christians are accused and slandered without mercy. Murderers and thieves receive better treatment than Christians. The world regards true Christians as the worst offenders, for whom no punishment can be too severe. The world hates the Christians with amazing brutality, and without compunction commits them to the most shameful death, congratulating itself that it has rendered God and the cause of peace a distinct service by ridding the world of the undesired presence of these Christians. We are not to let such treatment cause us to falter in our adherence to Christ. As long as we experience such persecutions we know all is well with the Gospel.

Jesus held out the same comfort to His disciples in the fifth chapter of St. Matthew. "Blessed are ye, when men shall revile you and persecute you, and shall say all manner of evil against you falsely, for my sake. Rejoice, and be exceeding glad; for great is your reward in heaven." The Church must not come short of this joy. I would not want to be at peace with the pope, the bishops, the princes, and the sectarians, unless they consent to our doctrine. Unity with them would be an unmistakable sign that we have lost the true doctrine. Briefly, as long as the Church proclaims the doctrine she must suffer persecution, because the Gospel declares the mercy and glory of God. This in turn stirs up the devil, because the Gospel shows him up for what he is, the devil, and not God. Therefore as long as the Gospel holds sway persecution plays the accompaniment, or else there is something the matter with the devil. When he is hit you will know it by the havoc he raises everywhere.

So do not be surprised or offended when hell breaks loose. Look upon it as a happy indication that all is well with the Gospel of the Cross. God forbid that the offense of the Cross should ever be removed. This would be the case if we were to preach what the prince of this world and his followers would be only too glad to hear, the righteousness of works. You would never know the devil could be so gentle, the world so sweet, the Pope so gracious, and the princes so charming. But because we seek the advantage and honor of Christ, they persecute us all around.

VERSE 12. *I would they were even cut off which trouble you.*

It hardly seems befitting an apostle, not only to denounce the false apostles as troublers of the Church, and to consign them to the devil, but also to wish that they were utterly cut off—what else would you call it but plain cursing? Paul, I suppose, is alluding to the rite of circumcision. As if he were saying to the Galatians: "The false apostles compel you to cut off the foreskin of your flesh. Well, I wish they themselves were utterly cut off by the roots."

We had better answer at once the question, whether it is right for Christians to curse. Certainly not always, nor for every little cause. But when things have come to such a pass that God and His Word are openly blasphemed, then we must say: "Blessed be God and His Word, and cursed be everything that is contrary to God and His Word, even though it should be an apostle, or an angel from heaven."

This goes to show again how much importance Paul attached to the least points of Christian doctrine, that he dared to curse the false apostles, evidently men of great popularity and influence. What right, then, have we to make little of doctrine? No matter how nonessential a point of doctrine may seem, if slighted it may prove the gradual disintegration of the truths of our salvation.

Let us do everything to advance the glory and authority of God's Word. Every tittle of it is greater than heaven and earth. Christian charity and unity have nothing to do with the Word of God. We are bold to curse and condemn all men who in the least point corrupt the Word of God, "for a little leaven leaveneth the whole lump."

Paul does right to curse these troublers of the Galatians, wishing that they were cut off and rooted out of the Church of God and that their doctrine might perish forever. Such cursing is the gift of the Holy Ghost. Thus Peter cursed Simon the sorcerer, "Thy money perish with thee." Many instances of this holy cursing are recorded in the sacred Scriptures, especially in the Psalms, e.g., "Let death seize upon them, and let them go down quick into hell." (Ps. 55:15.)

THE DOCTRINE OF GOOD WORKS

Now come all kinds of admonitions and precepts. It was the custom of the apostles that after they had taught faith and instructed the conscience they followed it up with admonitions unto good works, that the believers might manifest the duties of love toward each other. In order to avoid the appearance as if Christianity militated against good works or opposed civil government, the Apostle also urges us to give ourselves unto good works, to lead an honest life, and to keep faith and love with one another.

This will give the lie to the accusations of the world that we Christians are the enemies of decency and of public peace. The fact is we Christians know better what constitutes a truly good work than all the philosophers and legislators of the world because we link believing with doing.

VERSE 13. For, brethren, ye have been called unto liberty; only use not liberty for an occasion to the flesh, but by love serve one another.

In other words: "You have gained liberty through Christ, i.e., You are above all laws as far as conscience is concerned. You are saved. Christ is your liberty and life. Therefore law, sin, and death may not hurt you or drive you to despair. This is the constitution of your priceless liberty. Now take care that you do not use your wonderful liberty for an occasion of the flesh."

Satan likes to turn this liberty which Christ has gotten for us into licentiousness. Already the Apostle Jude complained in his day: "There are certain men crept in unawares...turning the grace of our God into lasciviousness." (Jude 4.) The flesh reasons: "If we are without the law, we may as well indulge ourselves. Why do good, why give alms, why suffer evil when there is no law to force us to do so?"

This attitude is common enough. People talk about Christian liberty and then go and cater to the desires of covetousness, pleasure, pride, envy, and other vices. Nobody wants to fulfill his duties. Nobody wants to help out a brother in distress. This sort of thing makes me so impatient at times that I wish the swine who trampled precious pearls under foot were back once again under the tyranny of the Pope. You cannot wake up the people of Gomorrah with the gospel of peace.

Even we creatures of the world do not perform our duties as zealously in the light of the Gospel as we did before in the darkness of ignorance, because the surer we are of the liberty purchased for us by Christ, the more we neglect the Word, prayer, well-doing, and suffering. If Satan were not continually molesting us with trials, with the persecution of our enemies, and the ingratitude of our brethren, we would become so careless and indifferent to all good works that in time we would lose our faith in Christ, resign the ministry of the Word, and look for an easier life. Many of our ministers are beginning to do that very thing. They complain about the ministry, they maintain they cannot live on their salaries, they whimper about the miserable treatment they receive at the hand of those whom they delivered from the servitude of the law by the preaching of the Gospel. These ministers desert our poor and maligned Christ, involve themselves in the affairs of the world, seek advantages for themselves and not for Christ. With what results they shall presently find out.

Since the devil lies in ambush for those in particular who hate the world, and seeks to deprive us of our liberty of the spirit or to brutalize it into the liberty of the flesh, we plead with our brethren after the manner of Paul, that they may never use this liberty of the spirit purchased for us by Christ as an excuse for carnal living, or as Peter expresses it, I Peter 2:16, "for a cloak of maliciousness."

In order that Christians may not abuse their liberty the Apostle encumbers them with the rule of mutual love that they should serve each other in love. Let everybody perform the duties of his station and vocation diligently and help his neighbor to the limit of his capacity.

Christians are glad to hear and obey this teaching of love. When others hear about this Christian liberty of ours they at once infer, "If I am free, I may do what I like. If salvation is not a matter of doing why should we do anything for the poor?" In this crude manner they turn the liberty of the spirit into wantonness and licentiousness. We want them to know, however, that if they use their lives and possessions after their own pleasure, if they do not help the poor, if they cheat their fellow-men in business and snatch and scrape by hook and by crook everything they can lay their hands on, we want to tell them that they are not free, no matter how much they think they are, but they are the dirty slaves of the devil, and are seven times worse than they ever were as the slaves of the Pope.

As for us, we are obliged to preach the Gospel which offers to all men liberty from the Law, sin, death, and God's wrath. We have no right to conceal or revoke this liberty proclaimed by the Gospel. And so we cannot do anything with the swine who dive headlong into the filth of licentiousness. We do what we can, we diligently admonish them to love and to help their fellow-men. If our admonitions bear no fruit, we leave them to God, who will in His own good time take care of these disrespecters of His goodness. In the meanwhile we comfort ourselves with the thought that our labors are not lost upon the true believers. They appreciate this spiritual liberty and stand ready to serve others in love and, though their number is small, the satisfaction they give us far outweighs the discouragement which we receive at the hands of the large number of those who misuse this liberty.

Paul cannot possibly be misunderstood for he says: "Brethren, ye have been called unto liberty." In order that nobody might mistake the liberty of which he speaks for the liberty of the flesh, the Apostle adds the explanatory note, "only use not liberty for an occasion to the flesh, but by love serve one another." Paul now explains at the hand of the Ten Commandments what it means to serve one another in love.

Galatians 5:14-26

Verse 14. For all the law is fulfilled in one word, even in this, thou shalt love thy neighbour as thyself.

It is customary with Paul to lay the doctrinal foundation first and then to build on it the gold, silver, and gems of good deeds. Now there is no other foundation than Jesus Christ. Upon this foundation the Apostle erects the structure of good works which he defines in this one sentence: "Thou shalt love thy neighbour as thyself."

In adding such precepts of love the Apostle embarrasses the false apostles very much, as if he were saying to the Galatians: "I have described to you what spiritual life is. Now I will also teach you what truly good works are. I am doing this in order that you may understand that the silly ceremonies of which the false apostles make so much are far inferior to the works of Christian love." This is the hall-mark of all false teachers, that they not only pervert the pure doctrine but also fail in doing good. Their foundation vitiated, they can only build wood, hay, and stubble. Oddly enough, the false apostles who were such earnest champions of good works never required the work of charity, such as Christian love and the practical charity of a helpful tongue, hand, and heart. Their only requirement was that circumcision, days, months, years, and times should be observed. They could not think of any other good works.

The Apostle exhorts all Christians to practice good works after they have embraced the pure doctrine of faith, because even though they have been justified they still have the old flesh to refrain them from doing good. Therefore it becomes necessary that sincere preachers cultivate the doctrine of good works as diligently as the doctrine of faith, for Satan is a deadly enemy of both. Nevertheless faith must come first because without faith it is impossible to know what a God-pleasing deed is.

Let nobody think that he knows all about this commandment, "Thou shalt love thy neighbour as thyself." It sounds short and easy, but show me the man who can teach, learn, and do this commandment perfectly. None of us heed, or urge, or practice this commandment properly. Though the conscience hurts when we fail to fulfill this commandment in every respect we are not overwhelmed by our failure to bear our neighbor sincere and brotherly love.

The words, "for all the law is fulfilled in one word," entail a criticism of the Galatians. "You are so taken up by your superstitions and cere-

monies that serve no good purpose, that you neglect the most important thing, love." St. Jerome says: "We wear our bodies out with watching,
fasting, and labor and neglect charity, the queen of all good works." Look
at the monks, who meticulously fast, watch, etc. To skip the least requirement of their order would be a crime of the first magnitude. At the same
time they blithely ignored the duties of charity and hated each other to
death. That is no sin, they think.

The Old Testament is replete with examples that indicate how much
God prizes charity. When David and his companions had no food with
which to still their hunger they ate the showbread which lay-people were
forbidden to eat. Christ's disciples broke the Sabbath law when they
plucked the ears of corn. Christ himself broke the Sabbath (as the Jews
claimed) by healing the sick on the Sabbath. These incidents indicate that
love ought to be given consideration above all laws and ceremonies.

Verse 14. For all the Law is fulfilled in one word.

We can imagine the Apostle saying to the Galatians: "Why do you get so
worked up over ceremonies, meats, days, places, and such things? Leave
off this foolishness and listen to me. The whole Law is comprehended
in this one sentence, 'Thou shalt love thy neighbour as thyself.' God is
not particularly interested in ceremonies, nor has He any use for them.
The one thing He requires of you is that you believe in Christ whom He
hath sent. If in addition to faith, which comes first as the most acceptable
service unto God, you want to add laws, then you want to know that all
laws are comprehended in this short commandment, 'Thou shalt love thy
neighbour as thyself.' "

Paul knows how to explain the law of God. He condenses all the laws
of Moses into one brief sentence. Reason takes offense at the brevity with
which Paul treats the Law. Therefore reason looks down upon the doctrine of faith and its truly good works. To serve one another in love, i.e.,
to instruct the erring, to comfort the afflicted, to raise the fallen, to help
one's neighbor in every possible way, to bear with his infirmities, to endure hardships, toil, ingratitude in the Church and in the world, and on
the other hand to obey government, to honor one's parents, to be patient
at home with a nagging wife and an unruly family, these things are not at
all regarded as good works. The fact is, they are such excellent works that
the world cannot possibly estimate them at their true value.

It is tersely spoken: "Love thy neighbour as thyself." But what more
needs to be said? You cannot find a better or nearer example than your
own. If you want to know how you ought to love your neighbor, ask yourself how much you love yourself. If you were to get into trouble or danger,
you would be glad to have the love and help of all men. You do not need
any book of instructions to teach you how to love your neighbor. All you
have to do is to look into your own heart, and it will tell you how you
ought to love your neighbor as yourself.

My neighbor is every person, especially those who need my help, as Christ explained in the tenth chapter of Luke. Even if a person has done me some wrong, or has hurt me in any way, he is still a human being with flesh and blood. As long as a person remains a human being, so long is he to be an object of our love.

Paul therefore urges his Galatians and, incidentally, all believers to serve each other in love. "You Galatians do not have to accept circumcision. If you are so anxious to do good works, I will tell you in one word how you can fulfill all laws. 'By love serve one another.' You will never lack people to whom you may do good. The world is full of people who need your help."

VERSE 15. But if ye bite and devour one another take heed that ye be not consumed one of another.

When faith in Christ is overthrown peace and unity come to an end in the church. Diverse opinions and dissensions about doctrine and life spring up, and one member bites and devours the other, i.e., they condemn each other until they are consumed. To this the Scriptures and the experience of all times bear witness. The many sects at present have come into being because one sect condemns the other. When the unity of the spirit has been lost there can be no agreement in doctrine or life. New errors must appear without measure and without end.

For the avoidance of discord Paul lays down the principle: "Let every person do his duty in the station of life into which God has called him. No person is to vaunt himself above others or find fault with the efforts of others while lauding his own. Let everybody serve in love."

It is not an easy matter to teach faith without works, and still to require works. Unless the ministers of Christ are wise in handling the mysteries of God and rightly divide the word, faith and good works may easily be confused. Both the doctrine of faith and the doctrine of good works must be diligently taught, and yet in such a way that both the doctrines stay within their God-given sphere. If we teach only words, as our opponents do, we shall lose the faith. If we only teach faith people will come to think that good works are superfluous.

VERSE 16. This I say then, Walk in the Spirit, and ye shall not fulfill the lust of the flesh.

"I have not forgotten what I told you about faith in the first part of my letter. Because I exhort you to mutual love you are not to think that I have gone back on my teaching of justification by faith alone. I am still of the same opinion. To remove every possibility for misunderstanding I have added this explanatory note: 'Walk in the Spirit, and ye shall not fulfill the lust of the flesh.'"

With this verse Paul explains how he wants this sentence to be understood: By love serve one another. When I bid you to love one another, this is what I mean and require, 'Walk in the Spirit.' I know very well you will not fulfill the Law, because you are sinners as long as you live. Nevertheless, you should endeavor to walk in the spirit, i.e., fight against the flesh and follow the leads of the Holy Ghost."

It is quite apparent that Paul had not forgotten the doctrine of justification, for in bidding the Galatians to walk in the Spirit he at the same time denies that good works can justify. "When I speak of the fulfilling of the Law I do not mean to say that you are justified by the Law. All I mean to say is that you should take the Spirit for your guide and resist the flesh. That is the most you shall ever be able to do. Obey the Spirit and fight against the flesh."

VERSE 16. *And ye shall not fulfill the lust of the flesh.*

The lust of the flesh is not altogether extinct in us. It rises up again and again and wrestles with the Spirit. No flesh, not even that of the true believer, is so completely under the influence of the Spirit that it will not bite or devour, or at least neglect, the commandment of love. At the slightest provocation it flares up, demands to be revenged, and hates a neighbor like an enemy, or at least does not love him as much as he ought to be loved.

Therefore the Apostle establishes this rule of love for the believers. Serve one another in love. Bear the infirmities of your brother. Forgive one another. Without such bearing and forbearing, giving and forgiving, there can be no unity because to give and to take offense are unavoidably human.

Whenever you are angry with your brother for any cause, repress your violent emotions through the Spirit. Bear with his weakness and love him. He does not cease to be your neighbor or brother because he offended you. On the contrary, he now more than ever before requires your loving attention.

The scholastics take the lust of the flesh to mean carnal lust. True, believers too are tempted with carnal lust. Even the married are not immune to carnal lusts. Men set little value upon that which they have and covet what they have not, as the poet says:

"The things most forbidden we always desire, And things most denied we seek to acquire."

I do not deny that the lust of the flesh includes carnal lust. But it takes in more. It takes in all the corrupt desires with which the believers are more or less infected, as pride, hatred, covetousness, impatience. Later on Paul enumerates among the works of the flesh even idolatry and heresy. The apostle's meaning is clear. "I want you to love one another. But you do not do it. In fact you cannot do it, because of your flesh. Hence we cannot be justified by deeds of love. Do not for a moment think that I am reversing myself on my stand concerning faith. Faith and hope must continue. By faith we are justified, by hope we endure to the end. In addition we serve each other in love because true faith is not idle. Our love, however, is faulty. In bidding you to walk in the Spirit I indicate to you that our love is not sufficient to justify us. Neither do I demand that you should get rid of the flesh, but that you should control and subdue it."

VERSE 17. For the flesh lusteth against the Spirit and the Spirit against the flesh.

When Paul declares that "the flesh lusteth against the Spirit, and the Spirit against the flesh," he means to say that we are not to think, speak or do the things to which the flesh incites us. "I know," he says, "that the flesh courts sin. The thing for you to do is to resist the flesh by the Spirit. But if you abandon the leadership of the Spirit for that of the flesh, you are going to fulfill the lust of the flesh and die in your sins."

VERSE 17. And these are contrary the one to the other; so that ye cannot do the things that ye would.

These two leaders, the flesh and the Spirit, are bitter opponents. Of this opposition the Apostle writes in the seventh chapter of the Epistle to the Romans: "I see another law in my members, warring against the law of my mind, and bringing me into the captivity to the law of sin which is in my members. O wretched man that I am! who shall deliver me from the body of this death?"

The scholastics are at a loss to understand this confession of Paul and feel obliged to save his honor. That the chosen vessel of Christ should have had the law of sin in his members seems to them incredible and absurd. They circumvent the plain-spoken statement of the Apostle by saying that he was speaking for the wicked. But the wicked never complain of inner conflicts, or of the captivity of sin. Sin has its unrestricted way with them. This is Paul's very own complaint and the identical complaint of all believers.

Paul never denied that he felt the lust of the flesh. It is likely that at times he felt even the stirrings of carnal lust, but there is no doubt that he quickly suppressed them. And if at any time he felt angry or impatient, he resisted these feelings by the Spirit. We are not going to stand by idly and see such a comforting statement as this explained away. The scholastics, monks, and others of their ilk fought only against carnal lust and were proud of a victory which they never obtained. In the meanwhile they harbored within their breasts pride, hatred, disdain, self-trust, contempt of the Word of God, disloyalty, blasphemy, and other lusts of the flesh. Against these sins they never fought because they never took them for sins.

Christ alone can supply us with perfect righteousness. Therefore we must always believe and always hope in Christ. "Whosoever believeth shall not be ashamed." (Rom. 9:33.)

Do not despair if you feel the flesh battling against the Spirit or if you cannot make it behave. For you to follow the guidance of the Spirit in all things without interference on the part of the flesh is impossible. You are doing all you can if you resist the flesh and do not fulfill its demands.

When I was a monk I thought I was lost forever whenever I felt an evil emotion, carnal lust, wrath, hatred, or envy. I tried to quiet my conscience in many ways, but it did not work, because lust would always come back and give me no rest. I told myself: "You have permitted this and that sin, envy, impatience, and the like. Your joining this holy order has been in vain, and all your good works are good for nothing." If at that time I had understood this passage, "The flesh lusteth against the Spirit, and the Spirit against the flesh," I could have spared myself many a day of self- torment. I would have said to myself: "Martin, you will never be without sin, for you have flesh. Despair not, but resist the flesh."

I remember how Doctor Staupitz used to say to me: "I have promised God a thousand times that I would become a better man, but I never kept my promise. From now on I am not going to make any more vows. Experience has taught me that I cannot keep them. Unless God is merciful to me for Christ's sake and grants unto me a blessed departure, I shall not be able to stand before Him." His was a God-pleasing despair. No true believer trusts in his own righteousness, but says with David, "Enter not into judgment with thy servant; for in thy sight shall no man living be justified." (Ps. 143:2) Again, "If thou, Lord, shouldest mark iniquities, O Lord, who shall stand?" (Ps. 130:3.)

No man is to despair of salvation just because he is aware of the lust of the flesh. Let him be aware of it so long as he does not yield to it. The passion of lust, wrath, and other vices may shake him, but they are not to get him down. Sin may assail him, but he is not to welcome it. Yes, the better Christian a man is, the more he will experience the heat of the conflict. This explains the many expressions of regret in the Psalms and in the entire Bible.

Everybody is to determine his peculiar weakness and guard against it. Watch and wrestle in spirit against your weakness. Even if you cannot completely overcome it, at least you ought to fight against it.

According to this description a saint is not one who is made of wood and never feels any lusts or desires of the flesh. A true saint confesses his righteousness and prays that his sins may be forgiven. The whole Church prays for the forgiveness of sins and confesses that it believes in the forgiveness of sins. If our antagonists would read the Scriptures they would soon discover that they cannot judge rightly of anything, either of sin or of holiness.

VERSE 18. But if ye be led of the Spirit, ye are not under the law.

Here someone may object: "How come we are not under the law? You yourself say, Paul, that we have the flesh which wars against the Spirit, and brings us into subjection."

But Paul says not to let it trouble us. As long as we are led by the Spirit, and are willing to obey the Spirit who resists the flesh, we are not under the Law. True believers are not under the Law. The Law cannot condemn them although they feel sin and confess it.

Great then is the power of the Spirit. Led by the Spirit, the Law cannot condemn the believer though he commits real sin. For Christ in whom we believe is our righteousness. He is without sin, and the Law cannot accuse Him. As long as we cling to Him we are led by the Spirit and are free from the Law. Even as he teaches good works, the Apostle does not lose sight of the doctrine of justification, but shows at every turn that it is impossible for us to be justified by works.

The words, "If ye be led of the Spirit, ye are not under the law," are replete with comfort. It happens at times that anger, hatred, impatience, carnal desire, fear, sorrow, or some other lust of the flesh so overwhelms a man that he cannot shake them off, though he try ever so hard. What should he do? Should he despair? God forbid. Let him say to himself: "My flesh seems to be on a warpath against the Spirit again. Go to it, flesh, and rage all you want to. But you are not going to have your way. I follow the leading of the Spirit."

When the flesh begins to cut up the only remedy is to take the sword of the Spirit, the word of salvation, and fight against the flesh. If you set the Word out of sight, you are helpless against the flesh. I know this to be a fact. I have been assailed by many violent passions, but as soon as I took hold of some Scripture passage, my temptations left me. Without the Word I could not have helped myself against the flesh.

VERSE 19. Now the works of the flesh are manifest, which are these.

Paul is saying: "That none of you may hide behind the plea of ignorance I will enumerate first the works of the flesh, and then also the works of the Spirit."

There were many hypocrites among the Galatians, as there are also among us, who pretend to be Christians and talk much about the Spirit, but they walk not according to the Spirit; rather according to the flesh. Paul is out to show them that they are not as holy as they like to have others think they are.

Every period of life has its own peculiar temptations. Not one true believer whom the flesh does not again and again incite to impatience, anger, pride. But it is one thing to be tempted by the flesh, and another thing to yield to the flesh, to do its bidding without fear or remorse, and to continue in sin.

Christians also fall and perform the lusts of the flesh. David fell horribly into adultery. Peter also fell grievously when he denied Christ. However great these sins were, they were not committed to spite God, but from weakness. When their sins were brought to their attention these men did not obstinately continue in their sin, but repented. Those who sin through weakness are not denied pardon as long as they rise again and cease to sin. There is nothing worse than to continue in sin. If they do not repent, but obstinately continue to fulfill the desires of the flesh, it is a sure sign that they are not sincere.

No person is free from temptations. Some are tempted in one way, others in another way. One person is more easily tempted to bitterness and sorrow of spirit, blasphemy, distrust, and despair. Another is more easily tempted to carnal lust, anger, envy, covetousness. But no matter to which sins we are disposed, we are to walk in the Spirit and resist the flesh. Those who are Christ's own crucify their flesh.

Some of the old saints labored so hard to attain perfection that they lost the capacity to feel anything. When I was a monk I often wished I could see a saint. I pictured him as living in the wilderness, abstaining from meat and drink and living on roots and herbs and cold water. This weird conception of those awesome saints I had gained out of the books of the scholastics and church fathers. But we know now from the Scriptures who the true saints are. Not those who live a single life, or make a fetish of days, meats, clothes, and such things. The true saints are those who believe that they are justified by the death of Christ. Whenever Paul writes to the Christians here and there he calls them the holy children and heirs of God. All who believe in Christ, whether male or female, bond or free, are saints; not in view of their own works, but in view of the merits of God which they appropriate by faith. Their holiness is a gift and not their own personal achievement.

Ministers of the Gospel, public officials, parents, children, masters, servants, etc., are true saints when they take Christ for their wisdom, righteousness, sanctification, and redemption, and when they fulfill the duties of their several vocations according to the standard of God's Word and repress the lust and desires of the flesh by the Spirit. Not everybody can resist temptations with equal facilities. Imperfections are bound to show up. But this does not prevent them from being holy. Their unintentional lapses are forgiven if they pull themselves together by faith in Christ. God forbid that we should sit in hasty judgment on those who are weak in faith and life, as long as they love the Word of God and make use of the supper of the Lord.

I thank God that He has permitted me to see (what as a monk I so earnestly desired to see) not one but many saints, whole multitudes of true saints. Not the kind of saints the papists admire, but the kind of saints Christ wants. I am sure I am one of Christ's true saints. I am baptized. I believe that Christ my Lord has redeemed me from all my sins, and invested me with His own eternal righteousness and holiness. To hide in caves and dens, to have a bony body, to wear the hair long in the mistaken idea that such departures from normalcy will obtain some special regard in heaven is not the holy life. A holy life is to be baptized and to believe in Christ, and to subdue the flesh with the Spirit.

To feel the lusts of the flesh is not without profit to us. It prevents us from being vain and from being puffed up with the wicked opinion of our own work-righteousness. The monks were so inflated with the opinion of their own righteousness, they thought they had so much holiness that they could afford to sell some of it to others, although their own hearts convinced them of unholiness. The Christian feels the unholy condition of his heart, and it makes him feel so low that he cannot trust in his good works. He therefore goes to Christ to find perfect righteousness. This keeps a Christian humble.

> VERSES 19, 20. *Now the works of the flesh are manifest, which are these: adultery, fornification, uncleanness, lasciviousness, idolatry, witchcraft...*

Paul does not enumerate all the works of the flesh, but only certain ones. First, he mentions various kinds of carnal lusts, as adultery, fornication, wantonness, etc. But carnal lust is not the only work of the flesh, and so he counts among the works of the flesh also idolatry, witchcraft, hatred, and the like. These terms are so familiar that they do not require lengthy explanations.

IDOLATRY

The best religion, the most fervent devotion without Christ is plain idolatry. It has been considered a holy act when the monks in their cells meditate upon God and His works, and in a religious frenzy kneel down to pray and to weep for joy. Yet Paul calls it simply idolatry. Every religion which worships God in ignorance or neglect of His Word and will is idolatry.

They may think about God, Christ, and heavenly things, but they do it after their own fashion and not after the Word of God. They have an idea that their clothing, their mode of living, and their conduct are holy and pleasing to Christ. They not only expect to pacify Christ by the strictness of their life, but also expect to be rewarded by Him for their good deeds. Hence their best "spiritual" thoughts are wicked thoughts. Any worship of God, any religion without Christ is idolatry. In Christ alone is God well pleased.

I have said before that the works of the flesh are manifest. But idolatry puts on such a good front and acts so spiritual that the sham of it is recognized only by true believers.

WITCHCRAFT

This sin was very common before the light of the Gospel appeared. When I was a child there were many witches and sorcerers around who "bewitched" cattle, and people, particularly children, and did much harm. But now that the Gospel is here you do not hear so much about it because the Gospel drives the devil away. Now he bewitches people in a worse way with spiritual sorcery.

Witchcraft is a brand of idolatry. As witches used to bewitch cattle and men, so idolaters, i.e., all the self-righteous, go around to bewitch God and to make Him out as one who justifies men not by grace through faith in Christ but by the works of men's own choosing. They bewitch and deceive themselves. If they continue in their wicked thoughts of God they will die in their idolatry.

SECTS

Under sects Paul here understands heresies. Heresies have always been found in the church. What unity of faith can exist among all the different monks and the different orders? None whatever. There is no unity of spirit, no agreement of minds, but great dissension in the papacy. There is no conformity in doctrine, faith, and life. On the other hand, among evangelical Christians the Word, faith, religion, sacraments, service, Christ, God, heart, and mind are common to all. This unity is not disturbed by outward differences of station or of occupation.

DRUNKENESS, GLUTTONY

Paul does not say that eating and drinking are works of the flesh, but intemperance in eating and drinking, which is a common vice nowadays, is a work of the flesh. Those who are given to excess are to know that they are not spiritual but carnal. Sentence is pronounced upon them that they shall not inherit the kingdom of heaven. Paul desires that Christians avoid drunkenness and gluttony, that they live temperate and sober lives, in order that the body may not grow soft and sensual.

> VERSE 21. Of the which I tell you before, as I have also told you in the past, that they which do such things shall not inherit the kingdom of God.

This is a hard saying, but very necessary for those false Christians and hypocrites who speak much about the Gospel, about faith, and the Spirit, yet live after the flesh. But this hard sentence is directed chiefly at the heretics who are large with their own self-importance, that they may be frightened into taking up the fight of the Spirit against the flesh.

> VERSES 22, 23. But the fruit of the Spirit is love, joy, peace, longsuffering, gentleness, goodness, faith, meekness, temperance.

The Apostle does not speak of the works of the Spirit as he spoke of the works of the flesh, but he attaches to these Christian virtues a better name. He calls them the fruits of the Spirit.

LOVE

It would have been enough to mention only the single fruit of love, for love embraces all the fruits of the Spirit. In I Corinthians 13, Paul attributes to love all the fruits of the Spirit: "Charity suffereth long, and is kind," etc. Here he lets love stand by itself among other fruits of the Spirit to remind the Christians to love one another, "in honor preferring one another," to esteem others more than themselves because they have Christ and the Holy Ghost within them.

JOY

Joy means sweet thoughts of Christ, melodious hymns and psalms, praises and thanksgiving, with which Christians instruct, inspire, and refresh themselves. God does not like doubt and dejection. He hates dreary doctrine, gloomy and melancholy thought. God likes cheerful hearts. He did not send His Son to fill us with sadness, but to gladden our hearts. For this reason the prophets, apostles, and Christ Himself urge, yes, command us to rejoice and be glad. "Rejoice greatly, O daughter of Zion; shout, O daughter of Jerusalem; behold, thy king cometh unto thee." (Zech. 9:9.) In the Psalms we are repeatedly told to be "joyful in the Lord." Paul says: "Rejoice in the Lord always." Christ says: "Rejoice, for your names are written in heaven."

PEACE

Peace towards God and men. Christians are to be peaceful and quiet. Not argumentative, not hateful, but thoughtful and patient. There can be no peace without longsuffering, and therefore Paul lists this virtue next.

LONGSUFFERING

Longsuffering is that quality which enables a person to bear adversity, injury, reproach, and makes them patient to wait for the improvement of those who have done him wrong. When the devil finds that he cannot overcome certain persons by force he tries to overcome them in the long run. He knows that we are weak and cannot stand anything long. Therefore he repeats his temptation time and again until he succeeds. To withstand his continued assaults we must be longsuffering and patiently wait for the devil to get tired of his game.

GENTLENESS

Gentleness in conduct and life. True followers of the Gospel must not be sharp and bitter, but gentle, mild, courteous, and soft-spoken, which should encourage others to seek their company. Gentleness can overlook other people's faults and cover them up. Gentleness is always glad to give in to others. Gentleness can get along with forward and difficult persons, according to the old pagan saying: "You must know the manners of your friends, but you must not hate them." Such a gentle person was our Savior Jesus Christ, as the Gospel portrays Him. Of Peter it is recorded that he wept whenever he remembered the sweet gentleness of Christ in His daily contact with people. Gentleness is an excellent virtue and very useful in every walk of life.

GOODNESS

A person is good when he is willing to help others in their need.

FAITH

In listing faith among the fruits of the Spirit, Paul obviously does not mean faith in Christ, but faith in men. Such faith is not suspicious of people but believes the best. Naturally the possessor of such faith will be deceived, but he lets it pass. He is ready to believe all men, but he will not trust all men. Where this virtue is lacking men are suspicious, forward, and wayward and will believe nothing nor yield to anybody. No matter how well a person says or does anything, they will find fault with it, and if you do not humor them you can never please them. It is quite impossible to get along with them. Such faith in people therefore, is quite necessary. What kind of life would this be if one person could not believe another person?

MEEKNESS

A person is meek when he is not quick to get angry. Many things occur in daily life to provoke a person's anger, but the Christian gets over his anger by meekness.

TEMPERANCE

Christians are to lead sober and chaste lives. They should not be adulterers, fornicators, or sensualists. They should not be quarrelers or drunkards. In the first and second chapters of the Epistle to Titus, the Apostle admonishes bishops, young women, and married folks to be chaste and pure.

VERSE 23. Against such there is no law.

There is a law, of course, but it does not apply to those who bear these fruits of the Spirit. The Law is not given for the righteous man. A true Christian conducts himself in such a way that he does not need any law to warn or to restrain him. He obeys the Law without compulsion. The Law does not concern him. As far as he is concerned there would not have to be any Law.

VERSE 24. And they that are Christ's have crucified the flesh with the affections and lusts.

True believers are no hypocrites. They crucify the flesh with its evil desires and lusts. Inasmuch as they have not altogether put off the sinful flesh they are inclined to sin. They do not fear or love God as they should. They are likely to be provoked to anger, to envy, to impatience, to carnal lust, and other emotions. But they will not do the things to which the flesh incites them. They crucify the flesh with its evil desires and lusts by fasting and exercise and, above all, by a walk in the Spirit.

To resist the flesh in this manner is to nail it to the Cross. Although the flesh is still alive it cannot very well act upon its desires because it is bound and nailed to the Cross.

VERSE 25. If we live in the Spirit, let us also walk in the Spirit.

A little while ago the Apostle had condemned those who are envious and start heresies and schisms. As if he had forgotten that he had already berated them, the Apostle once more reproves those who provoke and envy others. Was not one reference to them sufficient? He repeats his admonition in order to emphasize the viciousness of pride that had caused all the trouble in the churches of Galatia, and has always caused the Church of Christ no end of difficulties. In his Epistle to Titus the Apostle states that a vainglorious man should not be ordained as a minister, for pride, as St. Augustine points out, is the mother of all heresies.

Now vainglory has always been a common poison in the world. There is no village too small to contain someone who wants to be considered wiser or better than the rest. Those who have been bitten by pride usually stand upon the reputation for learning and wisdom. Vainglory is not nearly so bad in a private person or even in an official as it is in a minister.

When the poison of vainglory gets into the Church you have no idea what havoc it can cause. You may argue about knowledge, art, money, countries, and the like without doing particular harm. But you cannot quarrel about salvation or damnation, about eternal life and eternal death without grave damage to the Church. No wonder Paul exhorts all ministers of the Word to guard against this poison. He writes: "If we live in the Spirit." Where the Spirit is, men gain new attitudes. Where formerly they were vainglorious, spiteful and envious, they now become humble, gentle and patient. Such men seek not their own glory, but the glory of God. They do not provoke each other to wrath or envy, but prefer others to themselves.

As dangerous to the Church as this abominable pride is, yet there is nothing more common. The trouble with the ministers of Satan is that they look upon the ministry as a stepping-stone to fame and glory, and right there you have the seed for all sorts of dissensions.

Because Paul knew that the vainglory of the false Apostles had caused the churches of Galatia endless trouble, he makes it his business to suppress this abominable vice. In his absence the false apostles went to work in Galatia. They pretended that they had been on intimate terms with the apostles, while Paul had never seen Christ in person or had much contact with the rest of the apostles. Because of this they delivered him, rejected his doctrine, and boosted their own. In this way they troubled the Galatians and caused quarrels among them until they provoked and envied each other; which goes to show that neither the false apostles nor the Galatians walked after the Spirit, but after the flesh.

The Gospel is not there for us to aggrandize ourselves. The Gospel is to aggrandize Christ and the mercy of God. It holds out to men eternal gifts that are not gifts of our own manufacture. What right have we to receive praise and glory for gifts that are not of our own making?

No wonder that God in His special grace subjects the ministers of the Gospel to all kinds of afflictions, otherwise they could not cope with this ugly beast called vainglory. If no persecution, no cross, or reproach trailed the doctrine of the Gospel, but only praise and reputation, the ministers of the Gospel would choke with pride. Paul had the Spirit of Christ. Nevertheless there was given unto him the messenger of Satan to buffet him in order that he should not come to exalt himself, because of the grandeur of his revelations. St. Augustine's opinion is well taken: "If a minister of the Gospel is praised, he is in danger; if he is despised, he is also in danger."

The ministers of the Gospel should be men who are not too easily affected by praise or criticism, but simply speak out the benefit and the glory of Christ and seek the salvation of souls.

Whenever you are being praised, remember it is not you who is being praised but Christ, to whom all praise belongs. When you preach the Word of God in its purity and also live accordingly, it is not your own doing, but God's doing. And when people praise you, they really mean to praise God in you. When you understand this—and you should because "what hast thou that thou didst not receive?"—you will not flatter yourself on the one hand and on the other hand you will not carry yourself with the thought of resigning from the ministry when you are insulted, reproached, or persecuted.

It is really kind of God to send so much infamy, reproach, hatred, and cursing our way to keep us from getting proud of the gifts of God in us. We need a millstone around our neck to keep us humble. There are a few on our side who love and revere us for the ministry of the Word, but for every one of these there are a hundred on the other side who hate and persecute us.

The Lord is our glory. Such gifts as we possess we acknowledge to be the gifts of God, given to us for the good of the Church of Christ. Therefore we are not proud because of them. We know that more is required of them to whom much is given, than of such to whom little is given. We also know that God is no respecter of persons. A plain factory hand who does his work faithfully pleases God just as much as a minister of the Word.

VERSE 26. Let us not be desirous of vain glory.

To desire vainglory is to desire lies, because when one person praises another he tells lies. What is there in anybody to praise? But it is different when the ministry is praised. We should not only desire people to praise the ministry of the Gospel but also do our utmost to make the ministry worthy of praise because this will make the ministry more effective. Paul warns the Romans not to bring Christianity into disrepute. "Let not then your good be evil spoken of." (Rom. 14:16.) He also begged the Corinthians to "give no offense in anything, that the ministry be not blamed." (I Cor. 6:3.) When people praise our ministry they are not praising our persons, but God.

VERSE 26. Provoking one another, envying one another.

Such is the ill effect of vainglory. Those who teach errors provoke others. When others disapprove and reject the doctrine the teachers of errors get angry in turn, and then you have strife and trouble. The sectarians hate us furiously because we will not approve their errors. We did not attack them directly. We merely called attention to certain abuses in the Church. They did not like it and became sore at us, because it hurt their pride. They wish to be the lone rulers of the church.

GALATIANS 6:1-18

VERSE 1. Brethren, if a man be overtaken in a fault ye which are spiritual, restore such an one in the spirit of meekness.

If we carefully weigh the words of the Apostle we perceive that he does not speak of doctrinal faults and errors, but of much lesser faults by which a person is overtaken through the weakness of his flesh. This explains why the Apostle chooses the softer term "fault." To minimize the offense still more, as if he meant to excuse it altogether and to take the whole blame away from the person who has committed the fault, he speaks of him as having been "overtaken," seduced by the devil and of the flesh. As if he meant to say, "What is more human than for a human being to fall, to be deceived and to err?" This comforting sentence at one time saved my life. Because Satan always assails both the purity of doctrine which he endeavors to take away by schisms and the purity of life which he spoils with his continual temptations to sin, Paul explains how the fallen should be treated. Those who are strong are to raise up the fallen in the spirit of meekness.

This ought to be borne in mind particularly by the ministers of the Word in order that they may not forget the parental attitude which Paul here requires of those who have the keeping of souls. Pastors and ministers must, of course, rebuke the fallen, but when they see that the fallen are sorry they are to comfort them by excusing the fault as well as they can. As unyielding as the Holy Spirit is in the matter of maintaining and defending the doctrine of faith, so mild and merciful is He toward men for their sins as long as sinners repent.

The Pope's synagogue teaches the exact opposite of what the Apostle commands. The clerics are tyrants and butchers of men's conscience. Every small offense is closely scrutinized. To justify the cruel inquisitiveness they quote the statement of Pope Gregory: "It is the property of good lives to be afraid of a fault where there is no fault." "Our censors must be feared, even if they are unjust and wrong." On these pronouncements the papists base their doctrine of excommunication. Rather than terrify and condemn men's consciences, they ought to raise them up and comfort them with the truth.

Let the ministers of the Gospel learn from Paul how to deal with those who have sinned. "Brethren," he says, "if any man be overtaken with a fault, do not aggravate his grief, do not scold him, do not condemn him,

162

but lift him up and gently restore his faith. If you see a brother despondent over a sin he has committed, run up to him, reach out your hand to him, comfort him with the Gospel and embrace him like a mother. When you meet a willful sinner who does not care, go after him and rebuke him sharply." But this is not the treatment for one who has been overtaken by a sin and is sorry. He must be dealt with in the spirit of meekness and not in the spirit of severity. A repentant sinner is not to be given gall and vinegar to drink.

VERSE 1. Considering thyself, lest thou also be tempted.

This consideration is very much needed to put a stop to the severity of some pastors who show the fallen no mercy. St. Augustine says: "There is no sin which one person has committed, that another person may not commit it also." We stand in slippery places. If we become overbearing and neglect our duty, it is easy enough to fall into sin. In the book entitled "The Lives of Our Fathers," one of the Fathers is reported to have said when informed that a brother had fallen into adultery: "He fell yesterday; I may fall today." Paul therefore warns the pastors not to be too rigorous and unmerciful towards offenders, but to show them every affection, always remembering: "This man fell into sin; I may fall into worse sin. If those who are always so eager to condemn others would investigate themselves they would find that the sins of others are motes in comparison to their own."

"Wherefore let him that thinketh he standeth take heed lest he fall." (I Cor. 10:12.) If David who was a hero of faith and did so many great things for the Lord, could fall so badly that in spite of his advanced age he was overcome by youthful lust after he had withstood so many different temptations with which the Lord had tested his faith, who are we to think that we are more stable? These object lessons of God should convince us that of all things God hates pride.

VERSE 2. Bear ye one another's burdens, and so fulfill the law of Christ.

The Law of Christ is the Law of love. Christ gave us no other law than this law of mutual love: "A new commandment I give unto you. That ye love one another." To love means to bear another's burdens. Christians must have strong shoulders to bear the burdens of their fellow Christians. Faithful pastors recognize many errors and offenses in the church, which they oversee. In civil affairs an official has to overlook much if he is fit to rule. If we can overlook our own shortcomings and wrong-doings, we ought to overlook the shortcomings of others in accordance with the words, "Bear ye one another's burdens."

Those who fail to do so expose their lack of understanding of the law of Christ. Love, according to Paul, "believeth all things, hopeth all things, endureth all things." This commandment is not meant for those who deny Christ; neither is it meant for those who continue to live in sin. Only those who are willing to hear the Word of God and then inadvertently fall into sin to their own great sorrow and regret, carry the burdens which the Apostle encourages us to bear. Let us not be hard on them. If Christ did not punish them, what right have we to do it?

VERSE 3. For if a man think himself to be something, when he is nothing, he deceiveth himself.

Again the Apostle takes the authors of sects to task for being hard-hearted tyrants. They despise the weak and demand that everything be just so. Nothing suits them except what they do. Unless you eulogize whatever they say or do, unless you adapt yourself to their slightest whim, they become angry with you. They are that way because, as St. Paul says, they "think themselves to be something," they think they know all about the Scriptures.

Paul has their number when he calls them zeros. They deceive themselves with their self-suggested wisdom and holiness. They have no understanding of Christ or the law of Christ. By insisting that everything be perfect they not only fail to bear the burdens of the weak, they actually offend the weak by their severity. People begin to hate and shun them and refuse to accept counsel or comfort from them.

Paul describes these stiff and ungracious saints accurately when he says of them, "They think themselves to be something." Bloated by their own silly ideas and schemes they entertain a pretty fair opinion of themselves, when in reality they amount to nothing.

VERSE 4. But let every man prove his own work, and then shall he have rejoicing in himself alone, and not in another.

In this verse the Apostle continues his attack upon the vainglorious sectarians. Although this passage may be applied to any work, the Apostle has in mind particularly the work of the ministry.

The trouble with these seekers after glory is that they never stop to consider whether their ministry is straightforward and faithful. All they think about is whether people will like and praise them. Theirs is a threefold sin. First, they are greedy of praise. Secondly, they are very sly and wily in suggesting that the ministry of other pastors is not what it should be. By way of contrast they hope to rise in the estimation of the people. Thirdly, once they have established a reputation for themselves they become so chesty that they stop short of nothing. When they have won the praise of men, pride leads them on to belittle the work of other men and to applaud their own. In this artful manner they hoodwink the people who rather enjoy to see their former pastors taken down a few notches by such upstarts.

"Let a minister be faithful in his office," is the apostolic injunction. "Let him not seek his own glory or look for praise. Let him desire to do good work and to preach the Gospel in all its purity. Whether an ungrateful world appreciates his efforts is to give him no concern because, after all, he is in the ministry not for his own glory but for the glory of Christ."

A faithful minister cares little what people think of him, as long as his conscience approves of him. The approval of his own good conscience is the best praise a minister can have. To know that we have taught the Word of God and administered the sacraments rightly is to have a glory that cannot be taken away.

The glory which the sectarians seek is quite unstable, because it rests in the whim of people. If Paul had had to depend on this kind of glory for his ministry he would have despaired when he saw the many offenses and evils following in the wake of his preaching.

If we had to feel that the success of our ministry depended upon our popularity with men we would die, because we are not popular. On the contrary, we are hated by the whole world with rare bitterness. Nobody praises us. Everybody finds fault with us. But we can glory in the Lord and attend to our work cheerfully. Who cares whether our efforts please or displease the devil? Who cares whether the world praises or hates us? We go ahead "by honour and dishonour, by evil report and good report." (II Cor. 6:8.)

The Gospel entails persecution. The Gospel is that kind of a doctrine. Furthermore, the disciples of the Gospel are not all dependable. Many embrace the Gospel today and tomorrow discard it. To preach the Gospel for praise is bad business especially when people stop praising you. Find your praise in the testimony of a good conscience.

This passage may also be applied to other work besides the ministry. When an official, a servant, a teacher minds his business and performs his duty faithfully without concerning himself about matters that are not in his line he may rejoice in himself. The best commendation of any work is to know that one has done the work that God has given him well and that God is pleased with his effort.

VERSE 5. Every man shall bear his own burden.

That means: For anybody to covet praise is foolish because the praise of men will be of no help to you in the hour of death. Before the judgment throne of Christ everybody will have to bear his own burden. As it is the praise of men stops when we die. Before the eternal Judge it is not praise that counts but your own conscience.

True, the consciousness of work well done cannot quiet the conscience. But it is well to have the testimony of a good conscience in the last judgment that we have performed our duty faithfully in accordance with God's will.

For the suppression of pride we need the strength of prayer. What man even if he is a Christian is not delighted with his own praise? Only the Holy Spirit can preserve us from the misfortune of pride.

VERSE 6. *Let him that is taught in the word communicate unto him that teacheth in all good things.*

Now the Apostle also addresses the hearers of the Word requesting them to bestow "all good things" upon those who have taught them the Gospel. I have often wondered why all the apostles reiterated this request with such embarrassing frequency. In the papacy I saw the people give generously for the erection and maintenance of luxurious church buildings and for the sustenance of men appointed to the idolatrous service of Rome. I saw bishops and priests grow rich until they possessed the choicest real estate. I thought then that Paul's admonitions were overdone. I thought he should have requested the people to curtail their contributions. I saw how the generosity of the people of the Church was encouraging covetousness on the part of the clergy. I know better now.

As often as I read the admonitions of the Apostle to the effect that the churches should support their pastors and raise funds for the relief of impoverished Christians I am half ashamed to think that the great Apostle Paul had to touch upon this subject so frequently. In writing to the Corinthians he needed two chapters to impress this matter upon them. I would not want to discredit Wittenberg as Paul discredited the Corinthians by urging them at such length to contribute to the relief of the poor. It seems to be a by-product of the Gospel that nobody wants to contribute to the maintenance of the Gospel ministry. When the doctrine of the devil is preached people are prodigal in their willing support of those who deceive them.

We have come to understand why it is so necessary to repeat the admonition of this verse. When Satan cannot suppress the preaching of the Gospel by force he tries to accomplish his purpose by striking the ministers of the Gospel with poverty. He curtails their income to such an extent that they are forced out of the ministry because they cannot live by the Gospel. Without ministers to proclaim the Word of God the people go wild like savage beasts.

Paul's admonition that the hearers of the Gospel share all good things with their pastors and teachers is certainly in order. To the Corinthians he wrote: "If we have sown unto you spiritual things is it a great thing if we shall reap your carnal things?" (I Cor. 9:11.) In the old days when the Pope reigned supreme everybody paid plenty for masses. The begging friars brought in their share. Commercial priests counted the daily offerings. From these extortions our countrymen are now delivered by the Gospel. You would think they would be grateful for their emancipation and give generously for the support of the ministry of the Gospel and the relief of impoverished Christians. Instead, they rob Christ. When the members of a Christian congregation permit their pastor to struggle along in penury, they are worse than heathen.

Before very long they are going to suffer for their ingratitude. They will lose their temporal and spiritual possessions. This sin merits the severest punishment. The reason why the churches of Galatia, Corinth, and other places were troubled by false apostles was this, that they had so little regard for their faithful ministers. You cannot refuse to give God a penny who gives you all good things, even life eternal, and turn around and give the devil, the giver of all evil and death eternal, pieces of gold, and not be punished for it.

The words "in all good things: are not to be understood to mean that people are to give all they have to their ministers, but that they should support them liberally and give them enough to live well.

VERSE 7. Be not deceived; God is not mocked.

The Apostle is so worked up over this matter that he is not content with a mere admonition. He utters the threatening words, "God is not mocked." Our countrymen think it good sport to despise the ministry. They like to treat the ministers like servants and slaves. "Be not deceived," warns the Apostle, "God is not mocked." God will not be mocked in His ministers. Christ said: "He that despiseth you, despiseth me." (Luke 10:16.) To Samuel God said: "They have not rejected thee, but they have rejected me." (I Sam. 8:7.) Be careful, you scoffers. God may postpone His punishment for a time, but He will find you out in time, and punish you for despising His servants. You cannot laugh at God. Maybe the people are little impressed by the threats of God, but in the hour of their death they shall know whom they have mocked. God is not ever going to let His ministers starve. When the rich suffer the pangs of hunger God will feed His own servants. "In the days of famine they shall be satisfied." (Ps. 37:19.)

VERSE 7. For whatever a man soweth, that shall he also reap.

These passages are all meant to benefit us ministers. I must say I do not find much pleasure in explaining these verses. I am made to appear as if I am speaking for my own benefit. If a minister preaches on money he is likely to be accused of covetousness. Still people must be told these things that they may know their duty over against their pastors. Our Savior says: "Eating and drinking such things as they give; for the laborer is worthy of his hire." (Luke 10:7.) And Paul says elsewhere: "Do ye not know that they which minister about holy things live of the things of the temple?" and they which wait at the altar are partakers with the altar? Even so hath the Lord ordained, that they which preach the gospel should live of the gospel." (I Cor. 9:13, 14.)

VERSE 8. For he that soweth to his flesh shall of the flesh reap corruption; but he that soweth to the Spirit shall of the Spirit reap everlasting life.

This simile of sowing and reaping also refers to the proper support of ministers. "He that soweth to the Spirit," i.e., he that honors the ministers of God is doing a spiritual thing and will reap everlasting life. "He that soweth to the flesh," i.e., he that has nothing left for the ministers of God, but only thinks of himself, that person will reap of the flesh corruption, not only in this life but also in the life to come. The Apostle wants to stir up his readers to be generous to their pastors.

That the ministers of the Church need support any man with common sense can see. Though this support is something physical the Apostle does not hesitate to call it sowing to the Spirit. When people scrape up everything they can lay their hands on and keep everything for themselves the Apostle calls it a sowing to the flesh. He pronounces those who sow to the Spirit blessed for this life and the life to come, while those who sow to the flesh are accursed now and forever.

> VERSE . And let us not be weary in well doing: for in due season we shall
> reap, if we faint not.

The Apostle intends soon to close his Epistle and therefore repeats once more the general exhortation unto good deeds. He means to say "Let us do good not only to the ministers of the Gospel, but to everybody, and let us do it without weariness." It is easy enough to do good once or twice, but to keep on doing good without getting disgusted with the ingratitude of those whom we have benefited, that is not so easy. Therefore the Apostle does not only admonish us to do good, but to do good untiringly. For our encouragement he adds the promise: "For in due season we shall reap, if we faint not." "Wait for the harvest and then you will reap the reward of your sowing to the Spirit. Think of that when you do good and the ingratitude of men will not stop you from doing good."

> VERSE 10. As we have therefore opportunity, let us do good unto all men,
> especially unto them who are of the household of faith.

In this verse the Apostle summarizes his instructions on the proper support of the ministers and of the poor. He paraphrases the words of Christ: "I must work the works of him that sent me, while it is day: the night cometh, when no man can work." (John 9:4.) Our good deeds are to be directed primarily at those who share the Christian faith with us, "the household of faith," as Paul calls them, among whom the ministers rank first as objects of our well doing.

> VERSE 11. Ye see how large a letter I have written unto you with mine own
> hand.

With these words the Apostle intends to draw the Galatians on. "I never," he says, "wrote such a long letter with my own hand to any of the other churches." His other epistles he dictated, and only subscribed his greetings and his signature with his own hand.

VERSE 12. As many as desire to make a fair shew in the flesh, they constrain
you to be circumcised; only lest they should suffer persecution for the cross
of Christ.

Paul once more scores the false apostles in an effort to draw the Galatians away from their false doctrine. "The teachers you have now do not seek the glory of Christ and the salvation of your souls, but only their own glory. They avoid the Cross. They do not understand what they teach."

These three counts against the false apostles are of so serious a nature that no Christian could have fellowship with them. But not all the Galatians obeyed the warning of Paul.

The Apostle's attack upon the false apostles was not unjustified. Neither are our attacks upon the papacy. When we call the Pope the Antichrist and his minions an evil brood, we do not slander them. We merely judge them by the touchstone of God's Word recorded in the first chapter of this Epistle: "Though we, or an angel from heaven, preach any other gospel unto you than that which we have preached unto you, let him be accursed."

VERSE 13. For neither they themselves who are circumcised keep the law;
but desire to have you circumcised, that they may glory in your flesh.

In other words: "I shall tell you what kind of teachers you have now. They avoid the Cross, they teach no certain truths. They think they are performing the Law, but they are not. They have not the Holy Spirit and without Him nobody can keep the Law." Where the Holy Ghost does not dwell in men there dwells an unclean spirit, a spirit that despises God and turns every effort at keeping the Law into a double sin.

Mark what the Apostle is saying: Those who are circumcised do not fulfill the Law. No self-righteous person ever does. To work, pray, or suffer apart from Christ is to work, pray, and to suffer in vain, "for whatsoever is not of faith is sin." It does a person no good to be circumcised, to fast, to pray, or to do anything, if in his heart he despises Christ.

"Why do the false apostles insist that you should be circumcised? Not for the sake of your righteousness," although they give that impression, but "that they may glory in your flesh." Now what sort of an ambition is that? Worst of all, they force circumcision upon you for no other reason than the satisfaction they get out of your submission.

VERSE 14. But God forbid that I should glory, save in the cross of our Lord
Jesus Christ.

"God forbid," says the Apostle, "that I should glory in anything as dangerous as the false apostles glory in because what they glory in is a poison that destroys many souls, and I wish it were buried in hell. Let them glory in the flesh if they wish and let them perish in their glory. As for me I glory in the Cross of our Lord Jesus Christ." He expresses the same sentiment in the fifth chapter of the Epistle to the Romans, where he says: "We glory in tribulations"; and in the twelfth chapter of the Second Epistle to the Corinthians: "Most gladly, therefore, will I rather glory in my infirmities." According to these expressions the glory of a Christian consists in tribulations, reproaches, and infirmities.

And this is our glory today with the Pope and the whole world persecuting us and trying to kill us. We know that we suffer these things not because we are thieves and murderers, but for Christ's sake whose Gospel we proclaim. We have no reason to complain. The world, of course, looks upon us as unhappy and accursed creatures, but Christ for whose sake we suffer pronounces us blessed and bids us to rejoice. "Blessed are ye," says He, "when men shall revile you, and persecute you. and shall say all manner of evil against you falsely, for my sake. Rejoice, and be exceeding glad." (Matt. 5:11, 12.)

By the Cross of Christ is not to be understood here the two pieces of wood to which He was nailed, but all the afflictions of the believers whose sufferings are Christ's sufferings. Elsewhere Paul writes: "Who now rejoice in my sufferings for you, and fill up that which is behind of the afflictions of Christ in my flesh for his body's sake, which is the church." (Col. 1:24.)

It is good for us to know this lest we sink into despair when our opponents persecute us. Let us bear the cross for Christ's sake. It will ease our sufferings and make them light as Christ says, Matthew 11:30, "My yoke is easy, and my burden is light."

VERSE 14. By whom the world is crucified unto me, and I unto the world.

"The world is crucified unto me," means that I condemn the world. "I am crucified unto the world," means that the world in turn condemns me. I detest the doctrine, the self-righteousness, and the works of the world. The world in turn detests my doctrine and condemns me as a revolutionary heretic. Thus the world is crucified unto us and we unto the world.

The monks imagined the world was crucified unto them when they entered the monastery. Not the world, but Christ, is crucified in the monasteries.

In this verse Paul expresses his hatred of the world. The hatred was mutual. As Paul, so we are to despise the world and the devil. With Christ on our side we can defy him and say: "Satan, the more you hurt me, the more I oppose you."

VERSE 15. For in Christ Jesus neither circumcision availeth anything, nor uncircumcision, but a new creature.

Since circumcision and uncircumcision are contrary matters we would expect the Apostle to say that one or the other might accomplish some good. But he denies that either of them do any good. Both are of no value because in Christ Jesus neither circumcision nor uncircumcision avail anything.

Reason fails to understand this, "for the natural man receiveth not the things of the Spirit of God." (I Cor. 2:14.) It therefore seeks righteousness in externals. However, we learn from the Word of God that there is nothing under the sun that can make us righteous before God and a new creature except Christ Jesus.

A new creature is one in whom the image of God has been renewed. Such a creature cannot be brought into life by good works, but by Christ alone. Good works may improve the outward appearance, but they cannot produce a new creature. A new creature is the work of the Holy Ghost, who imbues our hearts with faith, love, and other Christian virtues, grants us the strength to subdue the flesh and to reject the righteousness of the world.

VERSE 16. And as many as walk according to this rule, peace be on them, and mercy.

This is the rule by which we ought to live, "that ye put on the new man, which after God is created in righteousness and true holiness." (Eph. 4:24.) Those who walk after this rule enjoy the favor of God, the forgiveness of their sins, and peace of conscience. Should they ever be overtaken by any sin, the mercy of God supports them.

VERSE 17. From henceforth let no man trouble me.

The Apostle speaks these words with a certain amount of indignation. "I have preached the Gospel to you in conformity with the revelation which I received from Jesus Christ. If you do not care for it, very well. Trouble me no more. Trouble me no more."

VERSE 17. For I bear in my body the marks of the Lord Jesus.

"The marks on my body indicate whose servant I am. If I was anxious to please men, if I approved of circumcision and good works as factors in our salvation, if I would take delight in your flesh as the false apostles do, I would not have these marks on my body. But because I am the servant of Jesus Christ and publicly declare that no person can obtain the salvation of his soul outside of Christ, I must bear the badge of my Lord. These marks were given to me against my will as decorations from the devil and for no other merit but that I made known Jesus."

Of the marks of suffering which he bore in his body the Apostle makes frequent mention in his epistles. "I think," he says, "that God hath set forth us the apostles last, as it were appointed to death: for we are made a spectacle unto the world, and to angels, and to men." (I Cor. 4:9.) Again, "Unto this present hour we both hunger, and thirst, and are naked, and are buffeted, and have no certain dwellingplace; And labour, working with our hands: being reviled, we bless; being persecuted, we suffer it; being defamed, we intreat: we are made as the filth of the world, and are the offscouring of all things unto this day." (I Cor. 4:11-13.)

VERSE 18. Brethren, the grace of our Lord Jesus Christ be with your spirit.
Amen.

This is the Apostle's farewell. He ends his Epistle as he began it by wishing the Galatians the grace of God. We can hear him say: "I have presented Christ to you, I have pleaded with you, I have reproved you, I have overlooked nothing that I thought might be of benefit to you. All I can do now is to pray that our Lord Jesus Christ would bless my Epistle and grant you the guidance of the Holy Ghost."

The Lord Jesus Christ, our Savior, who gave me the strength and the grace to explain this Epistle and granted you the grace to hear it, preserve and strengthen us in faith unto the day of our redemption. To Him, the Father and the Son and the Holy Spirit, be glory, world without end. Amen.